The Context of Language Teaching

CAMBRIDGE LANGUAGE TEACHING LIBRARY
A series of authoritative books on subjects of central importance for all language teachers.

In this series:

Teaching the Spoken Language: an approach based on the analysis of conversational English by Gillian Brown and George Yule

Communicative Methodology in Language Teaching: the roles of fluency and accuracy by Christopher Brumfit

Foreign and Second Language Learning: language-acquisition research and its implications for the classroom by William Littlewood

A Foundation Course for Language Teachers by Tom McArthur

The Context of Language Teaching by Jack C. Richards

Communicating Naturally in a Second Language: theory and practice in language teaching by Wilga M. Rivers

Speaking in Many Tongues: essays in foreign-language teaching by Wilga M. Rivers

Teaching and Learning Languages by Earl W. Stevick

The Context of Language Teaching

Jack C. Richards

University of Hawaii at Manoa

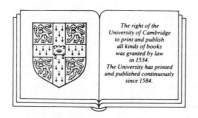

The right of the
University of Cambridge
to print and publish
all kinds of books
was granted by law
in 1534.
The University has printed
and published continuously
since 1584.

Cambridge University Press
Cambridge
London   New York   New Rochelle
Melbourne   Sydney

Published by the Press Syndicate of the University of Cambridge
The Pitt building, Trumpington Street, Cambridge CB2 1RP
32 East 57th Street, New York, NY 10022, USA
10 Stamford Road, Oakleigh, Melbourne 3166, Australia

First published 1985

Printed in the United States of America

Library of Congress Cataloging in Publication Data
Richards, Jack C.
The context of language teaching.
Bibliography: p.
Includes index.
1. Language and languages – Study and teaching.
I. Title.
P51.R47   1985   418'.007   84–21343
ISBN 0 521 26565 7 hardcover
ISBN 0 521 31952 8 paperback

Contents

Preface

In the last few years, my professional interests and activities have included classroom language teaching, studying and learning foreign languages, curriculum development and syllabus design, research, textbook writing, and lecturing to teachers in training. In order to obtain a better understanding of language teaching and learning, I have been obliged to immerse myself in its practical realities, to consult the findings of relevant theory and research, to undertake research, and to engage in speculation and theorizing. One result of this experience is the realization that there is still much to be learned about most aspects of language teaching. This is one of the frustrating consequences of working in a rapidly developing field; but it also means that there are fascinating issues to explore in almost any topic of interest. This, I hope, is demonstrated in *The Context of Language Teaching*. These essays illustrate both the scope of the applied linguistics of language teaching as well as the need for an integration of theory and practice in developing a fuller understanding of it.

Apart from three chapters written especially for this book (Chapters 1, 5, and 10), the essays represent attempts made at different times (from 1971 to the present) and in different locations (Quebec, central Java, Singapore, Hong Kong, and Honolulu) to develop a principled approach to practical issues in language teaching. This has involved questions of *approach* (as defined in Chapters 2 and 4), which is the realm of theories of the nature of language and language learning; those of *design*, which is concerned with developing a rationale for a language curriculum and syllabus; and *procedure*, the level at which questions of classroom techniques arise. The chapters hence deal with both "macro" and "micro" issues in language teaching. Although a topically organized collection of independently written papers inevitably deals with some issues more fully than others, it is hoped that the book will assist teachers, teachers in training, and students of applied linguistics to arrive at a clearer understanding of a wide range of important topics in the teaching of English as a second or foreign language.

In order to maximize the usefulness of the book, the chapters are grouped around several complementary themes. Chapters 1, 2, and 3 deal with curriculum and method issues. Chapter 1, "The Context of Language Teaching," gives an overview of language teaching and traces the ways in which language-teaching practices evolve, from the level of language policy through the curriculum and instructional process to evaluation. The main emphasis is the different levels of planning and organization that successful language teaching entails. Decisions made at one level inevitably produce repercussions elsewhere in what is essentially an interdependent system of curriculum, teaching, learning, and method variables.

The current interest in method and curriculum issues prompted me to write the next two chapters. In "Method: Approach, Design, and Procedure" (written with Ted Rodgers), we present a framework for the systematic description and comparison of methods. A method is defined in terms of three levels of theory and practice: approach, design, and procedure. *Approach* refers to the theory of language and language learning that underlies a method. *Design* refers to how this is operationalized in the form of a syllabus model and in terms of specific roles for teachers, learners, and teaching materials. *Procedure* is concerned with the teaching techniques and practices that a method employs in the classroom. The model is intended to enable methods to be understood and compared more easily, and its applications are illustrated with reference to recent method proposals. The chapter that follows, "The Secret Life of Methods," offers a complementary focus on methods. I compare methods according to whether they primarily represent innovations at the level of syllabus theory or instructional practice. A historical perspective is given and an attempt made to demythologize the method concept by showing how little evidence is available to substantiate the sometimes extravagant claims made for individual methods.

In Chapters 5 and 6, we turn to the theme of processes in second- and foreign-language learning. Chapter 4, "A Noncontrastive Approach to Error Analysis," is one of a group of papers by Corder, Selinker, myself, and others that appeared in the early seventies and began a paradigm shift in how second-language learning processes were viewed. This began with a questioning of some of the assumptions of contrastive analysis and led to a focus on learner error and learner language as evidence of success rather than failure. The terms *error analysis* and *interlanguage* were coined at this time and attracted considerable attention among researchers and teachers. The gradual evolution from an interest in error types and learner language to a more comprehensive approach to the study of second language learning is documented in Chapter 5, "Error Analysis, Interlanguage, and Second Language Acquisition: A Review," which discusses the emergence of the field of second language acquisition. Significant research issues and findings are presented, and the need for an integration of such research into a more comprehensive perspective on language learning is suggested. Such a view may be possible by considering the teaching/learning process in terms of input, process, task, and context variables and their inter-relationships.

The next four chapters shift from a psycholinguistic to a sociolinguistic focus and illustrate the relevance to language teaching of conversational analysis, discourse analysis, and speech-act theory. In Chapter 6, "Communicative Needs in Second- and Foreign-Language Learning," several components of communicative competence are discussed. Second- and foreign-language learning are seen to be influenced by communicative goals and processes. Strategies learners resort to in expressing meanings are shown to influence the nature of their discourse. The need for learners to acquire conventional ways of expressing meanings is discussed, as well as the importance of acquiring alternative ways of expressing speech acts. Conversation is seen as a process that reflects the interaction between the speaker, the hearer, language, and the message. In Chapter 7, "Answers to Yes/No Questions," a grammatical rule commonly taught in introductory ESL/EFL textbooks is tested against conversational and other data for its communicative authenticity. A considerable gap is found between the rules learners are required to master in textbooks and the rules native speakers use conversationally when they answer yes/no questions. This chapter offers a caution against relying on the intuitions of textbook writers when it comes to accurate representation of features of conversational discourse. In addition, it illustrates how teachers in training can be involved in data collection and discourse analysis as part of their preparation to teach English. Chapters 8 and 9, "Speech Acts and Second-Language Learning" (written with Richard Schmidt) and "Cross-Cultural Aspects of Conversational Competence" (written with Mayuri Sukwiwat), expand on some of the issues raised in Chapter 6. Conversational competence is discussed in terms of rules of speech-act and conversational management. Differences between English and the native language with respect to realization of speech acts, expression of directness, topic behavior, expression of politeness, and use of conversational routines are shown to have a potentially important influence on the processes of learning and communication.

The interest in communicative issues in language curriculum development in recent years, while necessitating a reevaluation of the role of grammar in language teaching, has not meant that grammatical questions are no longer of concern to teachers or textbook writers. Rather, questions concerning grammar are now typically dealt with in the context of the communicative treatment of particular language skills. Chapters 10, 11, and 12 deal with grammatical topics. In "The Status of Grammar in the Language Curriculum," grammar is discussed from the viewpoint of its contribution to language proficiency. A theory of language proficiency is seen as the starting point for curriculum development and for determining the importance of grammar at any given stage in a language curriculum. In the next two chapters, approaches to the teaching of grammar are considered. A case is made for sequencing and presenting the different meanings of the progressive and perfect aspects from an analysis of the notional and semantic meanings implicit in these grammatical distinctions. This is seen to involve minimizing potential learning problems by relating each grammatical form to uses where it is communicatively appropriate and functionally motivated.

The last two chapters consider the teaching of vocabulary and listening comprehension. In "Lexical Knowledge and the Teaching of Vocabulary," a consideration of what it means to know a word is discussed as a frame of reference for assessing vocabulary teaching. Linguistic, psycholinguistic, and discoursal aspects of vocabulary knowledge are examined. These include word frequency, collocation, register, case relations, associative meaning, and semantic networks. Teaching techniques are examined according to the way they attempt to build these aspects of vocabulary knowledge. In the final chapter, three dimensions in the teaching of listening comprehension are outlined. Initially, the nature of spoken discourse is described and a theory of listening processes developed. Then, from an analysis of listener needs, a taxonomy of listening micro-skills is developed. Finally, criteria for exercise types and teaching activities are presented.

In publishing this book, it is my hope that some of the insights I have gained from attempting to deal with specific issues may be helpful to teachers and others interested in the applied linguistics of language teaching. Rather than providing answers the essays suggest the sorts of questions that need to be asked and demonstrate ways of looking for solutions to both practical and theoretical questions. Throughout the period that the essays were being written, I have been fortunate to have found sympathetic listeners or readers in the form of friends and colleagues who were always ready to respond to ideas and proposals with constructive feedback and encouragement. Their support has been much appreciated. I owe a special debt of gratitude to James Alatis, Alison d'Anglejan, Chris Candlin, S. Pit Corder, Richard Day, H. V. George, Francis Johnson, R. Keith Johnson, Evelyn Hatch, Graeme Kennedy, Michael H. Long, Ted Rodgers, John Schumann, Richard Schmidt, Merrill Swain, H. H. Stern, Bernard Spolsky, Peter Strevens, Henry Widdowson and Richard Tucker, and to Peter Donovan and Ellen Shaw at Cambridge University Press for their support and effort in seeing the book through publication.

Chapter 2 is a jointly revised version (with Ted Rodgers) of a plenary address given at the Japan Association of Language Teachers' Convention in Nagoya, Japan, in November 1980. It was published in *TESOL Quarterly* 16 (2), June 1982, and is reprinted here with permission.

Chapter 3 was originally given as a plenary address at the 18th TESOL convention in Toronto, March 1983. It was subsequently published in *TESOL Quarterly* 18 (1), March 1984, and is reprinted here with permission. Chapter 4 was originally presented as a paper at the TESOL convention in San Francisco, March 1970. It was subsequently published in *English Language Teaching* 25, 1971, and is reprinted by permission of Oxford University Press. Chapter 6 was originally given as a plenary address at the Japan Association of Language Teachers' convention in Tokyo, November 1981. It was subsequently published in *English Language Teaching Journal* 37 (2), April 1983, and is reprinted by permission of Oxford University Press. Chapter 7 was originally published in *English Language Teaching* 31 (2), January 1977, and is reprinted by permission of Oxford University Press. Chapter 8 was originally published in *Applied Linguistics* 1 (2), 1980, and is reprinted by permission of Oxford University Press. Chapter 9 was originally published with the title "Language Transfer and Conversational Competence" in *Applied Linguistics* 2 (2), 1982, and is reprinted by permission of Oxford University Press. Chapter 11 was originally presented as a paper at the TESOL convention in Detroit, March 1981. It was subsequently published in *TESOL Quarterly* 13 (4), 1981, and is reprinted by permission. Chapter 12 was originally published in *TESOL Quarterly* 13 (4), 1979, and is reprinted by permission. Chapter 13 was originally published with the title "The Role of Vocabulary Teaching" in *TESOL Quarterly* 10 (1), 1976, and is reprinted by permission. Chapter 14 was originally published in *TESOL Quarterly* 17 (2), June 1983, and is reprinted by permission.

1 The context of language teaching

The teaching of second and foreign languages is a major international enterprise. The current status of English has turned a significant percentage of the world's population into part-time users or learners of English. The widespread need for English as a second or foreign language puts a considerable pressure on the educational resources of many countries. Problems relating to the teaching of English are discussed the world over. These range from practical questions concerning curriculum, methodology, and testing to more theoretical questions concerning the nature of second and foreign language learning and the role of cognitive and affective variables in the acquisition process. In this chapter, we will survey the nature and scope of English language teaching and consider the ways in which the field of Teaching English to Speakers of Other Languages (TESOL) deals with the practical realities of language teaching.

Uses and functions of English around the world

English as a mother tongue

English can be described as the mother tongue or first language of over 45 percent of the population in 10 countries; ranked according to greatest percentage of speakers of English these are the United Kingdom, Ireland, Australia, New Zealand, Barbados, Jamaica, Trinidad, the United States, Canada, and Guyana (Fishman et al. 1977). In English-speaking countries like these, English is not spoken in an identical manner, however. Different varieties or dialects of English exist, reflecting such factors as a person's degree of education, ethnic group, social class, or geographical location. A dialect may be distinguished by differences of vocabulary or grammar, but differences in pronunciation are generally its most recognizable feature and determine the speaker's accent, that is, the way his or her dialect is pronounced. The variety of English that is recognized by speakers of English as being the "correct" way of speaking, that is used as the basis for written English, and that is the variety generally used to teach English to those learning it as a second or foreign language is referred to as Standard English.

English as a second language (ESL)

In many countries a language that is not the mother tongue of the majority of the population may still function as an official language, that is, as the sole or major language of law, government, education, business, and the media. In countries where English has these functions it is usually referred to as a second language. English is an official (and hence second) language in Botswana, Cameroon, Fiji, Gambia, Ghana, India, Lesotho, Liberia, Malawai, Malta, Mauritius, Namibia, Nauru, Nigeria, Philippines, Zimbabwe, Sierra Leone, Singapore, South Africa, Swaziland, Tanzania, Tonga, Uganda, Western Samoa, and Zambia.

When English functions as a second language, that is, where it is used alongside other languages but is commonly the most important language of education, government, or business, it is often regarded by its users as a local rather than a foreign language (Richards 1979). Consequently, it is spoken in ways that mark its local status. Thus in countries like India, Nigeria, and Singapore people refer to their variety of English as Nigerian English, Indian English, or Singaporean English. These are legitimate varieties of English with a greater total number of users than the varieties of English spoken in countries where English is considered a native language (L. E. Smith 1981; Kachru 1982). They often serve as vehicles for the expression of literature and creative writing. In their written forms they are close to standard British or American English, but their spoken forms may be quite distinctive.

English as a foreign language (EFL)

In countries where English is not an official language it may still have a significant role to play. It may be an important school subject and it may be necessary to pass an examination in English to enter a university. It may be the language of certain courses at a university, or at least of a large percentage of the students' textbooks. It may be needed for people who work in tourism, business, and for some sections of the civil service. In countries where English has these functions, such as China, Japan, France, Germany, Mexico, Israel – that is, all those countries where English is not regarded as a second language – English is described as a foreign language.

In EFL countries, as they are sometimes referred to, English is increasingly the first foreign language studied at school or college. In China, English has replaced Russian as the most commonly studied foreign language. In many South American countries, it is replacing French as a foreign language in schools. In addition, over 50 percent of the world's non-English-speaking foreign students study in English-speaking coun-

2

tries. This has led to a greater need for English to be taught at the higher levels of education in EFL countries.

The language of the world's written information

Increasingly English is becoming the major international language of printed information. A great deal of the world's scientific, commercial, economic, and technological knowledge is written and published in English, though the writers may be Chinese, Swedes, or Italians. Publication in English ensures the widest possible readership for new findings and ideas. English is also an important language for the dissemination of news around the world. International newspapers, such as the *International Herald Tribune* – which is published in France, in English – are widely read and distributed. International news magazines, such as *Time* and *Newsweek*, have the majority of their readers in countries where English is not a mother tongue. In countries like China, Japan, and Indonesia, where the national language is not widely known outside the country, English-language newspapers are often used to present the official view of national and international events to the world.

A lingua franca

Finally, we must consider the function of English as a common language, or lingua franca, that is, a language that permits people who have no common language to communicate. Because English is widely taught or used as a second or foreign language, Japanese and German businessmen who meet, for example, use English as their business language. When Swedish tourists visit Italy, their travel language is English; when French tourists visit Bali, their hotel language is English. And English is the language that the English-speaking world uses to communicate with the rest of the world. The relative success with which people from non-English-speaking countries have learned to communicate in English has made native speakers of English in Britain, the United States, Australia, and elsewhere the world's most incompetent language learners. The pressure of some 300 million largely monolingual speakers of English in the economically and politically important English-speaking countries contributes another important dimension to the status of English in the world today and creates further reasons for others to learn it.

Having sketched some of the reasons for the current position of English as the world's most important second or foreign language, we can now consider how this need is acknowledged as an educational reality. The process by which a set of needs becomes translated into a reality is a complex one involving curriculum planning and development, teachers, formal instruction, textbooks, classrooms, and learners. It is the relative contribution of these dimensions of the teaching/learning process that we now consider.

The nature of language teaching

Language policies and goals

We have seen that the role of English and other second or foreign languages differs widely from one country to another, as do the reasons of particular groups of learners for studying them. A group of migrant children may be studying English in Australia in order to be able to enter a regular Australian high school. A Japanese steel company may engage foreign teachers to teach English to its employees to enable them to take part in international seminars and business meetings or to negotiate contracts with foreign clients. A group of Saudi university students may be studying English in order to read English textbooks in chemical engineering. Particular justifications for the teaching of English in different countries vary widely, but the factor common to all of them is that English is studied because the knowledge that it makes available is valued.

Any subject, whether English, history, music, or religion, enters the educational domain when it is found to be relevant to the demands and needs of a society. It is the task of educational and curriculum planners to examine these needs to determine what goals may be relevant to its educational system. The decision as to what the status of English will be within a society is a question of language policy. Language-policy decisions are made at the highest levels of national and educational planning. Such policies may specify (a) the aims or goals that serve as justifications for the teaching of English, and (b) the circumstances under which English will be taught. Examples of educational aims for the teaching of English might be

for appreciation of foreign cultures
for reasons of higher education
for scientific and technological advancement
for international commerce, trade, and communication.

Policy concerning the circumstances under which English will be taught may affect whether it will be taught in primary or in secondary school, the number of hours per week devoted to teaching it, and whether it will be made available to all or only certain students in the school system.

Language-policy decisions have repercussions across a wide spectrum of the educational system and ultimately determine how English is learned or taught. In Malaysia, for example, when language policy concerning the status of English was changed in 1973, English changed from being a medium of instruction to being a school subject. The requirement that a pass in English was needed to enter a university was also dropped. One result was that the reason for serious study of English was removed for many students. Performance on national English examinations dropped dramatically, and Malaysian universities now find it necessary to mount intensive courses for students who lack sufficient proficiency in English to complete their university courses. This is considered a price worth paying to bring about the democratization of education (i.e., by removing the barrier to education that English-medium instruction imposed on learners) and to enhance the use and status of the national language. Similar experiences are reported from the Sudan (Tucker 1978), where, in the northern provinces as a result of changes in language policy, Arabic replaced English as the medium of instruction; the time devoted to the study of English as a subject was reduced, and English was not required as a pass subject for the secondary school final examination. English however remained as the language of instruction at the country's main university, the University of Khartoum, thus creating the need for a new approach to the teaching of English at the tertiary level.

A number of facilities are available for the implementation of language policy (Noss 1967). These include:

1. Ministries of education; these are responsible for turning language policy into curriculum plans.
2. Curriculum development units and centers; these turn curriculum plans into curriculum content and courses.
3. Schools and educational institutions; these are responsible for teaching curriculum content.
4. The media; these may assist in the reception of policies, and provide auxiliary learning support.
5. Educational research institutions; these evaluate the degree to which policies are effective and are being successfully implemented.
6. Teacher training institutions; these prepare teachers to teach the curriculum.
7. Textbook bureaus; these prepare the necessary textbooks and support materials.
8. Testing and examination centers; these develop and sometimes administer tests and examinations based on the curriculum.
9. Translation bureaus; these provide specialized services for government and the private sector.
10. Foreign cultural organizations; organizations such as the British Council or the American Agency for International Development assist ministries of education, schools, teacher training institutions, and textbook bureaus in implementing language policies.

Language policy thus specifies the aims that a government or planning body sets for its educational system with respect to the role of languages in the educational system. How these aims are realized is the domain of what is known as curriculum development (D. Pratt 1980).

Language curriculum development

Curriculum development in language teaching is concerned with the following processes and activities (Richards 1984):

1. determining the needs a particular group of learners have for English instruction
2. developing objectives for a language course that will meet those needs
3. selecting teaching and learning activities and experiences that will enable these needs to be realized
4. evaluating the outcome.

The efficiency of a language teaching program depends upon how well these phases of curriculum development have been carried out. Let us consider each of them in turn.

NEEDS ANALYSIS

The goals of the needs-analysis phase of curriculum planning are to determine what a particular group of learners expect to use English for and what their present level of competence is. If a course is being designed for foreign students about to enter English-medium universities, needs analysis will focus both on determining the demands that will be made on first-year students in terms of reading, writing, listening, and speaking skills, and the learners' present abilities with respect to these demands. Needs-analysis procedures in this case involve gathering data from a variety of sources to find out, for example, the sorts of lectures students will have to attend, the types of reading and writing assignments they will have to carry out, and the types of study skills they need in order to be successful as students within a university setting.

Needs-analysis procedures may involve interviews with foreign students already in the university to determine perceptions of their major language difficulties, interviews with lecturers and instructors, observation of students in classes to observe how well they are able to carry out their assignments, examination of their lecture notes, essays, and so on, to determine their difficulties, as well as tests of different kinds to determine the students' level of proficiency in reading, writing, and note taking (Mackay and Palmer 1981). The aims of a needs analysis are thus to determine the types of situations in which learners will be using English, the tasks and activities they are expected to carry out or take part in in English, and their existing language skills or abilities with respect to those tasks (Munby 1978).

A course being designed for a foreign medical staff that needs an intensive English course in order to practice medicine in British hospitals, for example, would need to develop from an analysis of the type of communicative tasks the doctors will be expected to carry out (cf. Candlin et al. 1976). Techniques derived from discourse analysis (Coulthard

1977) may be needed to analyze the linguistic dimensions of such tasks as interviewing patients, understanding the instructions of air traffic controllers, or understanding instructions on the factory floor (Jupp and Hodlin 1975). In circumstances where English is being studied for more general purposes, such as a program for high school students in an EFL setting, needs analysis may focus on the sort of English language skills employers expect graduates to have mastered, and on the skills needed for further education.

GOAL SETTING

The results of the procedures of needs analysis enable goals to be set for a language program. Such goals must be realistic in terms of the setting and circumstances in which the program will be implemented, and relevant in terms of the language skills the learners will be expected to acquire. Particular constraints that result from the circumstances of the program define the parameters within which a language course operates. Key questions include: What facilities are available? Who will the teachers be and what is their degree of training and competence? Who is responsible for implementing and monitoring change? How much time is available? What are the limitations of the existing program? By examining the needs of the learners, according to priority, and by referring to the variables, general goals are turned into a more specific description of what the language program should set out to achieve.

The process by which increasingly specific goals are identified for a course of instruction is known as the setting of objectives (D. Pratt 1980). Objectives specify precisely what the learner should be able to do after a unit or period of instruction. They may be defined with reference to a unit of work within a course or to the course as a whole, and they serve to present the aims of the course in a form that can be taught, observed, and tested. Whereas the aims for a course in spoken English might be described simply as "to teach basic conversational skills," objectives would specify precisely what is meant by basic conversational skills. These might include:

ability to use a vocabulary of 2000 words commonly occurring in conversation; ability to give basic information and ask simple questions about topics concerned with family life, personal identification, place of work, place of residence, employment, hobbies, etc. (Van Ek and Alexander 1975).

SYLLABUS DESIGN

Objectives define the ends that the curriculum is designed to bring about, that is, the changes in knowledge and ability that the curriculum is expected to accomplish in learners. Subsequent phases in curriculum development are concerned with planning the means by which the objectives can be achieved. The process by which content is selected for a course of instruction in language teaching is generally referred to as syllabus design (Wilkins 1976). Generally, a syllabus represents a particular view of what is needed to attain an objective. For example, one syllabus for a conversation course might specify the topics, functions, and notions the learners are expected to master. Another might list conversational activities, such as "using the telephone" or "asking for directions," without specifying the language needed to carry out such activities. The form in which a syllabus specifies content will reflect how the syllabus will be used (Johnson 1981). If it is intended for use by classroom teachers as a basis for lesson planning, it may look very different from a syllabus primarily consulted by textbook writers in planning course books.

Theories of language syllabuses reflect current views of the nature of language and language learning and of the processes underlying reading, writing, listening, and speaking skills (Munby 1978, Yalden 1983; see also Chapters 2 and 3). Syllabus design in language teaching is hence an aspect of curriculum activity that depends upon findings in areas of applied linguistic research, such as second language acquisition, applied psycholinguistics, and discourse analysis. Current issues in syllabus design, such as the notional-functional syllabus (Wilkins 1976) and the product–process dichotomy in ESL writing curriculum theory (Murray 1980; Zamel 1982, 1983), demonstrate the impact of specific theories of language and language use on language curriculum and syllabus theory.

METHODOLOGY

Whereas the syllabus describes the content of a course of instruction (in terms of language items such as vocabulary, functions, notions, and grammar, or specific listening, speaking, reading, or composing skills), methodology in language teaching refers to the procedures and activities that will be used to teach the content of the syllabus. Methodology, syllabus design, and goal setting are interdependent, since our understanding of the psycholinguistic, interactional, linguistic, and cognitive nature of the content or processes identified in the syllabus serves as the rationale for selecting particular teaching techniques and learning experiences. This means that teaching techniques must be accountable in two ways. They must be accountable to theory (i.e., they must be justifiable in terms of current research, understanding, and theory about the nature of linguistic skills and processes) and they must be accountable in terms of the objectives they are designed to attain.

For example, a given instructional objective in a reading program may state: "Learners will be able to read materials at level 5 in the Longman

Graded Readers Series." Syllabus-design procedures should present this objective in terms of the linguistic skills and processes such an objective entails. These may include

ability to read at a reading speed of 350 words per minute with 85 percent comprehension;

ability to infer the meanings of unknown words from the contexts in which they occur;

ability to identify rhetorical structure of paragraphs and to locate topic and supporting sentences in paragraphs;

ability to distinguish between facts, opinions, and inferences in written materials.

At the level of methodology, these serve as justifications for the specific reading exercises and techniques that will be used in the course.

Ideally the techniques, classroom activities, and tasks that form the methodology of teaching different language skills should be designed by the teacher and should be perceived by the learner as a means toward an end, not merely as ends in themselves. Sometimes teaching techniques and classroom activities are regarded as ends in themselves, however, and both teachers and learners may be unclear about how they relate either to underlying processes or to longer-term goals and objectives. Students may see completion of the tasks and activities set by the teacher as the primary objective of learning. If this occurs, activities such as grammar study, memorization of word lists, or reciting of dialogues may become the objectives of the course in the minds of learners, when they should be viewed by both teachers and learners as a means to a broader goal.

EVALUATION

A language-teaching program that achieves its objectives can be considered successful to the degree that these objectives are valid. Evaluation is that phase of language program development that (a) monitors the teaching process in order to ensure that the system works, and (b) determines which phases of the system need adjustment when problems are detected (Jarvis and Adams 1979). Measuring the progress learners make toward objectives is clearly a crucial phase of evaluation, and the role of language tests is vital in the assessment of achievement. However, evaluation is concerned not only with the product or results of language teaching, but also with the processes by which language learning is accomplished (Long 1983). Its procedures include:

1. Analysis of the system through which the program is delivered, to determine if it represents the optimal structuring of time, resources, learners, teachers, and materials.
2. Analysis of the goals and objectives of the program to see if they are relevant and attainable.

3. Evaluation of the results of the program to see if the levels of performance attained are compatible with the program objectives.
4. Evaluation of results obtained to ascertain if these were achieved as a result of the program, or despite it. The fact that students make progress during a period of instruction, for example, does not enable one to conclude that this resulted from the program or methodology adopted. Students may learn independently of the method. To determine the degree to which the program is responsible for the results observed, research using a true experimental design may be needed, where the effects of a particular technique or method can be studied systematically.
5. Analysis of the process by which the program is implemented.

This may involve gathering data on the actual behavior of teachers and learners within classrooms during the course of instruction. This will provide a more detailed profile of teaching and learning behaviors, one from which it is possible to determine the degree of fit between the theory underlying a particular instructional philosophy and the actual teaching and learning behaviors that result from its implementation (Long 1983).

Too little time and too few resources are generally budgeted for evaluation in language-program development; consequently very few of the methods, procedures, and techniques described with such enthusiasm in the vast literature on language teaching have been subjected to detailed evaluation. Much of what is written about language-teaching methodology is consequently anecdotal rather than substantive in nature, characterized by assertions and proposals that have rarely been thoroughly tested and evaluated and for which there is little empirical evidence.

Methodology and methods

The domain of methodology in language teaching is concerned with developing and validating exercises and teaching activities by assessing the effect they have on the development of specific linguistic skills and abilities. Methodology is not developed independently of the processes of goal setting and syllabus design; it is but one phase in the sequence of activities known as language-program design. Teaching techniques can be assessed only if data are available on how they are used in the classroom, what sort of communicative, linguistic, and cognitive skills result from their use, and how they contribute to the learner's development of specific skills in listening, speaking, reading, or writing. In the teaching of writing, for example, one current methodological issue focuses on whether feedback on student writing (a) should be given at all, (b) should be given by the teachers, or (c) should be given by other learners via a peer-feedback format, and (d) whether a particular mode of giving feedback is superior in helping to develop composing skills. Prolonged discussion is always possible on such matters, but this debate can be resolved only by testing out and comparing the various possibilities in the classroom.

Currently, research directed to these issues does not provide straightforward answers to questions about the role of feedback in developing composing skills (Chaudron 1983a). Such research demonstrates that it is difficult to make strong, empirically based claims that can be widely generalized. Serious research into language-teaching methodology is still in its infancy. Until central issues concerning the fundamental processes involved in second language acquisition have been clarified, strong claims about the efficacy of specific instructional tactics cannot be made. Methodology issues must in general be resolved on a case-by-case basis and evaluated within the constraints of the situation in which they are used. For this reason, methodology is best considered an ongoing process, involving experimentation, data gathering, and evaluation, and informed by constant reference to target objectives and to research on underlying learning and communicative processes in second language acquisition.

Sometimes, however, global proposals for teaching are developed that derive from particular views of the nature of language and language learning and that relate to specific prescriptions as to how a language should be taught. These are referred to as methods. The Direct Method, for example, is based on a particular theory about how a foreign language can most effectively be learned and results in a specific set of principles and procedures being followed in the classroom. We discuss the assumptions behind methods in Chapters 2 and 3. Whereas methodology refers to language teaching within the context of language-program design, a method generally refers to language teaching outside the context of a broader framework of curriculum development; indeed, many method advocates promote their methods as substitutes for language curriculum development and say nothing about the broader issues of needs analysis, syllabus design, and evaluation, all of which are crucial phases in language program development.

Factors affecting the success of a language program

Language teaching is hence a complex issue, encompassing sociocultural, linguistic, psycholinguistic, as well as curricula and instructional dimensions. Planning a successful language program involves consideration of factors that go beyond the mere content and presentation of teaching materials. A large number of individual factors contribute to the dynamics of the teaching/learning process and provide reference points in discussions of language-teaching theory and practice. We will consider the impact of a number of these factors on the possible outcomes of a language course.

Sociocultural factors

The role English plays in a particular society, both pragmatically and symbolically, has an important influence both on language policies toward the teaching of English and on how the learning of English is viewed by members of a society. In some societies, knowledge of English is regarded as a sign of elitism. In others, successful acquisition of English is normal and inevitable for most members of society. It is sometimes remarked, for example, that Dutch, German, and Scandinavian students achieve a higher degree of proficiency in English than could be predicted from merely observing how they are taught English. This could be a reflection of the general expectation by students and parents that students should be able to leave school with a good knowledge of English (Strevens 1978). In countries where such an expectation is not present students may not achieve the same levels of proficiency, despite a similar exposure to English in school. The symbolic status of English likewise differs markedly across countries. In some, it has a largely pragmatic status, symbolizing internationalism and having a utilitarian appeal to learners. In others, particularly Third World countries, it may represent modernism, urbanization, wealth, and Western prosperity. English has come to symbolize modernization and technological sophistication and to correspond to a type of elitism, which in itself may create a special motivation for learning.

Teaching and learning styles

Education in different countries reflects culturally specific traditions of teaching and learning that may substantially shape the form and content of much school learning. This could be reflected in how the teacher's status and functions are viewed (i.e., as transmitter of knowledge, counselor, or helper), influence the dynamics of classroom interaction, and ultimately affect the amount of teacher talk versus pupil talk that characterizes classrooms. In some cultures students are encouraged to express opinion and disagreement, to display knowledge and verbal skills before peers and teachers. In others, a passive nonverbal mode is considered more normal. Learning styles may also reflect cultural traits. Rote memorization, for example, is a favored learning style in some Asian cultures but is not valued in many Western countries.

Learner factors

Students come to a language program with particular profiles of talents, interests, learning habits, and purposes that may crucially affect how well they do in a language course. They may differ with respect to personal goals and motivation. Some may be studying a language because they see its relevance to future occupational or educational goals. Others may be studying it to satisfy a curiosity and fascination with a foreign culture or cultural group. Such differences may substantially influence success in language learning, since they determine the criteria learners use to evaluate the relevance of the course, and consequently the amount of effort they are prepared to put into language learning. Students also differ with respect to the abilities they bring to the task. Some students have a good ear and pick up languages quickly. Others require much greater effort to achieve the same results. Learners also differ in how they go about the task of learning. Some learners are print-oriented and like to write down new words and sentences. Some worry when they do not understand something and look for explanations. Others are more prepared to tolerate ambiguity. Some seek out opportunities to use the language. Others may be shy about making errors and avoid such opportunities. Studies of the role of aptitude, motivation, and differences in cognitive style have done much to clarify the contributions of these factors to success or failure in second and foreign language learning (H. D. Brown 1980).

Program characteristics

A successful language program is dependent upon many factors. These relate to such elements as good management, planning, and administration, topics that are rarely included in TESOL training programs. Relevant factors include the following (Medley 1979).

DEGREE OF PREPARATION OF TEACHERS

Many attempts to implement change in language teaching have failed because insufficient attention was given to preparing teachers for change. Time and money invested in new syllabuses and curriculum may be wasted if teachers are not convinced of the need for change nor prepared for the different expectations made of them by a new method or curriculum policy. Uncoordinated development of syllabuses (by a team of foreign experts, for example) without consultation and input from the consumers (classroom teachers) may lead to creation of inapplicable materials and syllabuses.

13

How relevant is the existing curriculum? In one university language program for foreign students, students are required to take a listening comprehension course before being allowed to take graduate studies. They are placed in the course according to their score on a listening test. The test, however, is an inadequate measure of academic listening skills and deals mainly with memory and problem solving. Neither the instructors (hired on a term-by-term basis with no real commitment to the program) nor the program supervisor has a clear idea of what academic skills the students really need. Instructors are given few guidelines, either in the form of course objectives or methodology. The course is based on a text judged by students to be largely irrelevant to their needs. In this case, a program review is needed that includes (a) detailed needs assessment to determine the precise nature of the learners' academic listening problems; (b) development of a better test, based on criteria more relevant to academic listening; (c) preparation of detailed course objectives; (d) training and orientation for instructors; and (e) monitoring and evaluation of materials and activities selected to attain objectives.

CHARACTERISTICS OF THE STUDENT POPULATION

The successful implementation of a language program may depend on how well it matches the expectations, learning styles, and values of the learners. Many contemporary methods of language teaching make culturally based demands on teachers and learners. It is not a cultural universal, for example, that students should be talkative and communicative in classrooms. Teaching activities and procedures used in such contemporary methods as Counseling Learning, Communicative Language Teaching, and Silent Way derive from specific Western styles of classroom behavior that may be resisted in other cultural settings. In some societies, teachers are expected to be distant from students, and maintenance of status distinctions is obligatory. The use of skits, mime, and other activities may involve face-threatening behavior for teachers in some cultures, since they involve both teachers and learners in nontraditional roles.

SOFTWARE AND MATERIALS

In the absence of a carefully planned curriculum and syllabus, a well-chosen textbook may be the best alternative. A realistic budget for teaching materials may be the most crucial aspect of program planning in some settings. Even where syllabuses are well planned and teachers highly competent, materials are crucial. Too often, teacher time is dissipated by needless materials-preparation tasks when materials are available from publishers that far exceed the quality of materials teachers are capable of producing themselves. In many situations teacher energy might be better invested in adapting or modifying published materials to suit their particular needs rather than in attempting to write their own from scratch.

COORDINATION OF RESOURCES

Within any teaching institution, a considerable body of knowledge and experience exists. An effective administration will seek to ensure that this is optimally and cooperatively utilized rather than fruitlessly dissipated through uncoordinated individual efforts. Committee work on curriculum and materials projects is often the best way to ensure that available expertise is fully utilized and to give untrained teachers the opportunity for on-the-job training.

TESTING AND EVALUATION PROCEDURES

Testing is a vital component of curriculum development and evaluation. It affects how students are selected and placed in different levels in a program, how achievement is measured, and how learning problems are diagnosed and interpreted. Testing instruments must have adequate diagnostic and prognostic capabilities as well as provide reliable data on student progress. The degree to which tests relate to course content and program objectives is crucial in successful program development, yet testing is often regarded as an optional component of a language program rather than fundamental to its operation. Evaluation that is both based on test results and derived from classroom observation and teacher/student feedback should likewise be formalized, so that problems can be diagnosed and remedied as a program is developed and implemented.

In this chapter we have surveyed the scope of the teaching of English as a second and foreign language, as it affects educational planners, researchers, teachers, and learners; and we have looked at the different levels of planning, organization, instructional activity, and assessment that constitute the applied linguistics of language teaching. In subsequent chapters we will illustrate these processes in more detail.

2 Method: approach, design, and procedure

Jack C. Richards and Ted Rodgers

A comparison of the state of the art in language teaching today with the field as it was some twenty years ago reveals some interesting differences. In the fifties and sixties language teaching represented a reasonably unified body of theory and practice. It was clearly linked in its theoretical foundations to linguistics and psychology, particularly as these disciplines were represented in North America. The methodology of language teaching was identified with the orthodoxy of audiolingualism. Language teachers in the eighties, however, have a considerable array of theories and methods to choose from. Contemporary language teaching draws on a number of areas that were unknown or unconsulted by the linguists and psychologists of the fifties and sixties. These include (following Candlin 1976) studies in textual cohesion, language functions, speech-act theory, sociolinguistic variation, presuppositional semantics, interaction analysis, ethnomethodology and face-to-face analysis, ethnography of speaking, process analysis, and discourse analysis. Methodologies unheard of in the sixties are now familiar, at least by name: Silent Way, Total Physical Response, Communicative Language Teaching, Counseling Learning, Suggestopedia.

The practitioner is thus confronted with a somewhat bewildering set of options at the levels of both theory and practice. One conclusion might be that the field of language teaching has moved away from a generally accepted body of principles as a basis for the organization of language teaching. It is our belief, however, that current practices need not be seen as random or radical departures from the mainstream of applied linguistic thought and practice. Today's innovations in teaching practice represent variations on familiar themes, rather than radical departures or totally new practices. Given this point of view, we wish to outline a model for the systematic description and comparison of language-teaching methods in the hope that such a model may make it easier to understand recent developments in methodology in terms of some general principles.

As a point of departure we use a three-part distinction made some twenty years ago by Edward Anthony when he proposed an analysis of language-teaching practices using the terms *approach, method,* and *technique* (Anthony 1963). But since we prefer *method* as an umbrella term for the specification and interrelation of theory and practice, we find it

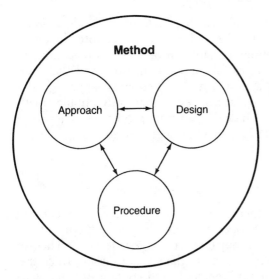

Figure 1

convenient to modify Anthony's terminology for the present purpose and speak of *approach, design,* and *procedure.*

These terms will be used to label three interrelated elements of organization upon which language-teaching practices are founded. The first level, *approach,* defines those assumptions, beliefs, and theories about the nature of language and the nature of language learning that operate as axiomatic constructs or reference points and provide a theoretical foundation for what language teachers ultimately do with learners in classrooms. The second level in the system, *design,* specifies the relationship of theories of language and learning to both the form and function of instructional materials and activities in instructional settings. The third level, *procedure,* comprises the classroom techniques and practices that are consequences of particular approaches and designs.

These three levels of organization form an interdependent system. When faced with a plethora of new language-teaching proposals, by focusing on the relationships between the levels of approach, design, and procedure, we can better understand the ways in which one method resembles or differs from another and hence more readily describe and evaluate the claims of different methods. We begin by defining the relevant elements of a teaching/learning system that form the basis for the description and comparison of methods. The system is illustrated in Figure 1.

We do not wish to imply that the ideal methodological development proceeds, rather neatly, from approach, to design, to procedure. It is not clear whether such a developmental formula is possible, and it certainly does not describe the typical case. Methodologies can develop out of any of the three categories (in Figure 1, clockwise, counterclockwise, or both). One can, for example, stumble on or invent a teaching procedure that appears to be successful on some measure and then later develop (counterclockwise) a design and a theoretical approach that explain or justify the given procedures. Several currently popular methods appear, in fact, to have been developed from procedure to approach (see, for example, Scovel's 1979 review of Suggestopedia).

Approach

Approach encompasses both theories of language and language learning. All language-teaching methods operate explicitly from a theory of language and beliefs or theories about how language is learned. Theories at the level of approach relate directly to the level of design, since they provide the basis for determining the goals and content of a language syllabus. They also relate to the level of procedure, since they provide the linguistic and psycholinguistic rationale for selection of particular teaching techniques and activities.

At least three different theoretical views of language explicitly or implicitly underlie currently popular language-teaching methods. The first and the most traditional of the three is the structural view, the view that language is a system of structurally related elements for the coding of meaning. The target of language learning is seen to be the acquisition of the elements of this system, which are generally defined in terms of grammatical units (clause, phrase, sentence) and grammatical operations (adding, shifting, joining elements). The second view of language is the functional view – the view that language is a vehicle for the expression of meaning. This approach emphasizes the semantic rather than the grammatical potential of language and leads to a specification and organization of language-teaching content by categories of function rather than by categories of form. A third view of language that informs some current methods of language teaching might be called the interactional view. It sees language as a vehicle for the realization of interpersonal relations and for the performance of social transactions between individuals. Areas of language inquiry that are being drawn on in the development of interactional language teaching include studies in interaction analysis, discourse analysis, ethnomethodology, and second language acquisition. Interactional theories focus on the patterns of moves, acts, and exchanges in communication. Language-teaching content, according to this view, may be specified and organized by patterns of exchange or may be left unspecified – to be shaped by the inclination of the learners as interactors.

Structural, functional, or interactional models of language (or variations on them) provide the axioms and theoretical framework of support underlying particular methods of language teaching. But in themselves they are incomplete and need to be complemented by theories of language learning. There often appear to be natural affinities between certain theories of language and theories of language learning; however, one can imagine different pairings of language theory to learning theory that might have worked as well as those we observe. The linking of structuralism (a linguistic theory) to behaviorism (a learning theory) produced audiolingualism. That particular link was not inevitable, however. Cognitive-code proponents, for example, have attempted to link structuralism to a more mentalistic and less behavioristic brand of learning theory.

Halliday (1975) has developed a theory of language focusing on "meaning potential," and he has proposed an account of how the capacity to use and understand the meaning potential of language develops in children. We can imagine a parallel account that describes the developmental stages by which meaning potential and communicative fluency are acquired by adult learners of a second language. Such an account would represent a learning model that might be paired with a notional/functional view of language.

Studies relevant to interactional models of learning are fewer and less developed than those relevant to interactional models of language. However, some proto-theories of interactive language learning are available, and others are imaginable. Weeks (1979) offers evidence of what we might call a *compulsion to converse* (our term), which she feels directs the course of language acquisition of young children. Curran (1972, 1976) speaks of a relationship of *redemptive convalidation* that exists between knower and learner. It is a state of interdependence that enables them to reach self-fulfillment. Human beings seek such redemptive convalidation, and Curran's Counseling-Learning identifies this as the driving force of language learning. Compulsion to converse or redemptive convalidation present proto-theories of interactive language learning that ultimately might support a theory of interactive linguistic organization as discussed earlier.

At the level of approach, we examine the theoretical principles underlying particular methods. With respect to language theory, we are concerned with a model of linguistic competence and an account of the basic features of linguistic organization. With respect to learning theory, we are concerned with an account of the central processes of language learning (e.g., memorization, inference, habit learning) and an account of the variables believed to promote successful language learning (e.g., frequency of stimulus, motivation, age, meaningfulness, type of learning, task, communality, activity).

Design

We now consider how the views of language and learning identified in a particular approach are linked to a design for language teaching. Such a design includes specification of (1) the content of instruction, that is, the syllabus, (2) learner roles in the system, (3) teacher roles in the system, (4) instructional materials types and functions.[1] Different approaches to language teaching manifest themselves in different design elements in language-teaching systems. Let us consider these elements, their relationship, and the outputs they determine.

Content choice and organization within the instructional system: the syllabus

All methods involve the use of the target language. All methods involve decisions concerning the selection of content that is to be used within the teaching program. Content concerns involve both subject matter and linguistic matter. In straightforward terms one makes decisions as to what to talk about (subject matter) and how to talk about it (linguistic matter). English for Specific Purposes and immersion courses, for example, are necessarily subject-matter focused. Structurally based courses are necessarily linguistically focused. Methods typically differ in what they see as the relevant language and subject matter around which language instruction should be organized and in the principles they make use of in structuring and sequencing content units within a course. These involve issues of selection and gradation that ultimately shape the syllabus adopted in a language course, as well as the instructional materials.

Within a design built on a structural theory of language, linguistic matter is identified with lexis and grammar, and the syllabus is an arrangement of linguistic units determined by such criteria as learnability, frequency of use, linguistic complexity, and so on. Within a design built on a functional theory of language, linguistic content is organized conceptually. An explicit notional syllabus, for example, would contain a specification of the propositional, conceptual, and communicative content of a language course, a selection of the linguistic means by which these are realized, and an organization of the product of such an analysis in terms of pedagogic priorities. Designs built on interactional theories of language and of language learning ostensibly use affective and interactive goals as organizing principles for the selection and structuring of

1 We acknowledge that some methods lack both teachers and teaching materials. A more general model of design would comprise: (1) knowledge considerations (content), (2) learner considerations, and (3) instructional considerations (presentation). However, since most current methods assume the existence of teachers and teaching materials, these are specified in the present model.

content. The progression within the course might be rationalized in terms of developing patterns of relationships between teachers and learners. An alternative solution for developing a syllabus within an interactional approach is illustrated by Community Language Learning (CLL). The emphasis in CLL is on having learners enter into a creative affiliation with other students and the teacher. To this end, CLL offers neither linguistic nor subject matter specification. Learners select content for themselves by choosing topics they wish to talk about. These are then translated into the target language and used as the basis for interaction and second-language practice and development.

Conceptions of syllabus thus range from code-based to relationship-based. These conceptions lead to different solutions to how the content of a course or textbook is to be chosen and organized (see Chapter 3). The evaluation and testing procedures and teacher-training proposals defined for a particular teaching method may also suggest the syllabus implicit in a particular method. A useful exercise we use in teacher training is to have trainees examine textbooks, course designs, language-learner protocols, and testing instruments in order to reconstruct the rationale for the selection and organization of content that has been followed. In the absence of these resources, trainees read what Asher, Curran, Gattegno, Candlin, and others have written about their own proposals for language teaching and then attempt to abstract specific principles for the selection and gradation of language content, that is, the actual criteria for syllabus design as specified or implied.

With respect to the selection and organization of content, design is thus the level that is concerned with the general objectives of a method (e.g., choice of language skills to be taught), the specific objectives of the method (e.g., target vocabulary or level to be taught in a conversation method), the criteria for the selection, sequencing, and organization of linguistic and/or subject matter content (e.g., frequency, learnability, complexity, personal utility), and the form in which that content is presented in the syllabus (e.g., grammatical structures, situations, topics, functions, exchanges).

Use of content in the instructional system: learners, teachers, and materials

The syllabus is the first component of the level of design. The other components concern the use of the syllabus in the system by the learners and teachers as they interact with the instructional materials. Design considerations thus deal with assumptions about the content and the context for teaching and learning – with how learners are expected to learn in the system and with how teachers are expected to teach with respect to a particular set of instructional materials organized according to the criteria of a syllabus.

Language-teaching methods differ in the weight they give to these variables and in the assumptions they make about them. A notional syllabus, for example, is rightly termed a syllabus and not a method. Discussions of notional syllabuses (e.g., Wilkins 1976) are directed to the organization of the linguistic content of language teaching. They say nothing about the roles of learners, teachers, or types of instructional materials. We might compare this to the Breen and Candlin discussion of communicative language teaching, for example, where they have tried to relate the syllabus to specific roles for learners, teachers, and materials (Breen and Candlin 1980). We discuss this in the three sections that follow. Individualized approaches to language learning have also redefined the roles of learner and teacher. This has led to a reconsideration of the kinds and uses of instructional materials and, in turn, to new requirements for specification of linguistic content, that is, new kinds of syllabuses for use in individualized instruction.

LEARNER ROLES

The majority of the world's population is bilingual, and formal classroom teaching has contributed only insignificantly to this statistic. Thus, it is easy to find successful language-learning situations that formally possess neither syllabus, teachers, nor instructional materials. It is difficult to imagine a language-learning situation without learners, however. Learners are the *sine qua non* of language learning.

What roles do learners play in the design of formal instructional systems? Many of the newer methodologies reflect a rethinking of the learner's contribution to the learning process and acknowledgment that the design of an instructional system will be much influenced by the kinds of assumptions made about learners. Such assumptions reflect explicit or implicit responses to such issues as the types of learning tasks set for learners, the degree of control learners have over the content of learning, the patterns of learner groupings recommended or implied, the degree to which learners influence the learning of others, the view of the learner as a processor, performer, initiator, problem solver, and so on.

Much of the criticism of audiolingualism came from the recognition of the very limited options available to learners in audiolingual methodology. Learners were seen as stimulus-response mechanisms whose learning was a direct product of repetitive practice. Newer methodologies customarily exhibit more concern for learner roles and variation among learners. Breen and Candlin describe the learner's role within a communicative methodology in the following terms. "The role of learner as negotiator – between the self, the learning process, and the object of learning – emerges from and interacts with the role of joint negotiator within the group and within the classroom procedures and activities which the group undertakes. The implication for the learner is that he should contribute as much as he gains, and thereby learn in an inter-dependent way" (1980: 110).

Johnson and Paulston (1976: 39–46) spell out learner roles in an individualized approach to language learning: (a) the learner is planner of his or her own learning program and thus ultimately assumes re-sponsibility for what he or she does in the classroom; (b) the learner is monitor and evaluator of his or her own progress; (c) the learner is a member of a group and learns by interacting with others; (d) the learner is a tutor of other learners; (e) the learner learns from the teacher, from other students, and from other teaching sources.

Counseling-Learning views learners as having roles that change de-velopmentally; indeed, Curran uses an ontogenetic metaphor to suggest this development. The developmental process is divided into five stages, extending from total dependency of the learner in Stage 1 to total in-dependence in Stage 5. These learner stages Curran (1976) sees as parallel to "the growth of a child from embryo to independent adulthood passing through childhood and adolescence."

TEACHER ROLES

Clearly linked to the roles defined for the learner are the roles the teacher is expected to play in the instructional process. Teacher roles, too, must ultimately be related both to assumptions about content and, at the level of approach, to particular views of language and language learning. Some instructional systems are totally dependent on the teacher as the source of knowledge and direction; others see the teacher's role as catalyst, consultant, diagnostician, guide, and model for learning; still others try to teacher-proof the instructional system by limiting teacher initiative and building instructional content and direction into texts or lesson plans. Teacher and learner roles define the type of interaction charac-teristic of classrooms in which a particular method is being used. Teacher roles in methods are related to the following issues: the types of functions teachers are expected to fulfill (e.g., practice director, counselor, model), the degree of control the teacher influences over learning, the degree to which the teacher is responsible for determining linguistic content, and the interactional patterns assumed between teachers and learners.

Typically methods turn most critically on teacher roles and their re-alization. In the classical audiolingual method the teacher is regarded as the source of language and learning. The teacher is the conductor of the orchestra, whose prime goal is to keep the players in tune and time, and without whom no music could be performed. Less teacher-conducted learning, however, still may have very specific and sometimes more demanding roles for the teacher. Such roles often require thorough training and methodological initiation on the teacher's part. Only the teacher who is thoroughly sure of the role to be filled, and of the concomitant learner's role, will risk departure from the security of traditional textbook-oriented learning.

For a functional/communicative method, the roles of the teacher have been described in the following terms:

The teacher has two main roles: the first role is to facilitate the communication process between all participants in the classroom, and between these participants and the various activities and texts. The second role is to act as an independent participant within the learning-teaching group. The latter role is closely related to the objectives of the first role and arises from it. These roles imply a set of secondary roles for the teacher; first, as an organizer of resources and as a resource himself, second as a guide within the classroom procedures and activities. . . . A third role for the teacher is that of researcher and learner, with much to contribute in terms of appropriate knowledge and abilities, actual and observed experience of the nature of learning, and organizational capacities. (Breen and Candlin 1980: 99)

Similarly, individualized approaches to learning define roles for the teacher that create specific patterns of interaction between the teachers and the learners in the classroom. These are designed to gradually shift responsibility for learning from the teacher to the learner (Johnson and Paulston 1976).

CLL sees the teacher (knower) role as that of psychological counselor – the effectiveness of the teacher role being a measure of counseling skills and attributes: warmth, acceptance, and sensitivity. As these examples suggest, the potential role relationships of learner and teacher are many and varied. These include asymmetrical relationships, such as those of conductor to orchestra member, therapist to patient, and coach to player. Some contemporary methodologies have sought to establish more symmetrical kinds of learner–teacher relationships such as friend to friend, colleague to colleague, teammate to teammate.

ROLE OF INSTRUCTIONAL MATERIALS

The fourth design component is concerned with the role of instructional materials within the instructional system. What is specified with respect to content (the syllabus) and with respect to learner and teacher roles suggests the functions for materials within the system. The syllabus defines linguistic content in terms of language elements: structures, topics, notions, functions, exchanges, or whatever. It also specifies the selection and ordering of particular language items to be taught that represent the elements. Finally, it defines the goals for language learning.

24

The instructional materials, in their turn, specify subject matter content (even where the syllabus may not). They also define or suggest the intensity of coverage for particular syllabus items: how much time, attention, and detail are devoted to specific language items. Finally, instructional materials define (or imply) the day-to-day learning objectives that (should) collectively constitute the goals of the syllabus. Materials designed on the assumption that learning is initiated and monitored by the teacher must meet quite different requirements from those materials designed for student self-instruction or for peer tutoring. Some methods require the instructional use of existing materials, found materials, and realia. Some assume teacher-proof materials that even poorly trained teachers with imperfect control of the target language can teach from. Some materials require specially trained teachers with near-native competence in the target language. Some are designed to enable learning to take place independently; that is, the materials are designed to replace the teacher. Some materials dictate various interactional patterns in the classroom; others inhibit classroom interaction; still others are noncommittal as regards interaction between teacher and learner or learner and learner.

The role of instructional materials within an instructional system will reflect decisions concerning the primary goal of materials (e.g., to present content, to practice content, to facilitate communication between learners, to enable the learners to practice content without the teacher, etc.), the form of materials (e.g., textbook, audiovisual, computer display, etc.), the relation materials hold to other sources of input (i.e., whether they serve as the major source of input, or only as a minor component of input), and the abilities of the teacher (e.g., competence in the language, degree of training, etc.).

A particular design for an instructional system may imply a particular set of roles for instructional materials in support of the syllabus and the teachers and learners. For example, the role of instructional materials within a functional/communicative methodology might be specified in terms such as the following:

1. The materials will facilitate the communicative abilities of interpretation, expression, and negotiation.
2. Materials will focus on understandable and relevant communication rather than on grammatical form.
3. Materials will command the learners' interests and involve their intelligence and creativity.
4. Materials will involve different types of text, and different media, which the participants can use to develop their competence through a variety of different activities and tasks.

By comparison, the role of instructional materials within an individualized instructional system might include such specifications as these:

1. Materials will allow learners to progress at their own rates of learning.
2. Materials will cater to different styles of learning.
3. Materials will provide opportunities for independent study and use.
4. Materials will provide for student self-evaluation and progress in learning.

The content of CLL is assumed to be a product of the interests of the learners. In that sense it would appear that no linguistic content or materials are specified within the method. On the other hand CLL acknowledges the need for learner mastery of certain linguistic mechanics, such as the learning of vocabulary, appropriate pronunciation, and grammatical rules. CLL sees these issues as falling outside the teacher/knower's central role as counselor. Thus, CLL has proposed the use of teaching machines and other learning apparatus to support the learning of such mechanics and free the teacher to function increasingly as a learning counselor.

Procedure

The last level of conceptualization and organization within an instructional system is what we refer to as procedure. Here the focus is on the actual moment-to-moment techniques, practices, and activities that operate in teaching and learning according to a particular method.

Many contemporary methods are characterized primarily by their techniques and practices. When we ask for impressions of these methods, we customarily get responses dealing with procedure rather than with approach or design. Free association to Silent Way elicits descriptions like "manipulating colored rods"; to Total Physical Response, "jumping up and down"; to Suggestopedia, "lying in a chaise longue listening to soothing music"; to Counseling-Learning, "sitting in a conversation circle"; and so forth. All of these responses deal with the procedural element of particular methods.

Differences in approach and design are likely to manifest themselves at the level of procedure in different types of activities and exercises in materials and in the classroom and in different uses for particular exercise types. Types of exercises include drill, dialogue, dictation, cloze sentence completion, (guided, semi-guided, and free) composition and conversation, role play, games, simulation. For a particular exercise type, procedure includes a specification of context of use and a description of precisely what is expected in terms of execution and outcome for each exercise type. For example, interactive games are often used in audiolingual methodology for motivation and change of pace from pattern-practice drills. In contemporary communicative methodology, the same games may be used to introduce or provide practice for particular types of interaction exchanges.

Within a particular version of a functional/communicative methodology, the following requirements have been specified for exercise type and use. Exercises must be interactive, authentic, purposive, and contextualized (cf. Palmer and Rodgers 1982). Thus the materials make use of dialogues as one exercise type, but the learner has to provide the content. The learner is asked to make decisions based on minimal clues rather than memorize prepackaged language because, it is argued, purposeful communication involves encoding meaning.

Another example of practices recommended within a particular method is seen in the types of drills proposed in the individualized instructional system advocated by Johnson and Paulston. Drills are permitted only if they pass a test of "responsiveness."

Practice is most effective when it is conducted in a responsive environment in which what is said by one learner matters to another or other learners, because they may in turn have to respond to what is said. . . . The most useful type of practice for developing communication skill is for the learner to say something and then have another learner respond entirely on the basis of what was said. It is apparent that in terms of responsiveness, the forms for practice easiest to provide in the classroom will be the request form and the question and answer form. A measure of effectiveness of practice will be the degree of responsiveness that a set of materials can incorporate into the practice of a sentence pattern. (Johnson and Paulston 1976: 31)

Procedure, then, is concerned with issues such as the following: the types of teaching and learning techniques, the types of exercises and practice activities, the resources – time, space, equipment – required to implement recommended practices.

We have now completed our discussion of the three elements and sub-elements that in their specification and interrelation constitute a statement of method. These elements and sub-elements are summarized in Figure 2. We conclude this chapter by suggesting several types of applications to which we think the model can usefully be put.

Applications

The model just discussed represents an attempt to provide a framework that can be used to describe, evaluate, and compare methods in language teaching. It attempts to define elements that are common to all methods and to highlight alternative realizations of these for particular methods. It is hoped that the model permits localization of points of similarity and difference between methods as well as identification of areas wherein particular methods may not have been defined with sufficient precision or detail. We can see that communicative language teaching, for example, was described initially at the level of approach (see Wilkins 1976, Breen

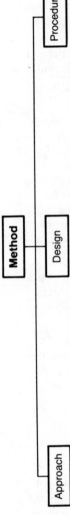

Method

Approach

Design

Procedure

a. *A Theory of the Nature of Language*
   - a model of linguistic competence
   - an account of the basic units of language structure

b. *A Theory of the Nature of Language Learning*
   - an account of the central processes of language learning
   - an account of what promotes success in language learning

a. *A Definition of Linguistic Content and Specifications for Selection and Organization of Content*
   - the general objectives of the method
   - the specific objectives of the method
   - criteria for the selection and organization of linguistic and/or subject matter content
     - a syllabus model
     - the form in which content is presented in the syllabus

b. *A Specification of the Role of Learners*
   - the types of learning tasks set for learners
   - the degree of control learners have over the content of learning
   - the patterns of learner groupings which are recommended or implied
   - the degree to which learners influence the learning of others
   - the view of the learner as a processor, performer, initiator, problem solver

c. *A Specification of the Role of Teachers*
   - the types of functions teachers fulfill
   - the degree of control of teacher influence over learning
   - the degree to which the teacher determines linguistic content
   - the types of interaction between teachers and learners

d. *A Specification of the Role of Materials*
   - the primary goal of materials
   - the form materials take (e.g., textbook, audio-visual format, etc.)
   - the relation materials have to other sources of input
   - the assumptions the materials make about teachers and learners

Descriptions of Techniques and Practices in the Instructional System
   - the types of techniques and tactics used by teachers for presenting and practicing language content
   - the types of exercises and practice activities that are used in materials or suggested for teachers to follow
   - the resources in terms of time, space, and equipment used to implement recommended classroom practices

Figure 2

and Candlin 1980) and has only recently been more fully elaborated at the levels of design (see Munby 1978) and procedure (Littlewood 1981, Johnson 1982).

We can superimpose the grid in Figure 2 on a particular methodological statement to determine the degree of specificity and adequacy with which the method has been described. As an example, let us briefly consider Asher's Total Physical Response (TPR) using this overlay technique. The method statement examined is that of Asher (1977).

TPR at the approach level

Asher's theory of language is implicit rather than explicit, but it appears to be based on a formalistic structural model of language focusing primarily on the form rather than the content of communication. It uses a surface-level concept of a grammatical system in which language is viewed as a code composed of structural elements that have to be mastered. Language is viewed as a vehicle for controlling the behavior of others, as a manipulative instrument.

Asher's learning theory is one based on the belief that language is learned through motor activity. In child language learning, "there is an intimate relationship between language and the child's body" (Asher 1977: 4), and this is the model for adult learning. Orchestrating language production with bodily movement is thought to promote success in learning, and this is the key to the method. There is a belief in transfer across skills, and skills acquired in speaking are thought to transfer to writing and reading.

TPR at the design level

The general objectives of TPR are to teach the spoken language to beginning-level students. Comprehension precedes production. Specific objectives are not elaborated. Because of the criteria for selection of language items, common conversational forms are not selected.

The syllabus is sentence-based, primarily lexical and grammatical. Items are selected according to the ease with which they may be used in the imperative form to initiate actions. "Most of the grammatical structure of the target language and hundreds of vocabulary items can be learned from the skillful use of the imperative by the instructor" (Asher 1977: 4). Vocabulary must be concrete and situational, and the verbs selected must be action verbs. The progression of items is from concrete to abstract, and syllabus items are presented in sentence patterns.

Learners mostly perform actions from commands given by the teacher. The emphasis is primarily receptive, and the learners have no control over what is said. At a more advanced level, learners may also give commands to other students. Learners learn in groups, but pair work is also possible at later stages. Learners typically learn from the teacher, and they are viewed as responders.

The teacher is the initiator of activities and communication. The teacher has considerable freedom of choice over what language is taught, provided the command-based mode of selection and practice is followed. Interaction is mainly nonreciprocal. The teacher commands and students react.

Teaching may proceed without materials. Materials play a primarily supplementary role (word charts, slides, pictures) and are teacher-produced.

TPR at the procedure level

The activities used are usually command-based drills. Meaning is communicated via gesture, mime, and demonstration. Written and spoken forms are presented at the same time. Both individual and group work are used. Errors are allowed and are not corrected initially. Comprehension is emphasized before production.

A fuller description of the Total Physical Response method would take into account all the elements of the model. The model, however, can also be used to compare and contrast methods. As an example, let us consider two methods: Total Physical Response and Community Language Learning.

Superficially the two methods seem antithetical. Comparing elements at the level of design, we find TPR typically has a written syllabus with paced introductions of structures and vocabulary. CLL has no syllabus and operates out of what learners feel they need to know. In TPR, the teacher role is one of drill master, director, and motivator. In CLL, the teacher/knower is counselor, supporter, and facilitator. TPR learners are physically active and mobile. CLL learners are sedentary and in a fixed configuration. TPR assumes that no particular relationship develops between learners and emphasizes the importance of individuals acting alone. CLL is rooted, as its title suggests, in a communal relationship between learners and teachers acting supportively and in concert. At the level of procedure, we find that TPR language practice is largely mechanical, with much emphasis on listening. CLL language practice is innovative, with emphasis on production.

The two methods do, however, have elements in common that can easily be overlooked. In approach, both TPR and CLL see stress, defensiveness, and embarrassment as the major blocks to successful language learning. They both see the learner's commitment, attention, and participation as a group member as central to overcoming these barriers. They both view the stages of adult learning as recapitulations of the stages of childhood learning. Both CLL and TPR consider mediation, memory, and recall of linguistic elements to be central issues and see physical activity as a way to facilitate these – CLL through manipulation of a button-operated, color-coded language item practice device, TPR through mimetic physical enactment. TPR holds with CLL that learning is multi-modal – that "more involvement must be provided the student than simply sitting in his seat and passively listening. He must be somatically or physiologically, as well as intellectually, engaged" (Curran 1976: 79). At the level of design, neither TPR nor CLL assumes method-specific materials, but both assume materials can be locally produced as needed.

Conclusion

The view of method we have outlined in this chapter relates theory to practice by focusing on assumptions and the programs and practices that relate to these assumptions. The model makes a claim as to what a descriptively adequate statement of method should comprise. It also shows how the reasonably fine-grained analysis that the present model directs can help provide important insights into the internal adequacy of particular methods, as well as into the similarities and differences that exist between alternative methods.

3 The secret life of methods

The history of language teaching is the history of ideas about what language is and how languages are learned. The application to language teaching of theories concerning the nature of language and language learning has led to a succession of different instructional methods. Although differences between methods often reflect opposing views of the nature of language and of language-learning processes, the reasons for the rise and fall of methods are often independent of either the theories behind those methods or their effectiveness in practice. To understand the role of language theory, instructional theory, and implementational factors in methods is to know their "secret life" and at the same time to discover the limitations of the "methods syndrome" in curriculum development.

Methods and language theory: how language content is defined

In using the term *method*, I refer to a language-teaching philosophy that contains a standardized set of procedures or principles for teaching a language that are based upon a given set of theoretical premises about the nature of language and language learning (see Chapter 2). There are essentially two routes to the development of methods in language teaching. One is through the syllabus, that is, the way language content is defined and organized. The other is through a theory of learning processes and instructional procedures. Although syllabuses and instructional procedures are often interdependent, they need not be, and the diverse methods options available today reflect the fundamentally different assumptions behind these two approaches to methods development.

The syllabus route

All methods are concerned with creating opportunities for learners to acquire language. But methods may define language differently. For some, language is identified with grammar and vocabulary. For others, it is an abstract set of semantic, syntactic, and lexical features. For still others, it is the ideas, concepts, and norms of social and linguistic behavior that humans exchange and manifest in daily life. Each of these is a particular view of what we ultimately teach, that is, a model of a language syllabus. Many current trends in language teaching, such as the notional/functional syllabus or the English for Specific Purposes (ESP) approach to program design, reflect the influence of particular accounts of language content and specific proposals as to what the language underlying a methods should contain.

The first major attempts to elaborate a systematic and rational foundation for methods in the twentieth century arose out of the movement toward vocabulary control in the 1920s and 1930s. This movement saw vocabulary as a major component of a language syllabus. It led to word frequency lists, to *Basic English* (Ogden 1930), to the *Interim Report on Vocabulary Selection* (Faucett, West, Palmer, and Thorndike 1936), and to the *General Service List* (West 1953). These were the products of people like Palmer and West, Bongers, and Ogden, who attempted to introduce a scientific or empirical basis to syllabus design (Mackey 1965).

Palmer had a parallel interest in grammar, but not the grammar of the grammar-translation method. For Palmer, grammar was the system underlying the patterns of speech. It led to his development of substitution tables and to his book, *A Grammar of Spoken English* (Palmer and Blandford 1939), and laid the foundations for work by Hornby, Mackin, and others on grammatical syllabuses (Hornby 1954). With the development of systematic approaches to the lexical and grammatical content of language courses, and with the efforts of specialists such as Palmer and West in using these resources as part of a comprehensive methodological framework for the teaching of English as a foreign language (TEFL), the foundations for the British approach to TEFL were firmly established. The graded sequence of sentence patterns and structures that served as syllabuses for courses and course materials was known as a *structural syllabus*. The use of such a syllabus together with a situational approach to contextualizing and practicing syllabus items became known as the *structural-situational approach*.

In the United States, the applied linguistic foundations of language teaching developed several decades later than the British effort but led to similar results. This time the word lists were produced by Charles Fries and his colleagues at the University of Michigan (Fries and Traver 1942), and the substitution tables became the "frames" that served as the basis for "pattern practice." The model of language content that Fries used, however, was more up to date, borrowed from a paradigm developed by American linguists in the 1930s and 1940s. Charles Fries was trained in structural linguistics, and when he became director of the University of Michigan's English Language Institute in 1939 – the first ELI in the United

States, he applied "structuralism" to language teaching and syllabus design. The result was the "aural-oral method" (Fries and Fries 1961).

The view that the content of language can be defined principally in terms of vocabulary and grammar has had a lasting influence on methods. It is basic to the views of such current methods "innovators" as Asher and Gattegno. It was embodied in the audiolingual method that swept foreign language departments in North America in the late 1950s and 1960s. It was only minimally affected by the views that Chomsky launched upon linguistics in the 1960s and that were manifested briefly in language teaching as the "cognitive-code" approach.

The first serious challenges to this view of language arose in the late 1960s, leading to the concept of notional syllabuses on the one hand (Wilkins 1976) and to the English for Specific Purposes movement on the other (Robinson 1980). Both reject the lexico-structural syllabus model and propose an alternative view of syllabus content. To understand the motivation for the rejection of the lexico-structural syllabus, we need to make explicit some of the assumptions behind it. The chief of these was that once the basic vocabulary and grammar of the target language had been learned, the learner would be able to communicate effectively in situations where English was needed for general, unspecified purposes. The structural/situational, aural/oral, and audiolingual methods were all designed to teach English for general purposes.

The notional syllabus proposed by Wilkins simply redefined the language content needed for English for general purposes to include not only grammar and vocabulary but also the notions or concepts the learner needs to communicate about, the functional purposes for which the language is to be used, the situations in which the language will be used, and the roles the learner might typically play. Such a view of language reflects a movement from a grammatical to a communicative account of what it means to know a language. In trying to put such a proposal into practice, the Council of Europe elaborated a now well-known version of such a syllabus – the *Threshold Level* (Van Ek and Alexander 1975). This is a description of the content of English to be taught for general communicative purposes.

In circumstances where English is taught for specific and narrowly defined purposes rather than for a more general communicative goal, the content of language can no longer be identified with the same grammar, vocabulary, notions, topics, and functions that serve the needs of English for general purposes. Rather, the specific linguistic requirements of the target learners will have to be determined as a basis for syllabus design, and this is the philosophy behind ESP. This approach to language teaching is cost-effective. It advocates teaching only the content that particular groups of learners require and begins not with an analysis of the language code but with a determination of the learner's communicative needs. Only then can the learner's language needs be determined.

Structural/situational, aural/oral, audiolingual, notional/functional, and ESP approaches to language teaching are seemingly odd bedfellows but do have one thing in common: They are built around content variables. They each make concrete proposals for a language syllabus, and the syllabus forms the basis for subsequently determined instructional procedures. But an alternative route to the development of methods is available, one based not on language content as the starting point but rather beginning from a theory of learning and teaching. Such methods as the Silent Way, Counseling-Learning (C-L), the Natural Approach, and Total Physical Response (TPR) have in common the fact that each is an outcome and an application of a particular theory of language learning and an accompanying body of instructional theory.

The instructional-theory route

An instructional theory in language teaching incorporates a psycholinguistic theory of language learning and a rationale for teaching procedures. It includes: (1) a psycholinguistic dimension, containing a theory of learning that describes learning strategies and processes and that specifies the conditions necessary for these processes to be effectively utilized by learners, and (2) a teaching dimension, containing an account of the teaching and learning procedures to be followed and of the role of teachers and learners in the instructional process (i.e., the types of tasks and activities they are expected to carry out, the role of learners as performers, initiators, and problem solvers, and their degree of independence and control over the content of what they learn and how they learn it).

We can classify methods according to whether they primarily represent reactions to content and syllabus issues or to instructional issues. A notional/functional view of a syllabus, for example, and an ESP approach to course design make no assumptions about instructional theory. It would not be logically inconsistent to have a notional/functional syllabus implemented through Silent Way procedures, since the concept of a notional syllabus is independent of any instructional theory. It is true that instructional procedures may appear to be wedded to particular syllabus models. For example, a notional/functional syllabus is often implemented via "communicative" procedures, and a structural syllabus via aural-oral/pattern practice techniques, but these pairings are by no means inevitable.

Such methods as Total Physical Response, the Natural Approach, and Counseling-Learning, on the other hand, operate without an explicit syllabus model. The contributions of methods developers like Asher (1977), Curran (1972), and Gattegno (1976) result from individual instructional philosophies and personal theories concerning the factors that promote successful learning. Asher, Curran, and Gattegno came to language teaching from backgrounds in different disciplines: psychology, counseling, and education. They were prompted not by reactions to linguistic or sociolinguistic theories but rather by their personal philosophies of how an individual's learning potential can be maximized.

Asher's Total Physical Response, for example, is designed to provide language-learning experiences that reduce the stress and anxiety adults experience in foreign language learning. "The task is to invent or discover instructional strategies that reduce the intense stress that students experience" (Asher 1977: 2). One way to reduce stress is to delay production and to build up receptive competence first. One of the primary conditions for success is through relating language production to physical actions, as Harold Palmer had advocated twenty years earlier:

In view of the fact that talking activities are invariably preceded by a more or less long period of purely receptive work, mostly in the form of reacting physically to verbal stimuli, it would seem to be no exaggeration to state that the execution of orders is a prerequisite to the acquiring of powers of expression ... no method of teaching foreign speech is likely to be economical or successful which does not include in the first period a very considerable proportion of that type of classroom work which consists of the carrying out by the pupil ... of orders issued by the teacher. (Palmer and Palmer 1959: 39)

Asher's view of language is not far removed from the lexico-grammatical conceptions of language current in the 1920s or 1930s. Asher accepts this as a given but proposes alternative procedures for teaching it. His method depends not on published materials, but rather allows teachers to develop their own syllabuses and materials as long as the recommended instructional procedures are followed.

Curran's Counseling-Learning is likewise predicated upon assumptions about how people best learn rather than on theories about the nature of language. It is based on Curran's "whole-person" model of learning and is an application of group counseling procedures. Curran saw the problems of adult foreign-language learning as resulting from emotional or affective barriers created by learners, and his method is designed to counter the anxiety and negative emotions of defense that he believed impede foreign-language learning in adults. For him, learning is a social phenomenon that takes place within the supportive environment of a "community" of fellow learners. Language learning involves a progression from total dependence on the teacher (the counselor, or "knower" in his terms) to a mature, independent relationship. As with Total Physical Response, Curran's approach provides neither a predetermined syllabus nor materials. Specific linguistic or communicative objectives are not provided, which means that it is ultimately a teacher-dependent approach in which procedure, rather than content, is specified.

Gattegno's Silent Way likewise draws on his individual philosophy of learning, which involves the conscious use of one's intelligence to heighten learning through listening, generalizing, and expressing oneself. The teacher is trained to engage students in experimenting, practicing, and problem solving, and the teacher is relatively silent for much of this process. Language is presented through pictures, objects, or situations to enable links to be made more directly between sounds and meanings. Word charts, pictures, and colored rods are used to stimulate speech. There is, however, a strong linguistic focus to Silent Way. Vocabulary, grammar, and accuracy are emphasized, although mastery of language is claimed not to be the only goal: "Learning is not seen as the means of accumulating knowledge but as the means of becoming a more proficient learner in whatever one is engaged in" (Gattegno 1972: 89).

I mention these methods not because they are any more or less convincing than proposals by Terrell, Lozanov, and others, but because they reflect so clearly a primary concern with instructional theory and procedures rather than with syllabus issues. Whereas in the case of structural/situational, aural/oral, or notional/functional approaches the development of classroom techniques follows the prior specification of objectives or syllabus content, with Total Physical Response, Counseling-Learning, and Silent Way the syllabus is an outcome of the instructional procedures. TPR and C-L allow teachers to develop their own syllabuses. What they and other learning-based methods have in common is a formula that links classroom procedures to language-learning assumptions. As Gattegno observes confidently of his own approach:

The proposals made ... work much better than any other currently available, because for the first time the learners in their concreteness are taken into account. This is a completely new idea in education. It was much easier to be concerned with languages and their steadiness than with moody and unpredictable boys and girls, and men and women whose appearances revealed nothing about their functionings. (1972: v–vi)

Implementation factors

So far my account of the two different kinds of issues that methods are a response to has not uncovered any dramatic secrets. But methods have a life beyond the classroom, beyond the questions of content, philosophy, and procedure that characterize them. The rise and fall of methods depends upon a variety of factors extrinsic to a method itself and often reflects the influence of fads and fashions, of profit seekers and promoters, as well as the forces of the intellectual marketplace. It is these factors that give a method its secret life, and to which we now turn.

The form a method takes

A crucial factor in determining the fate of a method is the form in which the method is available to those who wish to use it. Some methods exist primarily in the form of materials – that is, as a textbook that embodies the principles of selection, organization, and presentation of content the method follows, together with a set of specifications as to how the materials are to be used. Structural/situational, aural/oral, and notional/functional approaches to teaching or syllabus design provide principles that can be used in writing textbooks. This gives them a decided advantage over instructional philosophies that depend solely on the teacher's skill and ingenuity and that do not provide a basic text. The former – the text-based methods – can be used without additional training. The latter may require teachers to take special courses, involving an investment of both time and money. Consequently, methods that lead to texts have a much higher adoption and survival rate than those that do not. Audiolingual and communicative methods are widely known for this reason; they merely require that a teacher buy a text and read the teacher's manual. Methods such as those of Lozanov (Lozanov 1979) or Gattegno, on the other hand, are known in practice only to those who have received special training in their use.

Publish or perish

Where there are student texts and the possibility of widespread adoptions and sales, there are also publishers. If an abstract concept like that of a notional syllabus can be applied to the production of textbooks, publishers have everything to gain by making such concepts comprehensible and widely known. The terms *notional/functional* and *communicative* sell. Many an underpaid academic has consequently succumbed to attractive offers to lightly work over an audiolingual or structural course so that it can be published in a new edition bearing a notional/functional or communicative label. Publishers promote texts at conferences, book exhibits, and through direct visits to schools and institutions, and they finance workshops and lectures by authorities whose names lend credence to the philosophies behind the texts. The message is that anyone who has an innovative instructional philosophy to market had better make it dependent upon the use of a student text; otherwise, no major publisher will take it seriously. Publishers associated with notional/functional or communicative approaches in language teaching are major international publishing houses. The publishers of Asher's, Curran's, and Gattegno's works, on the other hand, are do-it-yourself presses like Sky Oaks Productions, Apple River Press, and Educational Solutions.

Support networks

Methods need more than the support of the publishing industry to gain credibility. They need to be acknowledged as legitimate and valid responses to genuine educational issues rather than as the personal beliefs of articulate and persuasive promoters. They need the support of academics and the sanction of professional teaching organizations; they need the visibility that adoptions by universities and educational agencies afford; with luck they may be prescribed by departments of education and even by governments.

In 1902, for example, the French Minister of Education gave official approval to the Direct Method. It became the only approved method for teaching foreign languages in France, and in the same year it also became the approved method in Germany. This could have meant a boon for publishers, except that the Direct Method was a philosophy of instructional procedures rather than a specification for syllabus design and materials production. Like the Silent Way and Counseling-Learning, it could not readily be translated into textbooks and materials, and this was one reason why it failed to survive despite the support it received in high places. More recently in France, the Audio-Visual Method received the sanction of the Département de la Coopération through its widespread use of the series *Voix et Images de France* for teaching French abroad. The Audio-Visual Method continues to enjoy the prestige that accrues from having been the "official" French method for so many years.

Universities and academics likewise play a crucial role in influencing the fate of methods. It is doubtful if Gattegno's Silent Way or Curran's Counseling-Learning would have attracted so much attention in the 1970s among the ESL profession in the United States without the sanction of Stevick's uncritical treatment of them in his books *Memory, Meaning, and Method* (1976) and *A Way and Ways* (1980). The Michigan methodology of the 1950s, embodied in the work of Charles Fries and Robert Lado and their Michigan associates, was sold as much on the basis of its association with that then-prestigious institution as through
its content. The well-known Michigan series – the blue, red, green, and yellow books, based on the principles of the aural/oral method – reflected the scientific principles that America's first English language institute proudly acknowledged. They were supported by Fries's definitive texts on language learning and teaching, and by Lado's work on contrastive analysis. The philosophy behind the materials was spread through the

pages of Michigan's own journal – *Language Learning*, the first journal devoted to the new "science" of applied linguistics. Consequently, in the 1950s, the Michigan approach and the Michigan materials became nothing less than the "American way," the orthodox methodology of American English specialists in both the United States and abroad. Under such circumstances, it was hardly courteous to question the soundness of the materials themselves. In the late 1950s and 1960s the same sense of American self-assuredness helped consolidate the status of another American orthodoxy – audiolingualism.

National styles of thought and practice have likewise played an important part in spreading British views of methodology, and British applied linguists have over the years advocated a relatively uniform view of methodology. This has been disseminated rapidly and in a relatively standardized manner through the auspices of a governmental agency of international scope – the British Council, which since the late 1930s has been actively involved in promoting the teaching of English the British way. Among the various activities of the council are involvement in the direct teaching of English in many parts of the world, advisory and consultancy services to governments and their agencies, and the joint publication with Oxford University Press of the *English Language Teaching Journal* – the British journal of English language teaching thought and practice.

The British Council has for many years served the interests of British methodologists by providing an instant and international outlet for their ideas, as well as funds to present their latest speculations at international forums and conferences. It is doubtful if communicative language teaching or the British approach to syllabus and program design could have been established so rapidly without the council's help. John Munby, for example, is a British Council employee. Even before the publication of his book *Communicative Syllabus Design* (1978), in which a model for the design of ESL courses is proposed, the Munby model had been presented in British Council-sponsored workshops and used as the basis for several council consultancy projects in different parts of the world. No one can blame the British for selling things British, but one wonders what the consequences might have been if, in the early 1970s, the council had adopted Curran's or Gattegno's methods as a basis for its global language teaching operations.

Curriculum and evaluation: the missing element

We have seen that there are many complex elements underlying the instructional system we refer to in language teaching as a method, and an equally complex set of factors comes into play in establishing a method and in giving it credibility and support within the language-teaching profession. But if the study of methods is to assume a more significant role within the applied linguistics of language teaching, it must focus on more than merely the descriptive and implementational aspects of methods. It must, above all, address the issue of accountability. What criteria can be used to assess and evaluate the often competing claims of methods and their advocates? Surely the claims of any method or approach are only as good as the evidence that can be found to support them. Yet very few methods developers or their supporters have made any attempt to gather evidence that could be used to evaluate their claims. It is rare to find methods writers even contemplating the possibility or desirability of evaluation through empirical studies and experimentation. Few suggest that their recommendations need anything other than instant implementation on a world-wide basis. Evaluation, however, has an established role within curriculum development, and evaluation procedures applied elsewhere in curriculum planning can serve the cause of methods evaluation equally well.

In curriculum development, the selection of the teaching method is but one phase in the curriculum development process. Curriculum development in language teaching includes the following additional procedures (see Chapter 1):

1. *Situational analysis*, in which the parameters of a language program are determined; relevant information about the learners, the teachers, constraints of time, money, and the institution defines a set of variables that can potentially play a crucial role in determining the success of any innovation in curriculum.
2. *Needs analysis*, in which the language needs of the learners are assessed through such means as diagnostic tests, interviews with learners and teachers, observation, and self-reports.
3. *Task analysis*, in which the task the learners will ultimately have to perform in the target language are determined, and the communicative and linguistic demands of the tasks ascertained.
4. *Goal setting*, in which both broad and specific program objectives are identified, reflecting the learners' entry level, communicative needs, and the program constraints.
5. *Selection of learning experiences*, in which teaching activities are developed that address the objectives established in (4) and that relate to the underlying skills, strategies, and processes that learners need to acquire in order to be able to perform their communicative needs in the target language.
6. *Evaluation*, both formative and summative, product- and process-oriented.

The literature on methods addresses almost exclusively the fifth procedure listed. But if language teaching is approached from the perspective of curriculum development, then goal setting, the development of ob-

41

jectives, the specification of the communicative and linguistic processes and skills needed to attain these objectives, the selection of teaching procedures, and the evaluation of the outcomes are seen to be interrelated aspects of the broader and more complex planning activity known as language-program design. The important issues, then, are not which method to adopt, but how to develop procedures and instructional activities that will enable program objectives to be attained. This is not a question of choosing a method but of developing methodology. This requires the use of accepted principles of program design and evaluation, from which gains in particular aspects of language proficiency can be demonstrated to result from particular program designs and instructional systems. The largely anecdotal and poorly researched literature on methods in language teaching demonstrates the need for a more informed approach to methods issues in our profession.

A claim that all methods make is that the adoption of a specific method will lead to higher levels of language achievement than the use of other methods. There are two ways to verify such claims: we can either look for evidence of the absolute effectiveness of the method, or we can seek evidence for its relative effectiveness (Long 1983). The first of these is concerned with whether students taught by the method (or program) make gains relative to their proficiency in the language at the start of the course of instruction. As Long points out, to demonstrate that it is necessary not only to compare pretest and posttest results but also to show that the results obtained were achieved as a result of the method or program rather than in spite of it. This involves using a true experimental design. To demonstrate the relative effectiveness of a method, on the other hand, we would have to demonstrate that the method produced better results than an alternative method or program.

An excellent example of the use of an experimental design to test the claims of a method is given in a study by Wagner and Tilney (1983). The method they examined was derived from Suggestopedy (Lozanov 1979) and Superlearning (Ostrander and Schroeder 1979). Suggestopedy is based on a learning theory known as Suggestology, which utilizes music, parapsychology, and other techniques to enhance the learning powers of students. Advocates of Superlearning claim that learners can learn 2,000 lexical items in 23 days by studying just three hours a day. Wagner and Tilney designed a study to evaluate these claims. In their study 21 subjects were randomly assigned to one of three experimental treatments or modes of vocabulary presentation. The experimental group received German language training with Superlearning methodology. A second group received the same Superlearning methodology but without the use of Baroque music – the use of which is a feature of Lozanov's method. A third group receiving language training in the classroom served as a no-contact control group. Levels of vocabulary learning in each group were compared. The results revealed no significant improvement across the five-week experimental period. When modes of presentation were compared, those subjects taught by a traditional classroom method learned significantly more vocabulary than those taught according to Superlearning principles.

Unfortunately, studies of this kind are all too rare in the vast promotional literature on methods. Too often, techniques and instructional philosophies are advocated from a philosophical or theoretical stance rather than on the basis of any form of evidence. Methods are promoted and justified through reference to intuitively appealing assertions and theories, which when repeated by those in positions of authority assume the status of dogma. Both the Natural Approach (Terrell 1977) and Communicative Language Teaching, for example, are based on the assumption that "communicative" classrooms provide a better environment for second language acquisition than classrooms dominated by formal instruction. Yet no studies have been undertaken by those promoting this view to demonstrate that classrooms in which learners are encouraged to use the target language for problem solving, communicative tasks, information exchange, and meaningful interaction are indeed more conducive to successful language learning than classrooms in which the teacher dominates much of the teaching time or where the primary focus of activities is on more controlled and less creative uses of language. Despite the intuitive appeal of claims for the value of natural communication in the classroom and the anecdotes used to support them, there is equally convincing anecdotal evidence to the contrary that suggests that such activities promote fossilization and pidginization by placing learners in situations where the demands of their performance soon outpace their grammatical competence (Higgs and Clifford 1982). The claims for the value of communicative classrooms, interactive games, and information-gap activities cannot be accepted without data on the types of language learning that result from such activities.

The need for rigorous evaluation procedures in planning methodological innovations is well demonstrated in the literature on "procedural syllabuses" (Johnson 1982, Prabhu 1983). Prabhu describes an "experiment" being conducted in Southern India to determine if "structure can best be learned when attention is focused on meaning" (cited in Johnson 1982: 135). The primary focus in the study Prabhu is directing is on whether students can learn English from an instructional program organized almost entirely around the use of communicative and problem-solving tasks and procedures (hence the term "task syllabus" or "procedural syllabus"). Prabhu has made several claims concerning the greater effectiveness of this approach when compared to conventional methods of language teaching. If the method is indeed more effective than traditional modes of instruction, it deserves to be taken seriously. But in order to be a candidate for serious consideration, a number of issues need to be identified as part of the evaluation process.

First, the goals and objectives of the program need to be described and criterion measures specified. Is the method primarily concerned with teaching grammar, as the quote from Prabhu suggests? If so, in order to determine the absolute effectiveness of the approach, pre- and post-testing would be required to determine if the students had indeed made gains during the period of instruction. Until the objectives for the program are specified, it is impossible to decide what criteria would be needed to judge the program's success or failure. As we have seen, however, gains in pre- and posttest scores would not in themselves enable us to determine if the method itself, rather than some factor extrinsic to the method, had been responsible for the gains. For this, a true experimental design would be required. If the hidden agenda of the program, on the other hand, is to develop more efficient learning strategies in learners (as some of Prabhu's recent pronouncements suggest), these strategies need to be specified as a basis for testing – also through a true experimental design. Unfortunately, in the Prabhu study neither objectives nor evaluation was incorporated into the program design. This makes any serious consideration of his claims impossible. Carefully designed research takes the same amount of time and effort to conduct as poorly designed research. In the case of carefully designed research, however, we are able to learn something from its results (Scovel 1979).

Once an instructional theory takes the form of a method, with theoretical bases in language and learning theory and operationalized practices in syllabus design and teaching procedures, claims made at each level of method organization must be regarded as hypotheses awaiting verification or falsification. If a method advocates providing a rich linguistic environment for learners and proposes specific techniques and tasks for generating such an environment (as do both the Natural Approach and Communicative Language Teaching), then data must be sought on the types of language and linguistic interaction that such activities actually generate when used with ESL learners in language classrooms. The language-teaching literature is full of books and articles about the value of games and group work in language teaching, for example, but few empirical studies have been carried out to provide data on the sort of interaction and language use such activities produce.

Likewise, if a method makes use of a particular kind of syllabus (e.g., grammatical, notional, lexical), how valid is the selection of items contained in the syllabus? Many communicative texts, for example, draw on the *Threshold Level* syllabus (Van Ek and Alexander 1975). But this is a subjective and speculative document based largely on the intuitions of its compilers. Is this all that is necessary to develop communicative syllabuses? The *Threshold* syllabus lacks any form of validation, and

even a cursory examination of it suggests that it contains major deficiencies. An example of the sort of research that is needed to help validate
such taxonomies is a study by Pearson (1983). She collected empirical
data on two speech acts from the *Threshold* list – agreement and disagreement. She collected data on how these speech acts were performed
conversationally by native speakers and compared her findings with the
way these speech acts are represented in communicative syllabuses and
texts. Not surprisingly, there was a low degree of fit between the empirical real-world conversational data and the ESL textbooks.

The supposed behaviors of teachers and learners in classrooms using
specific methods likewise cannot be accepted at face value. Long and
Sato (1983), for example, looked at language use in classes taught by
teachers trained in "communicative" methodology and compared it with
how native speakers conversed in non-classroom settings with non-
natives of the same level of proficiency as the classroom learners. They
found the type of language used by the "communicative" teachers to be
very different from the language of natural communication outside the
classroom. It shared many of the features of the mechanical question-
and-answer drills characteristic of audiolingual classrooms. Long (1983)
consequently advocates a process component in program and methods
evaluation that focuses on what actually goes on in ESL classrooms,
rather than just on the results of instruction (a product-approach to
evaluation).

Conclusion

We can see that the field of methods in language teaching has been
revitalized – by different theories concerning the nature of language, by
new theories concerning the central process of language acquisition, by
innovative proposals for syllabus development and the design of instructional systems, and by the use of a variety of novel practices, techniques,
and procedures in the language classroom. In discussing the secret life
of methods we have brought to light some facts about methods and
some less often talked-about aspects of their evolution. At the same time,
we have attempted to draw attention to the broader issues of curriculum
development in language program design and to the weak empirical
basis on which most methods are founded. If the methodology of language teaching is to move beyond speculation and dogma, its practitioners must become more seriously concerned with the issues of
accountability and evaluation than recent history has evidenced. This may
in turn mean shifting our attention to the relevant facts and procedures
of curriculum development, rather than concerning ourselves with the
unsubstantiated and often irrelevant claims of methods promoters.

4 A noncontrastive approach to error analysis

Identifying and analyzing interference between languages has traditionally been a central aspect of the study of bilingualism. The intrusion of features of one language into another in the speech of bilinguals has been studied at the levels of phonology, morphology, and syntax. The systems of the contact languages themselves have sometimes been contrasted, and an important outcome of contrastive studies has been the prediction of specific difficulties involved in acquiring a second language. "Those elements that are similar to the (learner's) native language will be simple for him, and those areas that are different will be difficult" (Lado 1957: 2). In the last two decades language teaching has derived considerable impetus from the application of contrastive studies. As recently as 1967, Politzer affirmed: "Perhaps the least questioned and least questionable application of linguistics is the contribution of contrastive analysis. Especially in the teaching of languages for which no considerable and systematic teaching experience is available, contrastive analysis can highlight and predict the difficulties of the pupils" (1967: 151).

Studies of second language acquisition, however, tend to imply that contrastive analysis may be most predictive at the level of phonology, and least predictive at the syntactic level. A recent study of Spanish-English bilingualism, for example, states:

Many people assume, following logic that is easy to understand, that the errors made by bilinguals are caused by their mixing Spanish and English. One of the most important conclusions this writer draws from the research in this project is that interference from Spanish is not a major factor in the way bilinguals construct sentences and use the language. (Smith 1969)

This chapter focuses on several types of errors observed in the acquisition of English as a second language, which do not derive from transfer from another language. Excluded from discussion are what may be called interlanguage errors, that is, errors caused by the interference of the learner's mother tongue. A different class of errors is represented by sentences like *did he comed, what you are doing, he coming from Israel, make him to do it, I can to speak French*. Errors of this nature are frequent, regardless of the learner's language background. They may be called intralingual and developmental errors. Rather than reflecting the learner's inability to separate two languages, intralingual and developmental errors reflect the learner's competence at a particular stage and illustrate some of the general characteristics of language acquisition. Their origins are found within the structure of English itself and through reference to the strategy by which a second language is acquired and taught (cf. Cook 1969; Stern 1969). A sample of such errors is shown in Tables 1–6 (see the appendix at the end of this chapter). These are representative of the sorts of errors we might expect from anyone learning English as a second language. They are the typical, systematic errors in English usage that are found in numerous case studies of the English errors of speakers of particular mother tongues. They are the sorts of mistakes that persist from week to week and that recur from one year to the next with any group of learners. They cannot be described as mere failures to memorize a segment of language or as occasional lapses in performance due to memory limitations, fatigue, and the like (Corder 1967). In some learners they represent final grammatical competence; in others they may be indications of transitional competence.

Tables 1–6 are taken from studies of English errors produced by speakers of Japanese, Chinese, Burmese, French, Czech, Polish, Tagalog, Maori, Maltese, and the major Indian and West African languages. From these sources I have selected those errors that occurred in a cross section of the samples. By studying intralingual and developmental errors within the framework of a theory of second-language learning, and through examining typical cases of the teaching of the forms from which they are derived, it may be possible to point the way toward teaching procedures that take account of the learner's strategy for acquiring a second language.

Types and causes of intralingual and developmental errors

An examination of the errors in Tables 1–6 suggests that intralingual errors are those that reflect the general characteristics of rule learning, such as faulty generalization, incomplete application of rules, and failure to learn conditions under which rules apply. Developmental errors illustrate the learner attempting to build up hypotheses about the English language from his limited experience of it in the classroom or textbook. For convenience of presentation, Tables 1–6 will be discussed in terms of (1) overgeneralization, (2) ignorance of rule restrictions, (3) incomplete application of rules, (4) false concepts hypothesized.

Overgeneralization

Jakobovits defines generalization or transfer as "the use of previously available strategies in new situations . . . . In second-language learning . . . some of these strategies will prove helpful in organizing the facts about the second language, but others, perhaps due to superficial similarities, will be misleading and inapplicable" (Jakobovits 1969a: 32; see also Jakobovits 1969b). Overgeneralization covers instances where learners create a deviant structure on the basis of their experience of other structures in the target language. For example (see Table 1, parts 1, 3, 4, 8), *he can sings, we are hope, it is occurs, he come from.* Overgeneralization generally involves the creation of one deviant structure in place of two regular structures. It may be the result of learners reducing their linguistic burden. With the omission of the third-person -*s*, overgeneralization removes the necessity for concord, thus relieving the learner of considerable effort. Dušková, discussing the omission of third-person -*s*, notes:

Since (in English) all grammatical persons take the same zero verbal ending except the third person singular in the present tense . . . omissions of the -*s* in the third person singular may be accounted for by the heavy pressure of all other endingless forms. The endingless form is generalised for all persons, just as the form *was* is generalised for all persons and both numbers in the past tense . . . . Errors in the opposite direction like *there does not exist any exact rules* may be explained either as being due to hypercorrection . . . or as being due to generalisation of the 3rd person singular ending for the 3rd person plural. (Dušková 1969: 20)

Overgeneralization is associated with redundancy reduction. It may occur, for instance, with items that are contrasted in the grammar of the language but that do not carry significant and obvious contrast for the learner. The -*ed* marker, in narrative or in other past contexts, often appears to carry no meaning, since pastness is usually indicated lexically in stories, and the essential notion of sequence in narrative can be expressed equally well in the present – *Yesterday I go to the university and I meet my new professor.* Thus the learner cuts down the tasks involved in sentence production. Ervin-Tripp suggests that "possibly the morphological and syntactic simplifications of second-language learners correspond to some simplification common among children (i.e., mother-tongue speakers) learning the same language" (Ervin-Tripp 1969: 33).

Certain types of teaching techniques increase the frequency of overgeneralized structures. Many pattern drills and transform exercises are made up of utterances that can interfere with each other to produce a hybrid structure:

Teacher	*Instruction*	*Student*
"*He walks quickly.*"	Change to continuous form	"*He is walks quickly.*"

This has been described as overlearning of a structure (Wolfe 1967: 180). At other times, *he walks* may be contrasted with *he is walking, he sings* with *he can sing,* and a week later, without any teaching of the forms the learner produces *he can sings, he is walks.*

Ignorance of rule restrictions

Closely related to the generalization of deviant structures is failure to observe the restrictions of existing structures, that is, the application of rules to contexts where they do not apply. *The man who I saw him* (Table 3, part 2) violates the limitation on subjects in structures with *who. I made him to do it* (Table 4) ignores restrictions on the distribution of *make.* These are again a type of generalization or transfer, since the learner is using a previously acquired rule in a new situation. Some rule-restriction errors may be accounted for in terms of analogy; other instances may result from the rote learning of rules.

Analogy seems to be a major factor in the misuse of prepositions (Table 4). The learner, encountering a particular preposition with one type of verb, attempts by analogy to use the same preposition with similar verbs. He *showed me the book* leads to *he explained me the book; he said to me* gives *he asked to me; we talked about it,* therefore *we discussed about it; ask him to do it* produces *make him to do it; go with him* gives *follow with him.* Some pattern exercises appear to encourage incorrect rules being applied through analogy. Here is part of a pattern exercise that practices *enable, allow, make, cause, permit.*

Expansion joints Safety valves We	*permit* *allow*	the pipes the steam the metal	*to*	expand or contract. escape from the boiler. cool slowly.
The heat Weakness in the metal	*made*	the metal melt. it fracture under tension.		
The heat Weakness in the metal	*caused*	the metal it	*to*	melt. fracture under tension.

It is followed by an exercise in which the student is instructed to complete a number of statements using verbs and prepositions from the table: *The rise in temperature – the mercury – rise up the tube. The risk of an explosion – the workers – leave the factory. The speed of the train – it – leave the rails on the curve . . . .*

From a class of twenty-three with mixed language backgrounds, no fewer than thirteen produced sentences like *The rise in temperature made the mercury to rise up the tube.* Practicing *make* in the same context as *allow it to, permit it to, enable it to,* precipitates confusion. Other instances of analogous constructions may be less easy to avoid. Table 3, part 2, includes *this is not fit to drink it, the man who I saw him*. By analogy with the learner's previous experience of subject + verb + object constructions, the learner feels that there is something incomplete about *that's the man who I saw*, and so adds the object, after the verb, as he has been taught to do elsewhere.

Failure to observe restrictions in article usage may also derive from analogy, with the learner rationalizing a deviant usage from his previous experience of English. This may happen even when the mother tongue is close to the English usage. F. G. French gives the following example of how a common article mistake is produced by rational analogy (French 1949). In English we say *The sparrow is a small bird. Sparrows are small birds*. Since the statements are exactly parallel, a logical substitute for the second language would be *The sparrows are small birds*. In Burmese, the equivalents would be

sa gale thi	nge thaw	nget	pyit thi
The sparrow	small	bird	is

and in the plural

sa gale mya thi	nge thaw	nget mya	pyit kya thi
The sparrows	small	birds	are

Instead of following the form of the mother tongue, however, the learner, having first produced *The sparrows are* from *The sparrow is*, sees a parallel between *sparrows* and *birds*, and produces the common error *The sparrows are the small birds*. A similar example is noted by Aguas involving Tagalog-speaking students (Aguas 1964).

Incomplete application of rules

Under the category of incomplete application of rules we may note the occurrence of structures whose deviancy represents the degree of development of the rules required to produce acceptable utterances. For example, across background languages, systematic difficulty in the use of questions can be observed. A statement form may be used as a question, one of the transformations in a series may be omitted, or a question word may simply be added to the statement form. Despite extensive teaching of both the question and the statement forms, a grammatical question form may never become a part of competence in the second language. Redundancy may be an explanatory factor. The second-language learner, interested perhaps primarily in communication, can achieve quite efficient communication without needing to master more than elementary rules in question usage. Motivation to achieve communication may exceed motivation to produce grammatically correct sentences. A further clue may be provided by classroom use of questions.

The use of questions is a common teaching device. Typically they are used not to find out something, but as a means of eliciting sentences. Alternatively, the statement form may be used as a means of eliciting questions through a transform exercise. Classroom observation suggests that the use of a question may be unrelated to the skills it is meant to establish. Here are some examples:

Teacher's question	*Student's response*
Do you read much?	Yes, I read much.
Do you cook very much?	Yes, I cook very much.
Ask her what the last film she saw was called.	What was called the last film you saw?
What was she saying?	She saying she would ask him.
What does she tell him?	She tell him to hurry.
What's he doing?	He opening the door.
Ask her how long it take.	How long it takes?
Will they soon be ready?	Yes, they soon be ready.
How much does it cost?	It cost one dollar.
What does he have to do?	He have to do write the address.
What does he ask his mother?	He ask his mother for the address.

As this sample illustrates, when a question is used to elicit a sentence, the teacher often has to correct the answer to counteract the influence of the teacher's question. Some textbooks proceed almost entirely through the use of questions; others avoid excessive use of questions by using signals to indicate the type of sentence required. These may reduce the total number of deviant sentences produced.

False concepts hypothesized

In addition to the wide range of intralingual errors that have to do with faulty rule-learning at various levels, there is a class of developmental errors that derive from faulty comprehension of distinctions in the target language. These sometimes result from poor gradation of teaching items. The form *was*, for example, may be interpreted as a marker of the past tense: *one day it was happened* (Table 1, part 2); and *is* may be understood to be the corresponding marker of the present tense: *he is speaks French* (Table 1, part 1). In Table 2, part 4, we find the progressive form instead of the simple past in narrative; elsewhere we encounter confusion between *too, so,* and *very,* between *come* and *go,* and so on. In particular instances I have traced errors of this sort to classroom presentation, and to presentation that is based on contrastive analysis of English and another language or on contrasts within English itself.

Here is an example of how the present progressive came to be understood as a narrative tense (see also Chapter 11). The simple present tense in English is the normal tense used for actions seen as a whole, for events that develop according to a plan, or for sequences of events taking place at the present moment (cf. Close 1959: 59; Hirtle 1967: 40–1). Thus the sports commentator's *Now Anderson takes the ball, passes it to Smith . . .* and the cooking demonstrator's *I take two eggs, now I add the sugar. . . .* How do we find this use represented in textbooks for teaching English as a second language?

Typically one finds that the progressive form has been used for these functions instead. A recent audiovisual course contains many sequences like the following: *The lift is going down to the ground floor. Ted is getting out of the lift. He is leaving the office building. Ted is standing at the entrance of the office building. He is looking up at the sky. . . .*

This is not a normal use of English. The usual tense for a sequence of events taking place "at the moment" is the present tense, the progressive form being used only when a single event is extracted from a sequence, the sequence itself being indicated by the present forms. This presentation of the progressive form led a number of students to assume that the progressive form in English is a tense for telling stories and for describing successions of events in either the present or the past.

The reason atypical verb use occurs in many textbooks appears to be related to a contrastive approach to language teaching. In this example, the course designer has attempted to establish the use of the progressive form in a context in which the present form is appropriate. It is often felt that a considerable amount of time should be devoted to the progressive form, since it does not exist in most learner's mother tongues. Excessive attention to points of difference at the expense of realistic English is characteristic of much contrastive-based teaching. My experience of such teaching confirms Ritchie's prediction: "A course that concentrates too much on 'the main trouble spots' without due attention to the structure of the foreign language as a whole, will leave the learner with a patchwork of unfruitful, partial generalizations" (Ritchie 1967: 129).

Many courses progress on a related assumption, namely, that contrasts within the language are an essential aid to learning. "Presenting items in contrast can lighten the teacher's and the student's work and consequently speed up the learning process" (Hok 1963: 129). Here are some examples of actual learning from materials thought out in terms of contrast.

George (1962) notes that a frequent way of introducing the simple and progressive forms is to establish the contrast:

is = present state, *is* + *ing* = present action.

This contrast is in fact quite false to English. When the past is introduced, it is often introduced as a past state. *He was sick.* This lays the groundwork for the learner to complete the picture of present and past in English by analogy:

is = present state, *is* + *ing* = present action,
was = past state ∴ *was* + *ing* = past action.

Thus *was* or *was* + *ing* may be used as past markers. (See Chapters 11 and 12.) Used together with the verb + *ed* this produces such sentences as *he was climbed the tree*. Interpreted as the form for "past actions" it gives *I was going downtown yesterday* instead of *I went downtown yesterday*.

Table 3 shows examples of the confusion of *too, so,* and *very*. Other substitutions are common, such as the use of *teach* for *learn*, of *do* for *make*, of *come* for *go*, of *bring* for *take*. Learners often feel that the members of such pairs are synonyms, despite every attempt to demonstrate that they have contrastive meanings. Such confusion is sometimes attributable to premature contrastive presentation.

Here are the occurrences of *too* and *very* in a first reader that tells the story of a group of children who light a fire in the snow in front of an old house: *The house is empty because it's old. . . . I'm very cold. England is too cold. . . . The fire is very big. . . . It's very big. It's a very big fire. The firemen are going to put water on the fire because it's too big.*

The course designers intended to establish a contrast between *too* and *very*, but in so doing they completely confuse the meaning of the two forms. From the presentation – and from the viewpoint of a young learner – they have the same meanings. Thus we have the parallelism between:

It's too big and it's dangerous.
The fire is dangerous. It's very big.

How could a child, following such a presentation, avoid saying *This is a too big house?* *Too* would be more safely taught out of association with *very*, and in contexts where it did not appear to be a substitute for *very*, as, for example, in a structure with *too* + adjective + infinitive – *this box is too heavy to lift.*

Other courses succeed in establishing confusion between *too, so,* and *very* by offering exercises like these:

1. Reword the following sentences using *too. This coffee is so hot that I can't drink it. I've got so fat that I can't wear this dress now.*
   Example: *This soup is very hot. I can't drink it. This soup is too hot (for me) to drink.*
2. Remake these sentences using *too. This hat is very big; he's only a little boy. This grammar is very difficult; a child can't understand it.*

53

This type of exercise leads to the errors described in Table 3, part 4. The common confusion of *since* and *for* (Table 4, part 4) is sometimes reinforced by similar exercises, such as those that require choosing the correct preposition in sentences like:

I have been here (for/since) a week.
We have been in Canada (for/since) 1968.

Constant attempts to contrast related areas of English can thus have results quite different from those we intend. As yet, there is no substantial confirmation that a contrastive approach to teaching is likely to be a priori more effective than any other approach. Classroom experience and common sense often suggest that a safer strategy for instruction is to minimize opportunities for confusion by selecting nonsynonymous contexts for related words, by treating them at different times and by avoiding exercises based on contrast and transformation.

Conclusion

An analysis of the major types of intralingual and developmental errors – overgeneralization, ignorance of rule restrictions, incomplete application of rules, and the building of false systems or concepts – may lead us to examine our teaching materials for evidence of the language-learning assumptions that underlie them. Many current teaching practices are based on the notion that learners will photographically reproduce anything that is given to them and that if they do not, it is hardly the business of the teacher or textbook writer. It has been remarked that

very surprisingly there are few published descriptions of how or what children learn. There are plenty of descriptions of what the teacher did and what materials were presented to the children, but little about what mistakes the children made and how these can be explained, or of what generalizations and learning strategies the children seem to be developing. . . . It may be that the child's strategy of learning is totally or partially independent of the methods by which he is being taught. (Dakin 1969: 107–11)

Interference from the mother tongue is clearly a major source of difficulty in second-language learning, and contrastive analysis has proved valuable in locating areas of interlanguage interference. Many errors, however, derive from the strategies employed by the learner in language acquisition, and from the mutual interference of items within the target language. These cannot be accounted for by contrastive analysis. Teaching techniques and procedures should take account of the structural and developmental conflicts that can come about in language learning.

Appendix: typical intralingual and developmental errors

Major sources for Table 1–6 are French 1949; Dušková 1969; Arabski 1968; Estacia 1964 (especially comments by Meyerstein and Ansre); Richards 1968; Bhaskar 1962; Grelier n.d.; Aguas 1964.

TABLE 1. ERRORS IN THE PRODUCTION OF VERB GROUPS

---

1. *be + verb stem* for *verb stem*

   We are live in this hut
   The sentence is occurs ...
   We are hope ...
   He is speaks French
   The telegraph is remain ...
   We are walk to school every day.

---

2. *be + verb stem +* for *verb stem + ed*

   Farmers are went to their houses
   He was died last year
   One day it was happened
   They are opened the door

---

3. Wrong form after *do*

   He did not found ...
   He did not agreed ...
   The man does not cares for his life
   He did not asks me
   He does not has ...

---

4. Wrong form after modal verb

   Can be regard as ...
   We can took him out
   I can saw it
   It can drawing heavy loads
   They can used it
   It can use in state processions
   She cannot goes
   She cannot to go
   They would became
   We must made
   We can to see
   We must worked hard

---

5. *be* omitted before *verb + stem + ed* (participle)

   He born in England
   It used in church during processions
   They satisfied with their lot
   He disgusted
   He reminded of the story

6. *ed* omitted after *be + participle verb stem*

   The sky is cover with clouds
   He was punish
   Some trees are uproot

7. *be* omitted before *verb + ing*

   They running very fast
   The cows also crying
   The industry growing fast
   At 10:30 he going to kill the sheep

8. *verb stem* for *stem + s*

   He alway talk a lot
   He come from India
   She speak German as well

TABLE 2. ERRORS IN THE DISTRIBUTION OF VERB GROUPS

1. *be + verb + ing* for *be + verb + ed*

   I am interesting in that
   The country was discovering by Columbus

2. *be + verb + ing* for *verb stem*

   She is coming from Canada
   I am having my hair cut on Thursdays

3. *be + not + verb + ing* for *do + not + verb*

   I am not liking it
   Correct rules are not existing
   In French we are not having a present continuous tense and we are not
     knowing when to use it

4. *be + verb + ing* for *verb + ed* in narrative

> ... in the afternoon we were going back. On Saturday we were going down-town, and we were seeing a film and after we were meeting my brother

5. *verb stem* for *verb + ed* in narrative

> There were two animals who do not like each other. One day they go into a wood and there is no water. The monkey says to the elephant ...

6. *have + verb + ed* for *verb + ed*

> They had arrived just now
> He had come today
> I have written this letter yesterday
> Some weeks ago I have seen an English film
> He has arrived at noon
> I have learned English at school

7. *have + be + verb + ed* for *be + verb + ed*

> He has been married long ago
> He has been killed in 1956

8. *verb + ed* for *have + verb + ed*

> We correspond with them up to now
> This is the only country which I visited so far

9. *be + verb + ed* for *verb stem*

> This money is belonged to me
> The machine is comed from France

TABLE 3. MISCELLANEOUS ERRORS

1. Wrong verb form in adverb clause of time

> I shall meet him before the train will go
> We must wait here until the train will return

2. Object omitted or included unnecessarily

> We saw him play football and we admired
> This is not fit to drink it
> This is the king's horse which he rides it every day
> That is the man who I saw him

3.   Errors in tense sequence

He said that there is a boy in the garden
When the evening came we go to the pictures
When I came back I am tired

4.   Confusion of *too, so, very*

I am very lazy to stay at home
I am too tired that I cannot work
I am very tired that I cannot go
When I first saw him he was too young
Honey is too much sweet
The man became so exhausted and fell on the floor

TABLE 4. ERRORS IN THE USE OF PREPOSITIONS

1.	*with* instead of	Ø	met with her, married with her
		from	suffering with a cold
		against	fight with tyranny
		of	consist with
		at	laughed with my words
2.	*in* instead of	Ø	entered in the room, in the next day
		on	in T.V.
		with	fallen in love in Ophelia
		for	in this purpose
		at	in this time
		to	go in Poland
		by	the time in your watch
3.	*at* instead of	Ø	reached at a place, at last year
		by	held him at the left arm
		in	at the evening, interested at it
		to	went at Stratford
		for	at the first time
4.	*for* instead of	Ø	serve for God
		in	one bath for seven days
		of	suspected for, the position for Chinese coolies
		from	a distance for one country to another
		since	been here for the 6th of June

5.	*on* instead of	Ø	played on the piano for an hour
		in	on many ways, on that place, going on cars
		at	on the end
		with	angry on him
		of	countries on the world
		to	pays attention on it
6.	*of* instead of	Ø	aged of 44, drink less of wine
		in	rich of vitamins
		by	book of Hardy
		on	depends of civilization
		for	a reason of it
7.	*to* instead of	Ø	join to them, went to home, reached to the place
		for	an occupation to them
		of	his love to her

TABLE 5. ERRORS IN THE USE OF ARTICLES

1. Omission of *the*

    (a) before unique nouns — Sun is very hot / Himalayas are ...

    (b) before nouns of nationality — Spaniards and Arabs ...

    (c) before nouns made particular in context — At the conclusion of article / She goes to bazaar every day / She is mother of that boy

    (d) before a noun modified by a participle — Solution given in this article

    (e) before superlatives — Richest person

    (f) before a noun modified by an *of-phrase* — Institute of Nuclear Physics

2. *the* used instead of Ø

    (a) before proper names — The Shakespeare, the Sunday

    (b) before abstract nouns — The friendship, the nature, the science

    (c) before nouns behaving like abstract nouns — After the school, after the breakfast

    (d) before plural nouns — The complex structures are still developing

    (e) before *some* — The some knowledge

3. *a* used instead of *the*

    (a) before superlatives   a worst, a best boy in the class
    (b) before unique nouns   a sun becomes red

---

4. *a* instead of Ø

    (a) before a plural noun qualified   a holy places, a human beings,
        by an adjective   a bad news
    (b) before uncountables   a gold, a work
    (c) before an adjective   ... taken as a definite

---

5. Omission of *a*

    before class nouns defined by   he was good boy
      adjectives   he was brave man

TABLE 6. ERRORS IN THE USE OF QUESTIONS

---

1. Omission of inversion

    What was called the film?
    How many brothers she has?
    What she is doing?
    When she will be 15?
    Why this man is cold?
    Why streets are as bright as day?

---

2. *be* omitted before *verb* + *ing*

    When Jane coming?
    What she doing?
    What he saying?

---

3. Omission of *do*

    Where it happened?
    How it looks like?
    Why you went?
    How you say it in English?
    How much it costs?
    How long it takes?
    What he said?

---

4. Wrong form of auxiliary, or wrong form after auxiliary

   Do he go there?
   Did he went?
   Did he finished?
   Do he comes from your village?
   Which road did you come by?

5. Inversion retained in embedded sentences

   Please write down what is his name
   I told him I do not know how old was it
   I don't know how many are there in the box

5 Error analysis, interlanguage, and second language acquisition: a review

A significant feature of the development of language teaching as a discipline since the 1960s has been the broadening of our understanding of teaching and learning processes. The expansion of knowledge and theory in issues concerning the nature of language and language learning has generated a different perception of many aspects of language teaching. In the mid-1960s, Mackey in his influential book *Language Teaching Analysis* (1965) argued that the process of language teaching cannot be understood or evaluated until it has been described. His book outlined a framework for describing and analyzing the method component of teaching. In the 1970s, a similar perspective emerged with respect to language learning. It was recognized that many issues in language teaching could not be resolved without a clearer understanding of the nature of second- and foreign-language learning. A focus on language learning thus emerged as a complementary perspective to teaching. Beginning with an interest in learners' errors as evidence of learning processes, it subsequently developed into what is now referred to as the field of second language acquisition (SLA). In this chapter we survey how this change came about and describe the major issues that error analysis and second language acquisition research have addressed.

Error analysis and interlanguage studies

The collection, classification, and analysis of errors in the written and spoken performance of second- or foreign-language learners has had a role in applied linguistics and language teaching since at least the 1950s. In the late 1960s, however, the study of learners' errors assumed a new significance. The fields of error analysis (EA) and interlanguage studies came into prominence. Their focus was the psycholinguistic processes of second language acquisition and the status of learner-language systems (Corder 1978). The data for this research came from language learners' sentences and utterances in the target language. These were examined for evidence of specific language-learning strategies and processes in an attempt to develop a more comprehensive theory of second- and foreign-language learning. Learner utterances were said to constitute an *interlanguage* – a term that came to refer to a dynamic and evolving linguistic system that the learner constructed from target-language input through the use of innate learning strategies and heuristics.

This perspective on learner errors was very different from that of the earlier contrastive analysis/audiolingual paradigm, which was central in language-teaching theory and practice in the 1950s. From that position, second language acquisition was seen to involve the juxtaposition of two linguistic systems. This led to intersystemic interference, which was seen as a barrier to successful language learning. Language-teaching syllabuses that derive from contrastive analysis of the native and target language systems, it was claimed, would allow such interference to be minimized. Initially, EA merely presented an alternative explanation for errors, but as interlanguage research developed throughout the 1970s, a more rigorous methodology for the study of second language acquisition developed and a richer theoretical perspective on language acquisition evolved.

Goals of error analysis and interlanguage studies

Nature of learner language systems

The applied-linguistic concept of error analysis was initially an application of concepts derived from linguistic theory of the 1960s and first-language acquisition research. One of the goals of error analysis was to help construct an account of the second-language learner's linguistic competence. "A learner's errors, then, provide evidence of the system of the language that he is using (i.e. has learned) at a particular point in the course" (Corder 1967). "An 'interlanguage' may be linguistically described using as data the observable output resulting from a speaker's attempt to produce a foreign norm, i.e. both his errors and non-errors. It is assumed such behavior is highly structured" (Selinker 1969: 71).

However, the concept of "system" or "competence" in linguistics was typically applied to a static, fully developed language code. Second-language learning on the other hand is characterized by a dynamic and changing set of variable rules (Corder 1979, Faerch 1979). Such terms as *transitional competence* (Corder 1967) and *approximative system* (Nemser 1971) reflect attempts to accommodate the concept of system to developmental data that by their very nature are fluctuating and changing. Various solutions to the problem of systematicity and variability in the description of learner-language systems were proposed, including probabalistic grammars and implication analysis.

Probabalistic grammars are formal grammars that assign indices to rules indicating their probability of application. They have been used in descriptions of the German acquired by Spanish and Italian migrant workers (Sankoff 1978). (For a variation on this technique see Tarone, Frauenfelder, and Selinker 1976, and for a critique and update see Bley-Vroman 1983.) Implicational analysis is a method of data analysis that enables systematic relationships between variable features to be determined and that allows for the reconstruction of developmental stages from variable data. Data from phonological errors (Dickerson 1975, Gatbonton 1975) and grammatical errors (Hyltenstam 1977, Andersen 1978) has been analyzed using this technique, allowing for the notion of system to accommodate unstable and changing rules. The investigation of the concept of systematicity continues as a significant issue in second language acquisition research. As Bley-Vroman observes:

If researchers are to make serious progress in the investigation of interlanguage...attention must be concentrated on the construction of linguistic descriptions of learners' languages which can illuminate their specific properties and their own logic. It is possible – even likely – that techniques and formal models of existing linguistic theories will prove to be insufficient for the task. (1983: 16)

Developmental stages

Important issues that emerged from error analysis and interlanguage studies were (a) whether learners passed through clearly identifiable stages in the acquisition of the grammar, phonology, and so forth of the target language; (b) whether learners with different mother tongues passed through the same developmental stages; and (c) whether L2 stages of development were the same as those observed among children acquiring English as a mother tongue (Brown 1973). Research addressed to these issues led to a great number of "morpheme order" studies in the mid-1960s, in which data were collected longitudinally on the order in which specific grammatical morphemes appeared in second-language learners. Examples of stages in interlanguage development were soon reported. These included:

1. use of do-support in yes/no questions before Wh-questions: that is, *Does he come?* before *What he did?* (Ravem 1974);
2. in Wh-questions, a stage in which the wh-words occur in sentence-initial position with the rest of the sentence in statement rather than in inverted form: *How he can do it? What she is doing?* (Ravem 1974);
3. Placement of the negative marker outside of the sentence: *I no like this one* (Cancino et al. 1974), *This is no have calendar* (Schumann 1978).

In a significant study, Dulay and Burt, studying a subset of the morphemes Brown had studied in first-language development, presented evidence suggesting a high degree of agreement between the order in which ESL learners acquired grammatical morphemes and that observed in L1 learners, although the two orders were not identical, as the following list shows:

First-language learners	Second-language learners
1. plural (-s)	1. plural (-s)
2. progressive (-ing)	2. progressive (-ing)
3. past irregular	3. contractible copula
4. articles (a, the)	4. contractible auxiliary
5. contractible copula	5. articles (a, the)
6. possessive	6. past irregular
7. third-person singular (-s)	7. third-person singular (-s)
8. contractible auxiliary	8. possessive ('s)

(Dulay and Burt 1974a)

Although studies such as these found some evidence of transfer from the first language, many tended to support the notion that second-language learners did indeed pass through stages in the acquisition of grammatical features, that these stages were similar to those observed in children acquiring English as a first language, and that the stages were similar for learners of different language backgrounds (see Dulay, Burt, and Krashen 1982; Hatch 1983). The primary effect of the first language seemed to be in determining how long it takes learners to pass through the various stages. Krashen (1982) hence supports the notion of a natural order for the acquisition of grammatical morphemes but stresses that this order is not identical to the order found in first-language acquisition of English and may appear only under certain conditions (it is more likely to be found in cases of naturalistic than instructed second-language acquisition). It should be pointed out, however, that there is much more to language acquisition than the mastery of twelve or so grammatical morphemes. Much of the SLA research of the 1970s consequently reflected an impoverished view of the nature of language proficiency. Language proficiency was viewed as mastery of grammar, and functional and communicative aspects of language development were ignored (see Chapter 10). Although the facts the morpheme studies demonstrated have not generally been disputed, their significance for a theory of second language acquisition is consequently limited.

Role of the mother tongue and language transfer

Error analysis and interlanguage analysis emerged as a reaction to the view of second-language learning proposed by contrastive analysis theory, which saw language transfer as the central process involved in second- and foreign-language learning. This view of transfer was often linked to behavioral views of learning. Error analysis and interlanguage analysis tried to account for learner performance in terms of the cognitive processes learners made use of in reorganizing the input they received from the target language. But the significance of language transfer could not be denied, and attempts were made to accommodate the concept of language transfer to more cognitively oriented theories of the nature of language transfer.

At present, language transfer is not viewed as the manifestation of a learner's inability to resist first-language patterns; instead, it is thought to interact with L2 developmental processes, in ways that are far from fully understood (Gass 1983). Differences between the L1 and the L2 may affect second-language learning in various ways: (a) They may influence the rate at which target-language features are acquired (Keller-Cohen 1979). (b) They may lead to the avoidance of certain target-language structures (Schachter 1974). (c) They may lead to the over-production of certain target-language forms, which are sometimes perceived as carrying L1 discourse functions. Schachter and Rutherford (1979), for example, show that learners with a topic-prominent first language, such as Japanese or Chinese, appear to over-use those English structures that appear to have a similar function, such as markers of extraposition – *It is fortunate that . . .* – and existential sentences – *There is . . .* (d) Language transfer may also constrain the acquisition processes. Schachter (1983) argues that transfer is not a process but that the L1 forms part of the learner's previous knowledge and thus constrains the hypotheses that the learner can make about the target language. In addition, learners' perceptions of what is transferable may result from what they perceive as language specific and language universal. Keller-man (1978) found that learners resist transferring items such as idioms, which are felt to be L1 specific and nontransferable, even where the native and target language share the same idioms.

The study of language transfer has consequently reemerged in inter-language and second language acquisition studies. As Gass observes, "in the past few years there has been a resurgence of interest in the phe-nomenon of language transfer, not as a mechanical transference of first language structures but as a cognitive mechanism involving many fac-tors" (Gass 1983: 10).

Communicative versus linguistic systems

As communicative competence theory assumed a more central role in applied linguistics in the 1960s and 1970s, so interlanguage and error analysis studies broadened in scope to include not only the nature and development of L2 linguistic systems (phonology, morphology, syntax) but also the interactional and communicative dynamics of L2 perfor-mance. Attention shifted to the functional, pragmatic, and social di-mensions of second language use and the effects of non-native communicative behaviors on native speaker (NS)–non-native speaker

(NNS) communication. Among issues that have been studied from this perspective are: (a) disfluency phenomena, which include studies of hesitations, corrections, repairs, repetitions, pausing, and other aspects of speech execution in L2 performance and their effects on NS–NNS communication and L2 discourse (Flick 1978a, b; Day et al. 1983), and (b) speech acts and rules of speaking, which includes studies of acquisition and use of such speech acts as apologies, requests, promises, complaints, compliments, and disagreements by L2 learners (Kasper 1977, Olshtain and Cohen 1983, Wolfson 1983; see also Chapters 8 and 9, this volume), and studies of turn taking, topic selection, openings and closings, gambits, presentation of self, and other aspects of conversational discourse. The focus of such studies has been on the discourse features and the tactics used by L2 learners to achieve particular communicative and illocutionary effects, and also on the pragmatic consequences of the use of nontarget-language communicative norms, which may result in misinterpretation and communication breakdown in cross-cultural settings (Gumperz and Roberts 1978, Scollon and Scollon 1983, J. Thomas 1983). Studies of the acquisition of such communicative and pragmatic skills as these have been necessary to complement the limited view of second-language proficiency seen in morpheme acquisition studies.

The nature of second-language learning processes

A primary focus of error analysis and interlanguage studies was on the evidence learner error and learner performance provides to an understanding of the underlying processes of second language acquisition. "They provide to the researcher evidence of how language is learned or acquired, what strategies or procedures the learner is employing in his discovery of the language" (Corder 1967). Learning processes were inferred from an examination of learner language protocols, study of learners' introspections, case studies and diary studies, classroom observations, and experimental studies (Long 1980, Faerch and Kasper 1983). Initially, attention was focused on error types, and classifications were set up that attempted to account for different types of errors on the basis of the different processes that were assumed to account for them (Selinker 1972). A basic distinction was made between *intralingual* and *interlingual* errors. Interlingual errors were accounted for by language transfer. Intralingual errors were categorized as *overgeneralizations* (errors caused by extensions of target language rules to inappropriate contexts [see Chapter 4]); *simplifications* (errors resulting from redundancy reduction [George 1972, Richards 1975]); *developmental errors* (those reflecting built-in stages of linguistic development [Corder 1967]); *communication-based errors* (errors resulting from strategies of communication [Selinker 1972, Tarone 1977]); *induced errors* (those derived from the sequencing and presentation of target language items [Stenson 1974]); *errors of avoidance* (failure to use certain types of target language features because of perceived difficulty [Schachter 1974]); and *errors of overproduction* (target language features produced correctly but used too frequently [Schachter and Rutherford 1979]). These and similar classifications have been used to account for errors at the levels of phonology, syntax, lexis, and speech acts.

Nevertheless, attempts to apply such categories to the classification of errors encountered problems in assigning errors to categories, because of a lack of precise criteria for classification, an overlapping of some of the categories, and the possibility of multiple explanations. Many error studies and classifications lacked reliability and had limited explanatory power. The need was acknowledged for enlarging the database in language acquisition studies to include not just learner errors but the learner's total linguistic performance in the target language. The term *performance analysis* was coined to suggest this difference in emphasis (Svartvik 1973, Faerch 1978). "To consider only what the learner produces in error and to exclude from consideration the learner's non-errors is tantamount to describing a code of manners on the basis of the observed breaches of the code" (Schachter and Celce-Murcia 1983: 276). Consequently a shift in perspective emerged in the mid-1970s with the emergence of what became known as the field of second language acquisition. Whereas error-analysis studies often focused primarily on describing the *products* of language learning in terms of error types, the focus on the field of second language acquisition was on *explaining* second-language learning in terms of more comprehensive theories of second-language learning processes.

Second language acquisition

Second language acquisition is now the preferred term for referring to the field within the applied linguistics of language teaching that studies the development of communicative competence in second- and foreign-language learners. The range of issues SLA research encompasses includes the development of second-language proficiency in both instructed (i.e., classroom) and noninstructed (naturalistic) settings, as well as the effects of instructional, social, cognitive, linguistic, and psychological variables on both the processes and products of second-language learning (Krashen 1982, Hatch 1983). Because the potential scope of SLA research is wide, the work that has been carried out in the last ten years appears somewhat fragmented. In an attempt to suggest how such research relates to a broader perspective on language learning, we will review major trends in SLA research according to how they relate to four interdependent variables. These are referred to as *input, process, task,* and *context.*

Input

The data for language learning, from any theoretical perspective, is provided by exposure to language. The relationship between what the learner receives as input and what he or she eventually learns is crucial both to theories of second- and foreign-language learning and to proposals for language-teaching syllabuses and methods. Issues that relate to input factors are: (a) Is the natural order observed in morpheme studies simply a reflection of the frequency with which morphemes occur in the input the learner receives? (b) Is what is learned a result of innate learning principles, independent of the structure of the input? (c) Is the form of input directed to second-language learners different in significant ways from the type of language addressed to native speakers, thus perhaps facilitating language acquisition? (d) What type of input is provided in language classrooms? It is to such issues that studies of input have been addressed. Results, however, are far from conclusive, as the following summary suggests.

THE FREQUENCY FACTOR

Studies of the relationship between the input the learner receives and subsequent interlanguage development have compared the frequencies of grammatical morphemes in NS speech with accuracy of use by L2 learners, or with the order in which target-language features are learned. Larsen-Freeman (1976a) found significant positive correlations between frequency rankings of grammatical morphemes in native-speaker input and learner's use of the same morphemes, and also examined frequency orders for morphemes in teacher speech with accuracy orders for L2 learners on a speaking task (1976b). In a more recent study, Hamayan and Tucker (1980) compared the frequency rate of nine structures in teacher's speech in French immersion programs with the use of these structures by learners in a story-telling task; their results support Larsen-Freeman's claim that frequency-of-input features affect production of specific linguistic features by second-language learners. Lightbown, however, has recently reexamined this issue (1983) and has found a low degree of correlation between the rank order of structures in the input that a group of L2 learners received and the order of accuracy for these structures in their speech. She suggests this may be partly because of a bias toward accuracy rather than communication in the instruction the learners received: that is, the input was distorted and students were following their own patterns of interlanguage development.

INPUT AND INNATENESS FACTORS

Most language-teaching methods are based on the assumption that learn-ing is facilitated by grading grammatical constructions so that there is a progression from simple to complex structures in the input that the text or method provides. If a similar order for development of mor-phemes were found in learners in both instructed and noninstructed settings, this would suggest that natural learning principles are more important in determining the outcome of learning than the sequencing and grading built in to the teaching materials themselves. Pienemann argues that "independently of the way of presenting input, classroom L2 learners produce the same type of (partly 'deviant') interlanguage structures as observed in natural acquisition. From this we may conclude that there is a set of developmental principles which apply to formal as well as natural L2 development" (Pienemann 1984: 26). Pienemann concludes that the concept of grading should not be abandoned but that principles of grading should reflect these developmental principles. Krashen (1982), on the other hand, argues that naturalistic language acquisition does not depend on presenting learners with input that has been consciously graded but results from providing learners with the right type of input. Such input (referred to as "optimal" input) should: (a) be comprehensible and interesting, (b) provide structures a little beyond the learner's current level of acquisition, (c) not be grammatically sequenced, and (d) focus on meaning, not form.

This type of input, according to Krashen, is provided in the classroom by naturalistic use of language. The issue that has consequently emerged from this discussion is the role of formal language instruction. Pienemann argues that there is a case for the effects of language instruction and that instruction will be beneficial to the degree that the learner is de-velopmentally ready to acquire a particular linguistic feature. Instruction may then affect (a) the speed with which a form is acquired, (b) the frequency with which a feature or rule is used, and (c) the range of contexts in which a form will be used (Pienemann 1984). Krashen's position reflects that of earlier theorists, who have argued that learners can acquire a language through using it and that formal presentation or sequencing of grammar is unnecessary (Newmark 1971, Krashen 1982). Despite the powerful arguments that have been advanced for and against the role of formal instruction in language learning, this is ultimately an empirical question, and both second language acquisition theorists and language-teaching methodologists concerned with this issue (e.g., Brum-fit 1984) will have to turn to empirical studies in order to provide a database to support their claims.

INPUT OR INTERACTION

If, as some SLA researchers believe, the "comprehensibility" and "naturalness" of the input is what is essential for successful language acquisition, a critical issue then becomes *how* input is made comprehensible. Research addressed to this issue has focused on the form and function of speech addressed to L2 learners, to determine if it has specific formal and interactional features that might be essential in order for second-language learning to take place. Such studies are a follow-up to earlier studies of the structure of "foreigner talk" (Ferguson 1971) and "caretaker speech" (Snow 1972) and other forms of speech addressed to nonproficient language users. These speech registers have been observed to differ in significant ways from normal discourse. They are said to be less complex syntactically, to use more frequent and more concrete vocabulary, to code topics and propositions more saliently, and, in addition, to employ prosodic and paralinguistic devices that serve to make input more comprehensible. Long (1981) considered whether it was modified input or modified interaction in NS–NNS discourse that facilitated comprehension and argues that the different interactional dimensions of NS–NNS discourse (because it contains more expansions, more repetitions, more comprehension checks, and clarification requests, etc.) facilitate the comprehensibility of such discourse.

CLASSROOM INPUT

The type of linguistic interaction between teachers and students in language classrooms generates another source of input to language learners, and the study of the nature of classroom language and classroom interaction has been an additional focus of SLA research. It is generally referred to as "classroom-centered research" and is motivated by an attempt "to look at the classroom as a setting for classroom language acquisition and learning in terms of the language input provided by the teacher's talk" (Gaies 1977). Issues investigated include:

1. *The nature of teacher talk.* Researchers have examined how speakers adjust their speech in communicating with learners (Gaies 1977). Chaudron (1979, 1983c) studied teacher-talk in ESL classrooms, looking at lexical simplifications, anaphoric reference, question usage, topic development, and explanations. He found that "the pressure to communicate appears to lead at times to ambiguous over-simplifications on the one hand, and confusingly redundant over-elaborations on the other."
2. *Feedback.* Studies have been carried out of the feedback given by teachers to learners and by learners to other learners. Chaudron (1977), observing teachers of adolescents in immersion programs, found that most teachers attend to content errors rather than grammatical ones. Fanselow (1977) found that 22 percent of errors produced by learners were not corrected.

Cathcart and Olsen (1976) found that in the adult ESL classroom, students reported that they preferred explicit correction of their oral errors and that they considered pronunciation and grammar errors important. Nystrom (1983) found three different styles of feedback to exist in the teachers she studied: overt corrective, covert corrective, and noncorrective, although the teachers varied as to how they gave feedback (see Gaies 1983 for a literature review).

3. *Studies of learner strategies in classrooms.* Beebe (1983) studied risk taking in an ESL classroom (the willingness to take chances and make choices where the outcome is uncertain). She looked at ESL students' willingness to use linguistic structures they were unsure of and found that risk taking and accuracy varied inversely with each other and with the ethnicity of the interviewer. Bailey (1983) used diary-study data to investigate the effect of competitiveness and anxiety in adult language learning. She suggests that anxiety can be caused and aggravated by competitiveness if learners perceive themselves as less proficient than fellow students. She suggests that anxiety may sometimes be facilitating, motivating the learner to greater effort, but debilitating if it is so severe as to cause the learner to withdraw from the language-learning experience.

4. *Classroom interaction and learner participation.* Seliger (1983) studied the relationship between student participation in the classroom and learner proficiency in the target language. He distinguished between "high-input generators" (those who are active in classrooms and get more input from the teacher) and "low-input generators," and looked at the role of learners in generating their own input and learning experience (1983: 142). Sato (1981) showed that student classroom participation may reflect ethnic differences in learning or communicative styles.

The emergence of classroom-centered research is a healthy sign. Much of the literature on language teaching consists of prescriptions for teaching different aspects of language proficiency, but very few studies have been undertaken of actual practices and processes. Research of the kind discussed in this chapter will hence lead to a better understanding of the nature of language teaching.

Process

We saw earlier that a primary motivation of error analysis and interlanguage studies was an attempt to infer the processes of second language acquisition. A consequence of this was a richer understanding of the nature of language transfer and its role in second language acquisition. The nature and relative contribution of language transfer continues to be an issue of interest to many researchers in SLA. In this section, however, we will review other process-related issues in SLA research.

By learning processes, researchers in SLA refer to both the conscious and the unconscious cognitive behaviors that learners engage in as they acquire and use a second or foreign language. These processes are generally assumed to involve (a) hypothesis formation and hypothesis testing; (b) synthesis, analysis, and abstraction, leading to long-term storage and representation of abstract information about the underlying systems of the target language; and (c) retrieval processes involved in accessing such information for use in different kinds of production and comprehension tasks (Ringbom 1983). Attempts to clarify the nature of such processes in second-language learning have led researchers and theoreticians to explore such dimensions as the role of long- and short-term memory in SLA (George 1972), the role of conscious and unconscious knowledge (Bialystock 1978, Krashen 1982), the effects of age and manner of learning on learning processes (Krashen 1982, Hatch 1983), and the role of the brain in such processes (Genesee 1982, Seliger 1982, Hatch 1983, Scovel 1982). As Wode observes, however,

no neurophysiological model of the functioning of the human brain, no linguistic theory, and no psychological learning theory – whether behavioristic, cognitive or other – is presently available which seems suited to describe the facts empirically observable when human beings learn languages. Consequently the results from [existing] studies on language acquisition are a great challenge for developmental psychology, brain research, language teaching and linguistic theorizing. (Wode 1982: 8)

In this section we will refer to several current conceptualizations of SLA processes, illustrating some of the problems and limitations of each theory.

LEARNING VERSUS ACQUISITION

In attempting to develop a process-based theory that explains the invariant order for L2 grammatical development found in many SLA studies – but that also accounts for significant departures from this order – Krashen made a distinction between acquisition and learning, seeing them as two distinct processes. He contrasted situations in which the learner's attention is consciously focused on formal features of the target language (learning) with situations in which the learner's subconscious processes are involved. In the latter, the learner is using the target language for authentic communication, and the focus is on meaning rather than on linguistic form (acquisition) (Krashen 1982). For Krashen, acquisition is the primary process; learning can contribute to language production only when learned information is engaged as a "monitor," editing the output of the acquired system in situations where the speaker is (a) focusing on formal features of the language, (b) knows the underlying rules, and (c) has time to apply this knowledge.

Krashen's distinction between acquisition and learning is linked to his input and monitor hypotheses as part of a comprehensive theory of second language acquisition; this theory has been put forward in numerous publications and has been used to support specific methodological practices (Krashen and Terrell 1983). Despite their intuitive appeal, however, it should be noted that little serious evidence has been advanced to support the various hypotheses Krashen's theory is based on, and some researchers doubt if the hypotheses themselves are empirically or even logically supportable (cf. Gregg 1984). For example, the distinction between acquisition and learning is central to Krashen's theory, yet neither term has been adequately operationalized. As Gregg points out, both terms are used loosely and ambiguously. Krashen's insistence that "learning" cannot become "acquisition" rests on the basis of tenuous and anecdotal evidence. Furthermore, if the criterion for acquisition is in the spontaneous and appropriate use of target language forms and utterances, counterexamples come readily to mind (equally as anecdotal as Krashen's own supporting "data"). For writers, for example, many of the conventions of spelling and punctuation were first taught and learned consciously, and later became automatic and, in most cases, unconscious; likewise, most second- or foreign-language learners can document instances where forms of address, correct pronunciations, colloquial phrases, conversational routines, and even verb forms and phrases, once consciously known, soon passed into immediate and automatic use. Krashen's view of "the monitor" is likewise an extremely limited and limiting view of the role of editing and revision processes in speech production, as is seen in the discussion in Morrison and Low (1983). Like his use of the terms *acquisition* and *learning*, Krashen's use of *monitor* refers to processes but does not describe them, and fails to explain how linguistic rules are accessed during comprehension or production.

CONSCIOUS AND UNCONSCIOUS KNOWLEDGE

Bialystock (1978, 1981) distinguishes between explicit knowledge (conscious facts we know about a language) and implicit knowledge (the intuitive information upon which the learner operates in order to produce language automatically and spontaneously). The system of explicit linguistic knowledge, according to Bialystock, contains generally simpler, less abstract rules about the target language, rules that are subject to conscious awareness and analysis. After continued use, information in the explicit system becomes automatic and is transferred to the system of implicit knowledge. In a number of studies, Bialystock investigated the relationship between different kinds of production and comprehension tasks and the use of implicit and explicit knowledge about language.

INFORMATION PROCESSING

A powerful alternative explanation of differences between monitored and spontaneous language use is proposed by McLaughlin, Rossman, and

McLeod (1983), who draw on an information-processing model. According to this theory, learning any complex task or form of behavior requires the integration of a number of subskills. In order to be able to handle recurring tasks and situations more efficiently, many of the underlying skills become routinized or automatic and are then generally performed without conscious attention. This is referred to as "automatic processing." In learning a particular task, such as conversational skills in a foreign language, subskills that are not yet part of automatic processing (e.g., handling the honorific system used in formal speech) may initially require conscious attention. They are under the domain of conscious processing at this stage. This may intrude on the ability to simultaneously perform other aspects of the task (for instance, maintaining tense distinction), which, in turn, could lead to the learner's control of grammar, fluency, and so on being affected. Gradually, controlled processes become automatic as the learner gains proficiency in the task. This is a different perspective from the acquisition/learning distinction proposed by Krashen, since both acquired or learned forms (in Krashen's sense) may come under controlled or automatic processing, depending on task demands.

DECOMPOSITION AND REINTEGRATION

Wode is a researcher who has attempted to go beyond categorizing learning processes and who takes account of the cognitive dimensions of processes. He posits that "within man's overall cognitive functioning there is a linguo-cognitive processing system or sets of systems, possibly a hierarchy of systems, which are especially geared to act upon incoming speech signals and to process them so that their information can be used by higher levels of cognitive functioning. These linguo-cognitive systems relate to perception, memory, and perhaps other cognitive domains" (1982: 299). Wode proposes that these systems fulfill two functions – they process speech data and they sustain development. His theory depends less on input features and more on innate cognitive processing as the source of SLA. Acquisition processes basically involve breaking down, or decomposing, the structures of the target language and then reintegrating the decomposed elements into target-like structures via developmental sequences. "What has been singled out via decomposition is reflected in the learner's productions, including his errors. The reintegration is mirrored in the respective developmental sequence" (Wode 1982: 303). Wode has investigated acquisition of grammatical and phonological features of various languages to show how these processes are reflected in both first-language and second-language developmental data.

NEUROLINGUISTIC EXPLANATIONS

Information on the functions of the human brain is clearly central to theories of L2 learning and developmental processes. Early speculations concerning the role of the brain in language learning (Penfield and Roberts 1959, Lenneberg 1967) identified a critical period during which language can be acquired most easily, occurring up to puberty. Beyond puberty, they said, language learning is more difficult because the brain has lost its "plasticity" – a result of lateralization (the establishment of language functions in a particular part of the left hemisphere). A review of Lenneberg's clinical data by Krashen (1973), however, did not lend support to such a conclusion.

Researchers in SLA have continued to explore such issues as what language functions are performed by the right hemisphere after language has become centralized in the left hemisphere, the relationship between the two hemispheres during language acquisition and processing, and the influence of age, manner of learning, and stage of learning on neuropsychological processes (Genesee 1982, Scovel 1982, Seliger 1982). Nonetheless, attempts to determine what cognitive functions and abstract processing abilities are associated with each hemisphere and whether such functions are uniquely under the control of a given hemisphere or brain area are not conclusive, and they certainly do not warrant the naive extensions to pedagogy sometimes made by language-teaching practitioners. Scovel consequently warns that the "pedagogical irrelevance of direct application of neuropsychological research emphasizes the ultimate futility of any attempts to seek a neurolinguistic reality to justify certain classroom techniques and behaviors" (Scovel 1982: 328).

Task

The third dimension involved in understanding second language acquisition is the role of tasks in language learning. By *task* I mean a specific goal or activity that is accomplished through the use of language. A learner may be engaged in such tasks as repeating a word or sentence, giving commands and instructions through the target language, reading a paragraph and answering questions about it, listening to a lecture and summarizing the main points, listening to instructions and carrying out an action as a result of what has been understood, working with another student and using the target language to solve a problem, writing a letter, or copying a paragraph from a book. Tasks differ according to the type of response they require from the learner, the type of interaction they engage the learner in (either with a text or with another learner), the level of language processing they require, and the type of language production they demand. Differences of these kinds may contribute in specific ways to learning.

In considering the role of tasks in SLA, then, we are concerned with their cognitive, linguistic, and communicative dimensions. The essential question is, How do particular tasks or activity types contribute to specific learning processes? Can learning be affected by manipulating tasks rather than input? From this perspective, input is considered too narrow a construct. It is not the input itself that may be important but what the learner does with it. The type of cognitive and linguistic processing the learner is engaged in depends upon the task that he or she is given.

In language teaching, tasks have traditionally been considered from a methods perspective. Many method writers have assumed that tasks are a critical variable in determining success in language learning. Writers on communicative language teaching, for example, advocate the use of tasks involving an "information gap" (i.e., where students each have different information and work in pairs or small groups to complete the task by sharing their information and negotiating). These kinds of tasks are said to be more successful in providing opportunities for language acquisition (Johnson 1982).

Likewise Silent Way (Gattegno 1976) is predicated upon the belief that specific pedagogic tasks – involving color charts to represent sounds and colored rods to represent words and grammatical relations, manipulated silently by the teacher to communicate sounds and meanings – are better at engaging learners' decoding and memory processes. There are no empirical data to demonstrate if there is indeed any relationship between task types and depth of cognitive processing or long-term retention, though such claims could readily be tested empirically. What is at issue is the degree to which the choice of task affects learning, a long-established concern in studies of the psychology of learning.

A similar case has been made by advocates of English for Specific Purposes and even immersion education programs. Widdowson (1968), for example, has argued that a second language is best learned by using it to study other subject matter. Similarly, a rationale for bilingual immersion programs has been that "the student can most effectively acquire fluency in a second language when the task of learning becomes incidental to that of gaining knowledge about a specific topic (geography, math, or basketball) via the target language through communicating with a native speaker" (d'Anglejan 1978: 227).

Several perspectives on the role of tasks in second-language learning have been considered by researchers in SLA.

TYPE OF PROCESSING INVOLVED

Language-teaching techniques have often been discussed according to the level of processing they involve. Drills in language teaching, for example, are sometimes classified according to whether they involve a mechanical, meaningful, or communicative response. A mechanical response involves low-level processing, mainly using short-term memory.

A communicative response requires the learner to respond appropriately, supplying both content and form (Paulston 1980). It is argued that drills and similar controlled-practice activities in language teaching should have a communicative dimension if they are to engage higher-level language acquisition processes. SLA researchers have also considered the type of processing involved in different language tasks. Chaudron (1983b), for example, discusses tasks in terms of the degree of linguistic production they involve (tasks may vary from nonverbal to highly verbal) and the degree of comprehension they demand (they may vary from low-level to high-level processing), and discusses measures of L2 proficiency according to the types of tasks they are based on.

Hosenfeld (1979) and Cohen and Hosenfeld (1981) have tried to investigate the relationship of tasks to processes by having learners reflect on and verbalize their observations as they carry out different kinds of classroom reading, writing, listening, speaking, vocabulary, and grammar tasks. They found that "(1) college students can verbalize and observe strategies that they use with many tasks commonly found in second language classrooms and (2) student's strategies are often quite different from strategies teachers assume they are using" (1981: 293). In studying a grammatical rule, for example, students tried to extrapolate to an imagined communicative situation where they might have to use the rule. In studies of differences between successful and unsuccessful readers based on students' descriptions of what they were doing as they performed reading tasks, it was found that "successful readers keep the meaning of the passage in mind, read in broad phrases, skip unessential words and guess from context the meaning of new words. In contrast, unsuccessful readers lose the meanings of sentences as soon as they decode them, read word-by-word in short phrases, rarely skip unessential words, and turn to the glossary for the meaning of new words" (Cohen and Hosenfeld 1981: 296). Such studies attempt to locate the strategies learners make use of in performing different kinds of pedagogic tasks (drills, reading comprehension exercises, etc.). Thus it becomes possible to assess the contribution different kinds of tasks make to second language acquisition.

TYPES OF LINGUISTIC STRUCTURES PRODUCED

A different focus on tasks concerns the types of linguistic forms learners practice or produce in carrying out specific tasks. Butler-Wall (personal communication) examined the relationship between different types of communicative tasks and the frequencies with which they elicited particular linguistic structures. The tasks studied were narrative, descriptive, expository, speculative, and cooperative tasks. Some structures (e.g., *there* insertion and passive voice) turned out to be relatively unaffected by tasks, whereas the frequency with which other structures were used (e.g., left-dislocation and extraposition) depended upon the task type. One possible application of such research would be in suggesting the sorts of communicative activities that could be used to teach or reinforce particular grammatical structures.

TYPE OF LINGUISTIC INPUT GENERATED

Some SLA researchers have looked more broadly at tasks in relation to input. How do different types of classroom tasks affect the sort of input the SL learner is getting? Many current language-teaching proposals (e.g., the Natural Approach and Communicative Language Teaching) emphasize the need for speaking practice, using such communicative classroom exchanges as information-sharing activities or dyadic problem-solving tasks. What sort of language do such tasks in fact generate when used by ESL learners?

Porter (1983) looked at communicative tasks according to the grammaticality of the language they generated, its interactional features, and its sociolinguistic appropriateness. She examined discussions during a problem-solving task between ESL learners and (a) native speakers, (b) advanced learners, and (c) intermediate learners. Analyzing the type of language generated, she concludes,

Simply practicing communicative activities in the classroom will not generate the type of sociocultural input that learners need. Though while doing problem-solving tasks they will get practice in expressing opinions, agreement, and disagreement, the way in which they express themselves is not the same as the language of native speakers. Thus the learner's language is inappropriate for use in other settings outside the classroom. (1983: 27)

However, although much of the language generated by ESL learners in carrying out the tasks was ungrammatical and sociolinguistically inappropriate, they did get practice in "repairs" and "prompts," that is, in communication strategies that may aid them in learning the target language. In addition, the quality of language they addressed to other learners was not different from the quality of language they addressed to native speakers. We may conclude that although teaching or contact with native speakers may be necessary to provide accurate grammatical and sociocultural input, "learners can offer each other genuine communicative practice, including the negotiations for meaning that may aid SLA" (Porter 1983: 29). Long (1981) likewise emphasizes that the interaction between learners can generate good data for second-language learning. He argues that tasks involving interaction and negotiation (and that therefore involve such devices as self- and other repetition, confirmation checks, and clarification requests) provide more comprehensible input and hence better input for second language acquisition.

Context

The last dimension of second-language learning we will consider is context. Here we are concerned with the effects of situational and contextual factors on language learning. Issues arising from this perspective are: (a) Do interlanguage processes vary according to the setting in which a language is being learned? (b) Are interlanguage features (i.e., the type and frequency of specific interlanguage characteristics) also influenced by the contexts in which a language is being learned? (c) How does the input that learners receive in informal settings differ from that in formal settings (e.g., classrooms) and what effects do such differences have on the success or failure of language learning?

The effect of context and situation for learning has long been of interest to researchers in bilingualism and second-language learning. The distinction between compound and coordinate bilingualism, for example (Ervin and Osgood 1954, Lambert 1961), rested upon an assumption that different settings for language learning may result in the development of different semantic systems in learners. A somewhat different interest in the effects of context on the products and processes of language learning has been evidenced in more recent second language acquisition research.

Variability in language performance according to setting and context has been observed in several SLA studies. Sampson (1971) suggests that the situation in which L2 data are collected (e.g., informal naturalistic conversation versus classroom language use) will lead to different kinds of errors and to different frequencies for particular error types. Ervin-Tripp suggests that language transfer is greater when the language is learned in situations such as foreign language classrooms, where the language "is not the language of the learner's social milieu so that the learning contexts are aberrant both in function and frequency of structure" (Ervin-Tripp 1974: 121). Pica (1983) investigated the effects of different contexts for language learning (formal classroom settings versus naturalistic non-instructional settings) on processes of language development as evidenced by differences in error types. She found morpheme oversuppliance and inappropriate distributions of morphemes were more prevalent in instructed students. Students acquiring English through naturalistic interaction used devices for marking plurality that were similar to processes observed in pidginization (using pre-modifying quantifiers instead of S-inflections). She suggests that one of the effects of instruction might therefore be to inhibit pidginization processes.

A different perspective on the effect of learning context on second language acquisition arose from studies of the social-psychological dimensions of second- and foreign-language learning. D'Anglejan (1978) reviews differences between language learning characteristics in classroom and nonclassroom settings. She compares the differing social, linguistic, communicative, and interactional characteristics of formal and informal learning contexts. She attributes failure in classroom language learning to the fact that it is often not embedded in the context of social interaction and focuses on language as an entity rather than on language as communication. Schumann (1975, 1978) argued that when learners are learning a language for restricted communicative purposes and are socially distant from speakers of the target language, as is the case with many immigrant minority groups and with migrant workers in various European countries, the process of pidginization is likely to occur (Schumann 1978). Pidginization is characterized by the development of an interlanguage marked by a lack of inflectional morphology and a restricted grammatical and lexical system. From this perspective, the degree of language development is seen as a reflection of the type of interaction between the learner and the target culture group. Schumann has speculated about the consequent affective and social barriers that impede language acquisition in such cases. His "acculturation model" posits acculturation (a grouping of social and affective variables) to be the major causal variable in second-language learning. Schmidt (1983b), however, investigates the case of a learner whose interlanguage reflects pidginization *despite* the fact that the learner is fully integrated into the target culture and uses English effectively for a wide range of communicative functions. This subject, Schmidt argues, constitutes serious counterevidence to the acculturation model. Schmidt concludes that "in addition to communicative effort, cognitive effort is a necessary condition for successful adult second language acquisition" (1983b: 109).

Conclusion

Error analysis, interlanguage analysis, and second language acquisition research have not been motivated by interest in issues of immediate practical application to language teaching. Many of the studies reviewed here have a descriptive and explanatory focus rather than a prescriptive one; therefore it would be inappropriate to expect SLA research to provide answers to many practical issues. Such research, however, has contributed to a broadening of our understanding of the "how" and the "why" of second- and foreign-language learning, and this makes possible a more informed and realistic understanding of the dimensions underlying many practical issues in language teaching. On the other hand, from an applied linguistics perspective, the applicability and value of much of the research surveyed here will ultimately depend on the degree to which it contributes to an integrated theory of language teaching and learning.

6 Communicative needs in second- and foreign-language learning

The theme of language and the learner's communicative needs is a familiar one in language teaching. In recent years, applied linguistics has been revitalized by attempts to describe how language reflects its communicative uses and by demonstrations of how syllabus design and methodology can respond to the need for communicative uses of language in classrooms and teaching materials. By considering some central aspects of communication, this chapter attempts to contribute to our general understanding of how language use reflects underlying communicative needs. Five assumptions about the nature of verbal communication will be discussed, namely, that communication is meaning-based, conventional, appropriate, interactional, and structured. These will be discussed in relation to the communicative needs of second- or foreign-language learners.

The meaning-based aspect of communication

Let us begin by examining basic "survival" language needs, those for example of a learner who has an active vocabulary of perhaps two hundred words, a minimal knowledge of the syntax of English, but who is in a situation where English is required for simple and basic communicative purposes. The most immediate need is to be able to refer to a core of basic "referents" or things in the real world, that is, to be able to name things, states, events, and attributes, using the words he or she knows. In addition, the learner must be able to link words together to make predications, that is, to express propositions. (A proposition is the linking of words to form predications about things, people, and events. For example, the words *book* and *red* constitute a proposition when we understand the meaning of *The book is red*.)

Propositions are the building blocks of communication, and the first task in learning to communicate in a language is to learn how to create propositions. Language is comprehensible to the degree that hearers are able to reconstruct propositions from the speaker's utterances (Wells 1981: 73–115). When the child says "hungry" to the mother, the mother understands "I am hungry"; from "no hungry" the mother understands the child's message as being "I don't want to eat." From these examples

82

we see that sentences do not have to be complete or grammatical for their propositional meaning to be understood. We often make good sense of a speaker who uses very broken syntax, just as we can understand a message written in telegraphese, for example, *no money send draft*.

Sentences may contain more than one proposition. *The girl picked the red flower* contains the propositions *the girl picked the flower* and *the flower is red*. Sentences may refer to the same proposition but differ in what they say about it. The following sentences all refer to the proposition *John married Mary*, but differ in what they say about it:

When did John marry Mary?
Why did John and Mary get married?
Mary and John have been married for ages.

"Survival level" communication in a foreign language, however, implies more than the construction of propositions. Speakers use propositions in utterances in a variety of ways. They may wish to ask a question about a proposition, affirm a proposition, deny or negate a proposition, or express an attitude toward a proposition. They may use propositions to communicate meanings indirectly, as when the speaker says *I'm thirsty* but means *I'd like a glass of water*, the latter being the "illocutionary effect" the speaker intends (see Austin 1962). Now, whereas adult native speakers of English can use the resources of adult syntax to encode propositions in the appropriate grammatical form and to communicate a wide range of illocutionary meanings, beginning foreign-language learners find that the demands of communication often exceed their knowledge of the grammar of English. The learners' immediate priority is to work out a way of performing such operations as stating, affirming, denying, or questioning propositions, as economically as possible, using only a partial knowledge of the vocabulary and syntax of the target language. Here learners have needs similar to children who are learning their mother tongue. Child language can be used to express complex meanings within the limits of a restricted grammatical system. "Mother talk" – that variety of speech which mothers use when talking to young children – is simplified to make propositions and illocutionary intentions more readily identifiable (Goody 1978:24). Mothers' questions to children, for example, contain far more yes/no questions than Wh-questions, because propositions are more readily identifiable in yes/no questions.

How do foreign-language learners communicate meaning when they lack the fully elaborated grammatical and discourse system of the target language? To answer this question, let us consider how a learner might try to express the meanings contained in the following sentences:

John ought to have come on time.
I regret I wasn't able to get to your class on time.
I can't afford to buy that dress.

One strategy learners adopt in communicating complex meanings like this is to "bring propositions to the surface" by expressing meanings and intentions *directly* rather than indirectly, and by expressing lexically aspects of meaning that in the target language are coded in the auxiliary system, in complex clauses, or by grammatical devices (Richards 1981; Dittmar 1981). The first sentence, for example, implies the proposition *John came late* and communicates the speaker's attitude toward this proposition. The meaning is roughly *Speaker disapprove that John came late.* This could be communicated by saying:

"Why John late?" (said with non-approving intonation)   or
"John late. That bad."

(The distinction between propositions that are expressed, and those that are presupposed, is an important one, but will not be pursued further here.) The second sentence contains the proposition *I am late*, together with the speaker's expression of regret. It might be communicated by saying:

"I late. So sorry."

I can't afford to buy that dress contains the propositions:

The dress is expensive. I don't have enough money to buy the dress.

It could be restated.

"The dress expensive. Cannot buy."   or
"Can't buy the dress. No money."

This type of "restructuring" is seen in the following examples, in which utterances in simplified learner syntax are compared with standard adult grammar.

Simplified Utterances	*Equivalent in standard adult syntax*
Mary lazy. No work hard.	Mary can work hard if she wants to.
Tomorrow I give money.	You will have your money tomorrow, I promise.
You no money. I lend you.	I will lend you some money if you need any.
This way. See the map.	According to the map, this ought to be the way.
One day I go England.	I would like to go to England some day.
	(De Silva: 1981)

Teachers too often resort to the type of language on the left in communicating with speakers of limited language proficiency. The following examples were produced by teachers who are native speakers of English:

1. A teacher is explaining the meaning of *wash*: "In your house, you...a tub...you (gestures) wash."
2. Here a teacher is explaining how to take telephone messages: "I want to speak other person. He not here. What good thing for say now?"
3. A teacher explaining an interview procedure produced: "Not other student listen. I no want. Necessary you speak. Maybe I say what is your name. The writing not important."
4. And here is a teacher reminding her students to bring their books to class: "The book...we have...(hold up book)...book is necessary for class. Right...necessary for school. You have book."

(Evelyn Hatch, personal communication.)

The preceding examples illustrate a linguistic system that can be used for communicating basic propositional meanings. Such a system is known as "child language" when it is produced by infants learning their mother tongue, "interlanguage" when it is produced by foreign-language learners, "teacher talk" when it is used by teachers, and "foreigner talk" when it is produced by native speakers communicating with foreigners. The linguistic system behind this type of communication is one that uses a basic "notional/functional" core of vocabulary items, a syntax that depends on simple word-order rules (such as negating by placing the negative word in front of the proposition), and in which the communication of meaning is not dependent on grammatical systems of tense or aspect, auxiliaries, function words, plural morphemes, and so forth.

The ability to use such a communicative system is crucial in the first stages of foreign-language learning. We should consequently be tolerant of grammatical "errors" from learners who are at this stage. They should not attempt active communication too soon, however. Before the learner is ready to begin speaking a foreign language, he or she should have a vocabulary of at least two hundred words and a feel for the basic word-order rules of the target language. The learner needs to develop a feel for the system of basic word order (in English: subject–predicate sentence order, adverb and adjectival positions, negation, question formation, etc.). When speaking is taught, the initial goal should be the production of comprehensible utterances through expressing basic propositional meanings and illocutionary intentions.

The conventional aspect of communication

Although much of the learner's efforts in speaking a foreign language center on developing the vocabulary and syntax needed to express propositional meanings, it is native-speaker syntax and usage that is ultimately the learner's goal. As language acquisition proceeds, the learner revises his or her ideas about how propositions are expressed in English.

The learner's syntax becomes more complex as his or her knowledge of negation, the auxiliary system, questions, word order, embedding, conjoining, and so on, expands. In short, the learner begins to develop grammatical competence.

Both linguists and applied linguists in recent years have emphasized the creative properties of grammatical systems. Language users were said to possess, as part of their grammatical competence, the ability to produce an infinite number of sentences, most of which are novel utterances. The learner's task was thought to be to "internalize" the rules needed to generate "any and all" of the possible grammatical sentences of English. The primary aim of language teaching was to create opportunities for these grammatical abilities to develop in language learners (this is dealt with more fully in Chapter 9).

The fact is, however, that only a fraction of the sentences that could be generated by our grammatical competence are actually ever used in communication. Communication largely consists of the use of language in conventional ways. There are strict constraints imposed on the creative–constructive capacities of speakers, and these limit how speakers encode propositional meanings. In telling the time, for example, we can say, *It's two forty* or *It's twenty to three*, but not *It's three minus twenty*, *It's ten after two thirty*, or *It's eight fives after twenty*. If I want you to mail a letter for me I may say, *Please mail this letter for me* or *Would you mind mailing this letter for me*, but I am unlikely to say, *I request you to mail this letter* or *It is my desire that this letter be mailed by you*. Although these sentences have been constructed according to the rules of English grammar, they are not conventional ways of using English. Though they are grammatically correct "sentences," they have no status as potential "utterances" within discourse, since they would never be used by native speakers of English.

This considerably complicates the task of foreign-language learning. Once learners have progressed to the stage where they are beginning to generate novel utterances, they find that many of their utterances fail to conform to patterns of conventional usage, although they are undoubtedly English sentences. Constraints that require speakers to use only *conventional* utterances affect both the lexical and grammatical structure of discourse. The constraints on lexical usage manifest themselves in idiosyncracies and irregularities that particularly affect verb, noun, preposition, and article usage, and are usually rationalized as "exceptions" or "collocational restrictions" in teachers' explanations.

Thus teachers must explain that *a pair of trousers* refers to one item, but *a pair of shirts* to two; that we can speak of a *toothache* or *a headache*, but not *a fingerache*; that someone may be *in church*, but not *in library*. Conventionalized language is seen in many other features of discourse. For example:

a. *Conversational openers: How are you?* may be used to open a conversation in English, but not *Are you well?* or *Are you in good health?*

b. *Routine formulas:* Some conventional forms are expressions whose use is limited to particular settings, such as *Check, please,* said when a bill is requested in a restaurant.

c. *Ceremonial formulas:* These are conventional phrases used in ritualized interactions, such as *After you,* said as a way of asking someone to go ahead of you when entering a room, and *How nice to see you,* said on encountering a friend after an absence of some time (Yorio 1980: 437).

d. *Memorized clauses (Pawley and Syder, 1983):* The concept of conventionalized language usage may be applied to a broader class of utterances. These are clauses that do not appear to be "uniquely generated" or created anew each time they are required in discourse, but that are produced and stored as complete units. Pawley and Syder cite the following examples:

Did you have a good trip?	Please sit down.
Is everything O.K.?	Call me later.
Pardon me?	I see what you mean.

They argue that speakers of a language regularly use thousands of utterances like these. Unlike novel utterances (those that speakers put together from individual lexical items), these are pre-programmed and run off almost automatically in speech production. Researchers in second language acquisition have observed that language learners also often use conventional formulas and memorized clauses as crutches in order to make communication easier. There is often a high frequency of them in their speech in the early stages of conversational competence (Schmidt 1983a).

The fact that language is conventional has important implications for language teaching. First, it suggests that there is reason to be skeptical of the suggestion that language cannot be taught but only acquired. Many of the conventional aspects of language usage are amenable to teaching. Second, applied linguistic effort is needed to gather fuller data on such forms (through discourse analysis and frequency counts, for example) with a view to obtaining useful information for teachers, textbook writers, and syllabus designers.

The appropriateness aspect of communication

Mastery of a foreign language requires more than the use of utterances that express propositional meanings and are conventional. The form of utterances must also take into account the relationship between speaker and hearer, and the constraints imposed by the setting and circumstances in which the act of communication is taking place. *What's your name?* is a conventional utterance, for example, but it is not an appropriate way of asking the identity of a telephone caller; in this case, *May I know who is calling?* is considered more appropriate.

Communicative competence (Hymes 1972) includes knowledge of different communicative strategies or communicative styles according to the situation, the task, and the roles of the participants. For example, if a person wanted to get a match from another person in order to light a cigarette, he or she might take one of the following courses of action, according to the person's judgment of its appropriateness:

1. Make a statement of need: "I need a match."
2. Use an imperative: "Give me a match."
3. Use an embedded imperative: "Could you give me a match?"
4. Use a permission directive: "May I have a match?"
5. Use a question directive: "Do you have a match?"
6. Give a hint: "The matches are all gone, I see."

(Ervin-Tripp 1976:29)

Young children learning their mother tongue soon become skilled at using communicative strategies appropriately. Thus a child who wants something done may bargain, beg, name-call, or threaten violence in talking to other children; reason, beg, or make promises in talking to parents; or repeat the request several times, or beg, in talking to grandparents.

The choice of an appropriate strategy for performing a communicative task or speech act depends on such factors as the age, sex, familiarity, and roles of speaker and hearer, which will determine whether a speaker adopts conversational strategies implying either *affiliation* or *dominance*. In the former case, "Got a match?" may be considered an appropriate way of requesting a match, and in the latter, "I wonder if I could bother you for a match?" (Brown and Levinson 1978). Foreign-language learners typically have fewer alternatives available to them for performing speech acts appropriately. They may use what they consider a polite or formal style for all situations, in which case people may find them overformal; or they may create novel ways of encoding particular speech acts, such as using *please + imperative* to make requests, regardless of whom they are talking to. An example of this would be, "Please, you carry this suitcase," said by a non-native speaker to a friend, where "How about carrying this suitcase for me?" would be a more appropriate form; or "Please. Bring more coffee," said to a waitress, where a more appropriate form would be "Could I have another cup of coffee, please?" (Schmidt 1983a).

Canadian researchers have investigated the problems that non-native speakers have when they are put in a situation where they feel they lack the means of speaking appropriately (such as when a person who has been taught to use a formal type of French needs a style of speaking suitable for communication in informal situations). It was predicted that speakers would show considerable discomfort in using a casual style and that this discomfort would cause them to downgrade the personality of the inter- locutor and to judge that the interlocutor had formed a bad impression of them. It was argued that such speakers would have some awareness that they were not speaking in a suitably friendly and casual manner, and would conclude that they really did not like the person they were speaking to. The results of the study supported this prediction. "These findings have certain implications for second language learners who have only mastered basic vocabulary and syntax in their new language but have not developed skills in the domain of linguistic variability. Such people may find social interaction with native speakers in their new language to be a relatively negative experience and may become discouraged from pursuing language practice with native speakers" (Segalowitz and Gatbonton 1977: 86). Lan- guage-learning texts have only recently begun to focus on the strategies learners need to perform various types of speech acts appropriately. In these texts the emphasis is not simply on teaching functions and their exponents, but on selecting appropriate exponents in different types of communicative situations. Textbooks thus need to give practice in per- forming particular speech acts with interlocutors of different ages, ranks, and social status, and practice in selecting language according to these variables. (Speech-act theory is dealt with more fully in Chapter 8.)

The interactional aspect of communication

The use of utterances that take appropriate account of the speaker's and the hearer's roles implies that conversation is often just as much a form of social encounter as it is a way of communicating meanings or ideas. This may be described as the interactional function of conversation. It is the use of language to keep open the channels of communication between people and to establish a suitable rapport. Goffman has argued that "in any action, each actor provides a field of action for the other actors, and the reciprocity thus established allows the participants to exercise their interpersonal skills in formulating the situation, presenting and enacting a self or identity, and using strategies to accomplish other interactional ends" (cited in Watson 1974: 58). We see evidence of this at many levels within conversation. In the initial stages of conversation with a stranger, for example, speakers introduce uncontroversial topics into the conversation, such as the weather, the transport system, and so forth. These topics are carefully chosen so that there is a strong likelihood of mutual agreement. "The raising of safe topics allows the speaker the

89

right to stress his agreement with the hearer, and therefore to satisfy the hearer's desire to be right or to be corroborated in his opinions...The weather is a safe topic for virtually everyone, as is the beauty of gardens, the incompetence of bureaucracies, and so on" (Brown and Levinson 1978:117). These are examples of what has been called *phatic communion*. "Much of what passes for communication is rather the equivalent of a handclasp, or an embrace; its purpose is sociability" (Bolinger 1975: 524).

The mechanisms of phatic communion include (a) the speaker's repertoire of verbal and visual gestures, which signal interest in what his or her conversational partner is saying (such as the use of *mmm, uh-uh, yeah, really,* etc.); (b) the speaker's stock of "canned topics" and formulaic utterances, which are produced at relevant points in discourse, such as the small talk that is required to make brief encounters with acquaintances comfortable and positive; and (c) awareness of when to talk and when not to talk, that is, appropriate use of turn-taking conventions.

Adequate management of these conversational resources is essential if we are to create a sense of naturalness in conversational encounters. Nonnative speakers who lack the ability to use small talk and to exploit the interactional aspects of communication may find many encounters awkward and may avoid talk where talk would be appropriate. For example, a foreign couple with a good command of English but lacking the ability to participate in ongoing small talk were judged as cold, standoffish, and reserved by their American relatives (personal observation).

Communication as interaction is thus aimed largely at the need of speaker and hearer to feel valued and approved of. If our conversation-teaching materials primarily emphasize transactional skills, such as how to ask directions, how to order a meal, and so forth, learners may not have the chance to acquire the interactional skills that are also an important component of communicative competence.

The structured aspect of communication

The last aspect of communication I wish to consider is its ongoing organization. This can be looked at from two perspectives: a "macro" perspective, which reveals the differences in rhetorical organization that reflect different discourse genres or tasks; and a "micro" perspective, which shows how some of the processes by which discourse is constructed out of individual utterances are reflected in speech.

Task structure

Communication consists of different genres of discourse, such as conversations, discussions, debates, descriptions, narratives, and instructions. These different rhetorical tasks require the speaker to organize utterances in ways that are appropriate to that task. When we tell a story, for example, we follow certain conventions. Stories consist of a setting, followed by episodes. The setting consists of statements in which time, place, and characters are identified. Episodes consist of chains of events and conclude with reactions to events. Most stories can be described as having a structure of this type, and it is this structure that gives them coherence. Just as a sentence is grammatical to the extent that it follows the norms of English word order and structure, so a story is coherent to the extent that it follows the norms of semantic organization used in English.

Other types of rhetorical acts derive coherence from norms of structural organization. When we describe something, for example, coherence in our description is determined by how appropriately we deal with such elements as the level of the description, the content, the order in which items are described, and the relations between items mentioned in the description (Clark and Clark 1977: 232). In describing a landscape, for example, the writer must decide on the appropriate level of the description and decide whether to focus on the general impressions of the scene or on every detail (as for example in a police report). The writer must also make decisions concerning content, which will determine which elements of the scene to include or exclude. Then the elements must be arranged in an appropriate order and the relations between the things mentioned must be decided. Some objects may be highlighted in the description, for example, and other items related to them. The result will be a coherent description, one that is organized according to appropriate norms for this type of discourse. Similar decisions must be made when we describe people, rooms, states, or events. If we adopt solutions that are conventional, we create rhetorical acts that are coherent.

Other types of rhetorical acts also develop in ways that are organized and structured. Conversations, for example, begin with greetings and progress through various ordered moves: the speaker's and hearer's roles are ascertained, topics are introduced, rights to talk are assumed, new topics are raised, and, at an appropriate time, the conversation is terminated in a suitable manner. The development of communicative competence in a foreign language is crucially dependent on the speaker's ability to create discourse that is coherent. Schmidt (1983a), in his study of the development of communicative competence in a Japanese adult, studied how the subject's ability to perform coherent narratives and descriptions developed. At an early stage in his language development, the subject's attempts to narrate events suffered through the inclusion of excessive details presented in a random order, which made comprehension difficult.

Process structure

When we talk, much of our discourse is made up of words and phrases that indicate how what we are going to say relates to what has already been said. For example, our reaction to an idea or opinion may be to expand it, to add something to it, to disagree with it, to substantiate it, to give a reason for it, or to explain it. The following are examples of phrases or lexical items that may serve these or related functions:

When it comes to that	yes but
and another thing	well maybe
all the same	actually
consequently	anyway
in my case	as a matter of fact
to give you an idea	to begin with

These have been termed *conversational gambits* (Keller 1981), and they signal directions and relations within discourse. Evidence suggests that these contribute significantly to an impression of fluency in conversation. Course materials are now available that focus on these aspects of conversational competence. They are inappropriate, however, if they are used too often or in the wrong places, as in the following example:

To my mind I'll have another cup of coffee.

Conclusion

Theories about how we teach a foreign language reflect our view of the nature of language. Although it is no innovation to define language as a system of communication, the way the dynamics of the communicative process influence the form of verbal communication is seldom fully appreciated. ESL/EFL materials too often focus only on the finished *products* of communication, rather than on the *processes* by which people communicate. A deeper understanding of the effects of communicative needs on non-native speaker discourse should make us more understanding of our students' difficulties in using English, and happier with their partial successes.

7 Answers to yes/no questions

The use of questions in the language classroom is one of the oldest techniques of language teaching. Questions are used to provide models for transformation, repetition, and manipulation exercises, to test comprehension, and to maintain an acceptable ratio of student–teacher participation in the learning process. Despite the extensive use of questions in language teaching, their role in normal communication appears to have been little studied. Most textbooks divide questions into two classes: Wh-questions, which begin with a wh-word such as *who, when,* or *why,* and yes/no questions, which begin with an auxiliary verb. Although there is no grammatical limitation to the type of answer possible as a reply to a Wh-question, teachers and textbooks often demand that a yes/no question be answered with *yes* or *no* and repetition of the verb or auxiliary used in the question: *Is John smiling? Yes, he is. Are these apples? Yes, they are.*

The justification usually offered for this practice is that (a) this is the way people speak and (b) this is an easy and useful pattern for the learner to acquire. My experience with elementary language classes does not confirm the second of these assumptions, since the learner must attempt to manipulate a complex grammatical feature involving correct production of the verb used in the question (*do, did, is, are, were,* etc.). A great deal of time and energy is spent mastering the ability to produce the same verb that occurred in the question. Once the "rule" is learned, however, it tends to inhibit natural conversation, leading to stilted exchanges, such as the following:

A: Are you a student?
B: Yes, I am.
A: Do you like studying?
B: Yes, I do.
A: Are you French?
B: Yes, I am.
A: Are you from Paris?
B: Yes, I am.
A: Is that a nice place to live?
B: Yes, it is.

An attempt to find out if this is typical of normal conversation prompted the study described here. How do people usually deal with a yes/no

93

question? In order to answer this question, a survey was made of answers to yes/no questions in a corpus of written and spoken English. The answers native speakers gave to yes/no questions were observed and analyzed, and the information obtained compared with typical textbook treatment of yes/no questions.

The corpus

Two registers of English were examined for data on normal answers to yes/no questions. A written English corpus was studied, consisting of a sample of modern novels and plays whose authors attempt to represent normal spoken English in their writing. (The written English corpus consisted of the following texts: Graham Greene, *The Power and the Glory*; Ernest Hemingway, *A Farewell to Arms, A Moveable Feast*, and *The Old Man and the Sea*; Somerset Maugham, *The Razor's Edge*; Keith Waterhouse, *Billy Liar*; Arthur Miller, *All My Sons*; Tennessee Williams, *The Glass Menagerie*; and Somerset Maugham, *Collected Short Stories*.) Each consecutive occurrence of a yes/no question was noted, providing a total of 575 questions and their answers. A spoken English corpus was obtained through recording informal interviews with four native speakers. They were told only that they were being interviewed to find out about life in their countries and their reactions to living in Southeast Asia. Some 70 yes/no questions were put to each subject.[1] We also examined the answers to yes/no questions in six widely used textbooks.

Classification of the data

A formal classification of the answers obtained was then made. Although we were primarily interested in comparing the frequency of answers with *yes* or *no* + verb repetition with other answers in general, after a preliminary examination of the data six classes of answers were established. According to this classification, the question *Are you British?* might be answered in any of the following ways:

(a) Yes./No.   (Class I)
(b) Yes, I am./No, I'm not.   (Class II)
(c) Yes. From London.   (Class III)
(d) I am.   (Class IV)
(e) Of course.   (Class V)
(f) I was born in England.   (Class VI)

---

1 The counting and interviewing was done by my students in a methods course at Satya Wacana University, Salatiga, Indonesia; Sisworahardjo, Hari Subekti, Hirawati Rahardjo, Theresia Tristiowati, Eveline Christianto.

Class I consists of the words *yes, yes please, no, no thank you.* The following are typical of Class I answers, and are taken from the corpus:

(a) Don't you like to sit on the floor? No.
(b) Are you sure his name is Jim O'Connor? Yes.
(c) Is your wife an American? Yes.

Class II consists of *yes* or *no* + repetition of the verb or auxiliary verb in the question. Examples from the corpus are:

(a) Didn't we have a class or something together? Yes, we did.
(b) Is there to be mass in the morning, Father? Yes, there is to be mass.
(c) Did you enjoy living in Philadelphia? Yes, I did.

Class III includes replies which contain *yes* or *no* without repetition of the verb or auxiliary, but with additional information confirming, supporting, denying, modifying, or commenting on the question:

(a) Aren't you going to have any? No, I never eat asparagus.
(b) Did you stop in Rome? Yes, I spent a week there.
(c) Are foreign languages compulsory in school? No, it depends on the school.

Class IV consists of answers where the verb or auxiliary verb is repeated without *yes* or *no*. Additional qualifying, supporting, denying, or affirming information may be given.

(a) You are not going? I am.
(b) She is not in Paris? She is indeed.
(c) Are the students generally well paid? The men are; the women aren't.

Class V includes synonyms for *yes* or *no*. This class consists of lexical items or idioms which have the meaning of *yes* or *no* or some intermediate shade of meaning between these two categories. If we arrange some of the commonest items from our data on a scale ranging from those meaning approximately *yes* to those meaning approximately *no*, together with items falling between these two positions, we come up with the representative examples in Table 1. Representative samples from the corpus are:

(a) Are you feeling all right? Of course, darling.
(b) Has he money? Plenty.
(c) Is he in his bedroom? I don't know.

Class VI is closely related to Class V, and consists of replies in which a positive, negative, or neutral reply is inferred from the general context of the answer, although the question is not answered directly. Confirmation, agreement, denial, and so on, are communicated by inference from the context of the reply, or the reply may take the form of a comment or a request for clarification. Examples from the corpus are:

95

TABLE 1. REPRESENTATIVE EXAMPLES OF SYNONYMS FOR "YES" AND "NO"

(yes)				*(no)*
uh huh	mostly	maybe	not that	of course not
certainly	as usual	perhaps	I know	never
of course	rather	fairly	not well	nothing
sure	I think so	sometimes	I don't	not a bit
why not	I believe so	I don't know	think so	
terribly	I suppose so		I don't	
very	I expect so		believe so	
very much			not really	
definitely			not much	
plenty				
perfectly				

(a) Has something happened, mother? I'll be all right in a minute.
(b) Are you going at once? As soon as possible.
(c) Did you talk to any girls? Only the waitress when we went out for coffee.

Having considered the different classes of answers found in our corpus, we will now turn to the statistical results of the survey.

Results of the survey

Table 2 summarizes the results of the survey, giving the frequencies for each class of answer in the written and spoken English corpus, and in the six textbooks that were analyzed. The percentage represented by each class of answer is also given. The results can be summarized as follows.

In ordinary English, the most usual way of replying to a yes/no question seems to be a reply in which the question is not answered directly with *yes* or *no*, but from the answer it is clear whether the question has been answered positively, negatively, or in some other way. This is shown in the answers to Classes V and VI in the corpus, which together make up nearly 60 percent of the written corpus and nearly 50 percent of the spoken English corpus. If we add Class III, which consists of replies containing *yes* or *no* together with additional information but without auxiliary or verb repetition, almost 80 percent of the written corpus is included and over 70 percent of the spoken corpus. Replies containing auxiliary or verb repetition (Classes II and IV) make up less than 10 percent of the written corpus and less than 20 percent of the spoken corpus.

When we look at textbooks for the teaching of English, however, we find that the most frequent type of answer practiced is *yes* or *no* with repetition of the verb auxiliary (Class II). Some textbooks, such as text

TABLE 2. RESULTS OF SURVEY ON YES/NO QUESTIONS

The corpus	I Yes/No	II Yes/No + repetition of auxiliary	III Yes/No + additional information	IV Auxiliary repeated without Yes/No (+ additional information)	V Synonyms of of Yes/No[a]	VI Context	Total no. of questions counted
Written English corpus							
Total	78	22	104	28	117	226	575
%	13.56	3.83	18.09	4.87	20.35	39.30	100
Spoken English corpus							
Total	27	32	68	20	50	89	286
%	9.44	11.19	23.78	6.99	17.48	31.12	100
Textbook A (1st year)							
Total	5	135	9	20	18	33	220
%	2.27	61.37	4.09	9.09	8.18	15.00	100
Textbook A (2nd year)							
Total	2	44	11	45	19	4	125
%	1.60	35.20	8.80	36	15.20	3.20	100

TABLE 2 (CONT.)

The corpus	I Yes/No	II Yes/No + repetition of auxiliary	III Yes/No + additional information	IV Auxiliary repeated without Yes/No (+ additional information)	V Synonyms of Yes/No[a]	VI Context	Total no. of questions counted
Textbook B							
Total	30	229	19	40	21	50	389
%	7.71	58.57	4.89	10.28	5.43	12.85	100
Textbook C							
Total		122	94			1	217
%		56.22	43.32			0.46	100
Textbook D							
Total		994					994
%		100					100
Textbook E							
Total		718	11			1	730
%		98.35	1.51			0.14	100

[a] E.g., certainly, of course (not), adverbs of frequency and manner.

D, practice this type of answer exclusively. Such answers, however, are not typical of normal English. This is not perhaps surprising, since in ordinary conversational exchanges, more is usually expected from the participants than could be communicated by simply using *yes* or *no* with verb or auxiliary repetition.

Recommendations for the teacher and textbook writer

In this survey of answers to yes/no questions, we found a marked difference between the structures of answers in normal English and in textbooks. Teachers and textbooks too often demand that yes/no questions be answered with yes/no plus verb or auxiliary repetition. Such answers are not typical of real English. The complex grammatical manipulation required by this type of answer poses unnecessary difficulties for students and does not lead them toward normal uses of English. Although it is quite reasonable for textbook writers and teachers to present beginning students with regularized and graded English from which unnecessary difficulties have been removed, the need for auxiliary or verb repetition in answering a yes/no question is not justified by the norms of spoken English. Nor is it of any real value to the learner. Simple yes/no answers are sufficient at the elementary stages of language learning. Later, when sufficient vocabulary has been acquired, textbooks should gradually introduce some of the range of answers illustrated in this study, without dwelling unnecessarily on yes/no plus verb repetition.

8 Speech acts and second-language learning

Richard W. Schmidt and Jack C. Richards

Several new paradigms have emerged within applied linguistics in recent years. The Chomskyan paradigm has had a marked influence on theories of language and language learning. The goal of language learning within the Chomskyan approach is identified with the acquisition of underlying linguistic categories and systems, from which surface forms are derived through the application of transformational and other rules and processes of a universal type. Despite the addition of a philosophical framework for the theory, and although the Chomskyan concept of language knowledge is quite different in its own terms from the concept of language knowledge implicit in pre-Chomskyan theory, it is only a partial account of the knowledge required to *use* a language. This chapter considers other areas of knowledge that constitute an equally important dimension of the task of learning a language, with particular reference to second- and foreign-language learning.

Sociolinguists and others have long acknowledged the limitations in the Chomskyan formulation of competence and have stressed the need to include knowledge of the rules of use and communicatively appropriate performance. Bruner, writing of first-language learning, has argued that mother-tongue acquisition should be looked at not as a solo flight by the child in search of disembodied rules of grammar but as a problem-solving transaction. The essential problems to be solved by mother and infant have to do with "how to make our intentions known to others, how to communicate what we have in our consciousness, what we want done on our behalf, how we wish to relate to others, and what in this or other worlds is possible" (Bruner 1978). In this chapter we will consider second language acquisition from a similar perspective to that advocated by Bruner for first language acquisition, focusing on the development of communicative rather than linguistic or grammatical competence. Although communicative-competence theory covers a range of different dimensions of language behavior in the individual and in the speech community, we will focus on one aspect of communicative competence, namely, speech acts, and consider the contribution of speech-act theory to our understanding of second language acquisition.

What is a speech act?

Speech-act theory has to do with the functions and uses of language; so in the broadest sense we might say that speech acts are all the acts we perform through speaking, all the things we *do* when we speak. Such a definition is too broad for most purposes, however, because we use speech in most human activities. We use language to build bridges, to consolidate political regimes, to carry on arguments, to convey information from one person to another, to entertain – in short, to communicate. We use speech in ceremonies, games, recipes, and lectures. On some occasions, for example, social gatherings, we use language successively to introduce one person to another, carry on conversations, tell jokes, criticize and praise third parties both present and absent, expound on favorite topics, seduce or attempt to seduce, and say farewell. We could extend such lists indefinitely, but as Halliday (1973: 18, 28) has pointed out, such lists do not by themselves tell us very much, for the innumerable social purposes for which adults use language are not represented directly, one-to-one, in the language system.

Hymes (1972) has proposed a useful distinction between speech situations, speech events, and speech acts. Within a community one finds many *situations* associated with speech, such as fights, hunts, meals, parties. But it is not profitable to convert such situations into part of a sociolinguistic description by simply relabeling them in terms of speech, for such situations are not in themselves governed by consistent rules throughout. The term *speech event* can be restricted to activities that are directly governed by rules or norms for the use of speech, events such as two-party conversations (face-to-face or on the telephone), lectures, introductions, religious rites, and the like. This notion of speech event is related to the traditional concept of genre, though Hymes argues that the two must be treated as analytically independent, and a great deal of empirical research is needed to clarify the relationship between the terms. *Speech acts* (in a narrow sense now) are the minimal terms of the set: speech situation/event/act. When we speak we perform acts, such as giving reports, making statements, asking questions, giving warnings, making promises, approving, regretting, and apologizing.

Sinclair and Coulthard (1975), who have analyzed classroom transcripts, also propose a "top-down" analysis, beginning with the social occasion (the lesson) as the outermost analytic frame and successively dividing and subdividing the sequence of discourse down to the smallest unit, the *act*, which they define as the most minimal unit of speaking that can be said to have a function. Acts are labeled according to discourse function, for example, elicitation, question.

In this chapter we focus primarily on individual speech acts. However, it is necessary to look somewhat beyond the isolated act represented by the individual sentence, primarily the verb. Austin (1962) pointed out that there are many speech acts (illocutionary acts, in his terminology), and in English there are many verbs that refer to them. Consider for example just the related set: *ask, request, direct, require, order, command, suggest, beg, plead, implore, pray.* Austin claimed that there are over a thousand such verbs in English. But although English verbs provide a useful initial taxonomy for speech acts, the acts are not in fact equivalent to the verbs that frequently name them. Searle (1976) points out that many verbs are not markers of illocutionary force but of some other feature of the speech act. *Insist* and *suggest*, for example, mark degree of intensity but do not mark separate speech-act functions or illocutionary points. Both may be used with directive function ("I suggest/insist that we go to the movies") or with representative function ("I suggest/insist that the answer is found on page 16"). We need to recognize also that speech acts are not identifiable with the sentence or with any other level of grammatical description. Hymes's (1972) position is that the level of speech acts mediates between the usual levels of grammar and the rest of a speech event in that it implicates both linguistic form and social norm. Whether or not a particular utterance has the status of a request, for example, may depend upon a conventional linguistic formula ("How about picking me up early this afternoon?"), but it may also depend upon the social relationship between speaker and hearer.

It needs to be recognized too that speech acts occur within discourse, and that the interpretation and negotiation of speech-act force is often dependent on the discourse or transactional context. As a minimum, we need to consider the fact that talk is often organized into two-part exchanges. As Goffman (1976) points out, this organizing principle follows from very fundamental requirements of talk as a communication system. A speaker needs to know whether his message has been received and understood; a recipient needs to show that he has received and understood the message. We therefore must recognize such "adjacency pairs" as summons–answer (Schegloff 1968), statement–reply (Goffman 1976), question–answer, request–refusal of request, and the like.

An investigation of speech acts therefore leads naturally into questions of act sequencing (events) and contexts (speech settings or situations). Rehbein and Ehlich, quoted in Candlin (1978), list the different operations that may take place inside a restaurant when the activity is ordering a meal: entering, looking around, judging, taking a seat, wanting the menu, asking for the menu, wanting information, asking for information, consulting, deciding, ordering, transmission, production, delivery, serving, consuming, wanting to pay, asking for the bill, drawing up the account, getting/presenting the bill, accepting the bill, paying, leaving. Norms of linguistic behavior identify various parts of the sequence.

Different participants have different amounts and different types of talking to do, as well as different topics to talk about. Within speech events there are norms for opening and closing sequences, sequencing rules, and distribution frequencies and probabilities for particular speech acts. "Assigning the value *command* to any of a range of possible utterances ('hot dog'; 'that one'; 'please bring me X'; a deictic gesture) is a function of recognizing the social world of the restaurant with the rights, duties and social relationship between the participants, as well as that of being aware of the discoursal position of the 'act of commanding' within the transactional process" (Candlin 1978: 17).

Both speech acts and speech events have been studied extensively in recent years and have constituted topical focuses for scholars from a great number of disciplines. Speech events have been investigated by anthropologists and ethnographers (Albert 1964, Gumperz and Hymes 1972, Sanches and Blount 1975), folklorists (Abrahams 1962, Dundes, Leach, and Ozkok 1972), literary critics (M. Pratt 1977), and sociologists (Allen and Guy 1974). The most detailed and perhaps the most provocative analyses of speech events have been provided by those sociologists who work within the area of sociology termed ethnomethodology, the primary goal of which is to give rigorous sociological formulation to the interactional basis of the things people say and do in the settings of everyday life. Working primarily from transcripts of natural conversations, characterizations have been developed for a variety of conversational activities: turn taking (Sacks, Schegloff, and Jefferson 1974), story telling and identity negotiations (Sacks 1972), opening and closing conversations (Schegloff and Sacks 1973), telephone conversations (Schegloff 1968), and many other aspects of the establishment and management of social relations through conversational roles (Garfinkel 1967, Goffman 1972 and 1976, Sudnow 1972, Schenkein 1978). Speech acts, on the other hand, have been studied primarily by philosophers of language (Austin 1962, Grice 1968 and 1975, Searle 1969 and 1976) and linguists (Ross 1970, Gordon and Lakoff 1971, Cole and Morgan 1975).

Theoretical questions

The following are some of the major theoretical issues discussed in the speech-act literature.

Units and categories

For linguistic analysis, the units of concern are sentences. Contrasts between well-formed and ill-formed (ungrammatical) sentences are primary data. Although the grammatical paradigm has been followed by many linguists who have dealt with issues in speech-act theory (see most of the papers in Cole and Morgan 1975) and although basic semantic differences are indeed likely to have syntactic consequences (Searle 1976), speech acts are in essence *acts*, not *sentences*. Speech acts cannot be equated with *utterances* either, for we often perform more than one act (e.g., inform and request) with a single utterance: for example, "I'm hungry." Finally, speech acts cannot be equated with the notion of *turn* as an interactional unit, as it may take several speaker turns to accomplish a single act, or, conversely, several acts may be performed within a single speaker turn.

So far we have presented only a very vague description of what speech acts *are*. Perhaps the notion is best clarified by examples, with some effort to group together illocutionary acts into major types.

Searle (1976) presents the clearest taxonomy. For Searle, the basis for classification is "illocutionary point" or purpose of the act, from the speaker's perspective. According to Searle, speech acts can be grouped into a small number of basic types based on speaker intentions:

Representatives. One of the basic things we do with language is tell people how things are. We *assert, claim, say, report*, and the like. The point or purpose of this class of representatives is to commit the speaker in varying degrees (*suggest, doubt*, and *deny* are members of this class also) to the truth of something. One test of a representative is whether it can be characterized as true or false.

Directives. When we use language, we do not just refer to the world and make statements about it. Among our most important uses for language is trying to get people to do things. The class of directives includes all speech acts whose primary point is that they count as attempts on the part of the speaker to get the hearer to do something. Suggestions, requests, and commands are all directives. They differ in the force of the attempt but are all attempts by the speaker to get the hearer to do something.

Commissives. Commissives are those illocutionary acts whose point is to commit the speaker to do something. Promises and threats both fall into this category, the difference between them being the speaker's assumption about whether or not the promised action is desired by the hearer.

Searle makes the interesting point that there is a difference in the direction of fit between the words of a speech act and the state of affairs in the world when comparing representatives with directives and commissives. With representatives the direction of fit is words-to-world, that is, what is at issue is whether the words uttered ("The world is flat") match the world. With both representatives and commissives the direction of fit is world-to-words. Future actions are to be done in accordance with words previously uttered. The basic distinction between requests and commissives is that hearer actions are the point of requests and other directives, whereas speaker actions are the issue with promises and other commissives.

Expressives. The point of this class is to express feelings and attitudes about states of affairs. We *apologize* for things we have done, *deplore* other people's actions, regret, thank, welcome, and so on. With expressives there is no direction of fit, but the state of affairs specified in the following proposition is simply assumed to be true. Note also that although representatives, directives, and commissives are all associated with a consistent psychological dimension (belief, wish, and intent, respectively), the psychological states expressed by expressives are extremely varied.

Declarations. Some speech acts bring about changes in the world simply through their successful execution. "You're fired," says the boss, and the employee must start the search for a new position. "I do," say the bride and groom, and after the presiding official's (secular or clerical) speech the marriage has taken place. The defining characteristic of this class is that the performance brings about the correspondence between the words and the world. This class is closest to Austin's (1962) original notion of a performative, an act of doing something in the world rather than an act of saying alone.

OTHER CLASSES, MAJOR AND MINOR

Several taxonomies have been proposed in addition to that of Searle. Fraser (1975) adds a few categories. In addition to *acts of asserting* (= Searle's representatives), he includes *acts of evaluating,* the point of which is to express the speaker's assessment of the truth of a proposition and the basis of the judgment, for example, *analyze, conclude, hypothesize.* In addition to acts of requesting (= Searle's directives), Fraser has a category of acts suggesting, for example, *recommend, suggest, urge.* *Acts of stipulating* express a speaker's desire for the acceptance of a naming convention expressed by the proposition, for example, *call, classify, designate.* Hancher (1979) has suggested two additional kinds of acts, those that combine commissive with directive illocutionary force (e.g., offering, inviting, challenging) and those that require two participants (e.g., giving, selling, contracting).

Although the great majority of speech acts can probably be analyzed as examples of Searle's major classes, or of Fraser's somewhat longer list, there are doubtless some speech acts that are outside these particular taxonomies. Greetings and farewells, for example, constitute a small category (or categories) of acts that are not generalizable as major classes but that deserve attention. It is also useful to mention such acts as *refusal of a request,* although utterances that fall into such a category will in

105

most cases already be classifiable in terms of the basic act types: "I'm sorry, but I can't" = expressive + representative; "I'll be able to see you tomorrow" (not today) = commissive; "Do it yourself" = directive.

PERFORMATIVE VERBS

From Austin's original notion of a performative come the current and important terms *performative verb* and *explicit performative* (sentence or utterance). These are verbs (sentences, utterances) that explicitly name the acts being performed, for example, "I promise to be there," an explicit performative that can be contrasted with the implicit "I'll be there." There are certain syntactic requirements generally assumed to hold for a verb to function performatively, such as the requirements that the subject (if expressed) be first person, the addressee (if expressed) second person, and that the verb be in the present tense. Thus "I promise you that I'll be there" is explicitly performative, but "He promised that he'd be there" is not – in fact it is not a promise (commissive) at all, but rather a report (representative). Most authors see the performative as a sentence type with such syntactic requirements, but Fraser (1975) demurs, arguing that strict syntactic requirements cannot be proved and favoring instead a distinction between strongly performative examples (those that are easily seen as counting as the act denoted by the verb) and weakly performative examples.

How to perform a speech act

Searle (1965) has attempted to provide analyses of various illocutionary acts, asking what conditions are necessary and sufficient for a particular act to have been performed by the uttering of a particular sentence. For promises, the conditions are identified as follows:

Normal input and output conditions obtain, that is, the speaker and hearer are not insane, they are not play acting, and so on.

A speaker expresses a sentence, the propositional content of which predicates a future act of the speaker.

The hearer would prefer the speaker's doing the act to his not doing the act, and the speaker believes this. Searle calls this a preparatory condition.

It is not obvious to both speaker and hearer that the speaker will do the act in the normal course of events.

The speaker intends to do the act. This is the illocutionary point of promising, which Searle calls the sincerity condition.

The speaker intends that the utterance of the sentence will place him under an obligation to do the act. This is called the essential condition.

The general type of analysis carries over to other speech acts as well. For assertions, for example, one condition is that the speaker must have some basis for supporting the assertions to be true, the sincerity condition is that he must believe it to be true, and the essential condition is that the utterance counts as an attempt to inform and convince.

These conditions do not tell us how speech acts are actually used and understood, however; and the question of how the speaker and hearer assign appropriate illocutionary value to a speech act remains a topic for speculation among linguists, philosophers and ethnomethodologists. Goffman (1976) has pointed out that a classification of speech acts provides us with an opportunity to see that how an interchange unfolds will depend somewhat on the type of speech act involved, but that an attempt must be made "to uncover the principles which account for whatever contrast is found on a particular occasion between what is said, what is usually meant by this, and what in fact is meant on that particular occasion of use."

Searle (1975) talks of inferential strategies and suggests how the second of the following statements could be taken as a rejection of the proposal made in the first statement.

Student X: Let's go to the movies tonight.
Student Y: I have to study for an exam.

Searle (1975: 63) reconstructs the steps necessary to derive the intended meaning in the following way (without proposing that these are conscious operations).

Step 1:   I have made a proposal to Y, and in response he has made a statement to the effect that he has to study for an exam (facts about the conversation).

Step 2:   I assume that Y is cooperating in the conversation and that therefore his remark is intended to be relevant (principles of conversational cooperation).

Step 3:   A relevant response must be one of acceptance, rejection, counterproposal, further discussion, and so on (theory of speech acts).

Step 4:   But his literal utterance was not one of these, and so was not a relevant response (inference from Steps 1 and 3).

Step 5:   Therefore, he probably means more than he says. Assuming that his remark is relevant, his primary illocutionary point must differ from his literal one (inference from Steps 2 and 4).

Step 6:   I know that studying for an exam normally takes a large amount of time relative to a single evening, and I know that going to the movies normally takes a large amount of time relative to a single evening (factual background information).

Step 7:   Therefore he probably cannot both go to the movies and study for an exam in one evening (inference from Step 6).

Step 8:   A preparatory condition on the acceptance of a proposal, or on any other commissive, is the ability to perform the act predicated in the propositional content condition (theory of speech acts).

Step 9: Therefore, I know that he has said something that has the consequence that he probably cannot consistently accept the proposal (inference from Steps 1, 7, and 8).

Step 10: Therefore, his primary illocutionary point is probably to reject the proposal (inference from Steps 5 and 9).

Grice's (1975) "general principles of co-operative behaviour" likewise attempt to identify presuppositions that enable the participants in a speech event to assign appropriate illocutionary value to utterances. Grice refers to four maxims:

Maxim of Quantity: Make your contribution (just) as informative as is required.
Maxim of Quality: Make your contribution one that is true.
Maxim of Relation: Be relevant.
Maxim of Manner: Avoid obscurity and ambiguity; be brief and orderly.

Grice gives the following example.

Suppose that A and B are talking about a mutual friend C, who is now working in a bank. A asks B how C is getting on in his job, and B replies: "Oh, quite well, I think; he likes his colleagues, and he hasn't been to prison yet." At this point A might well enquire what B was implying, what he was suggesting, or even what he meant by saying that C had not yet been to prison...in a suitable setting A might reason as follows: (1) B has apparently violated the maxim "Be relevant" and so may be regarded as having flouted one of the maxims conjoining perspicuity; yet I have no reason to suppose that he is opting out from the operation of the Cooperative Principle; (2) given the circumstances I can regard his irrelevance as only apparent if and only if I suppose him to think that C is potentially dishonest; (3) B knows that I am capable of working out step (2). So B implicates that C is potentially dishonest.

Meaning, deep structure, and surface structure

One of the most controversial aspects of speech-act theory has to do with whether illocutionary point is part of the "meaning" of a sentence and whether that aspect of meaning ought to be represented in the grammar of a language, in the deep structure.

THE PERFORMATIVE ANALYSIS

In traditional school grammars of English, there is an assumed fit between sentence type and illocutionary point, to wit: declarative sentences (a grammatical sentence type) are used for making assertions (a speech-act category); imperative sentences are used for orders; interrogative sentences are used for asking questions (requests for verbal responses).

The "performative analysis" is essentially an attempt to capture this relationship, by position for all imperative sentences, for example, a highest performative clause "I order you" in the deep structure.

Ross (1970) has claimed that declarative sentences must be derived from deep structures containing an explicitly represented performative "I say (assert, state, etc.) to you X." Ross presents a large number of syntactic arguments to support the existence of both pronouns in the higher clause, such as pseudo-reflexives in sentences like "This paper was written by Ann and myself." Ross does not attempt to prove that the highest performative is a specific English verb, like *say* or *state*, but simply asserts that it must be [+ performative], [+ communication], [+ linguistic], and [+ declarative].

In its simplest form, the performative analysis does not take us very far in understanding the relationship between linguistic form and illocutionary point. Ross's syntactic arguments have been strongly criticized (see Matthews 1972), and there are obvious problems with the assumed fit between sentence type and illocutionary force on semantic grounds. Declarative sentences are not always assertions, but can function as questions (when the hearer rather than the speaker is assumed to have knowledge about the proposition – Labov 1972) or as orders ("No one will leave this room, and that means you!"). Syntactic imperatives may function as other speech acts than orders, as in a sentence like "Spare the rod and spoil the child." In general the fit between sentence type and function is only typical, not absolute (Bolinger 1967).

Sadock (1970) first tackled the problem of what he called "whimperatives," sentences that have imperative force but question form, for example, "Will you close the door please?" Sadock analyzed such constructions as conjunctions of questions and imperatives. Other analyses are possible. Whimperatives could be analyzed as ordinary questions (thus failing to take any account of the imperative force, but leaving this to pragmatic, extragrammatical explanations), or one could analyze them as identical in deep structure to imperatives (Heringer 1972). One could claim that forms like "Will you shut up?" are merely simple imperatives ("Shut up") to which tags have been added and then preposed (Green 1975).

CONVERSATIONAL POSTULATES

An entirely different approach to the analysis of whimperatives and other indirect speech acts has been proposed by Gordon and Lakoff (1971). Following Grice (1968), they argue that sentences may convey more than their literal meaning. The sentence "It's cold in here," when spoken by a superior to a subordinate, may convey the meaning of "Close the window," but that does not mean that the analysis of "It's cold in here" should include positing an imperative force-indicating device in the deep structure. Gordon and Lakoff propose that speakers and hearers interpret such sentences by reference to conversational postulates. Thus whimperatives are to be analyzed grammatically as simple questions, but interpreted as imperatives by means of a conversational postulate or entailment rule, such as: A speaker can convey a request by asking if the hearer intends to do the act, as in "Will you close the door?"

The conversational postulates proposed by Gordon and Lakoff are both highly predictive and intuitively satisfying. They directly relate the philosophical analyses of what is involved in certain speech acts with the forms of language. For requests, the full form of the conversational postulate is that one can convey a request by either asserting a speaker-based condition or questioning a hearer-based condition. Thus we have the following forms:

I'd like you to go now.	Asserts speaker-based sincerity condition S wants H to do A.
Could you be a little quieter?	Questions hearer-based preparatory condition H is able to do A.
Well, are you going to help me?	Questions hearer-based preparatory condition. It is not obvious to both S and H that H will do A in the normal course of events.

It is clear that the conversational postulates are not quite as neat as Gordon and Lakoff suggest. For example, one can convey requests by asserting hearer-based conditions as well as by questioning them, for example, "You could be a little quieter, you know," "From now on, when I say *jump* you will jump." But as Clark and Clark (1977) have pointed out, it is an extraordinary correspondence when speakers make indirect requests by making use of the social conventions that cover the proper use of requests.

SURFACE STRUCTURES AND CONTEXTS

Ervin-Tripp (1976) has proposed a strikingly different analysis of English directives. Ervin-Tripp argues that although native speakers' understanding can be treated as inferences from literal interpretations, social factors are what determine the actual choice of directive type. Based on a number of empirical studies, Ervin-Tripp reports that need statements ("I need a match") occur between persons differing in rank. Permission directives, sentences that look like requests for permission but in fact require action on the part of the hearer ("Can I have my record back?"), are usually directed upward in rank, when the hearer controls resources. Hints, which do not include a literal expression of the act desired, are frequent in families and communal groups. The social variables that affect directive choice include age, rank, familiarity, presence of outsiders, territorial location, the seriousness of the service asked, and many others. Moreover, Ervin-Tripp claims that directives do not require inference from literal interpretations. Where knowledge of obligations and prohibitions is shared, simple interpretation rules allow prompt understanding.

Reviewing the linguistic debate over the incorporation of illocutionary point in the analysis of sentences, Sadock (1975) suggests two methods of removing arbitrariness from current descriptions. One would eliminate all transderivational constraints that state an interaction between logic and language; the other would require a logicogrammatical treatment wherever it is possible to provide one. Sadock recognizes that the result would be two very different interpretations of sentence meaning, one very shallow and one very deep, but states that "I am not sure that anything at all rides on this difference." Does the difference matter for our view of the teaching/learning process? For teaching purposes, especially the preparation of materials, both the deep structure analysis of Gordon and Lakoff and the surface structure–oriented analysis of Ervin-Tripp provide valuable source material. But when we consider the implications of the different models for our view of language learning, there does appear to be a difference. The logicogrammatical "deep" model would force us to view the acquisition of grammatical competence and the acquisition of communicative competence as essentially the same thing, whereas the "shallow" model would allow us to consider the development of grammatical forms quite distinctly from the pragmatic ability to match linguistic forms with appropriate social contexts.

Universals

For the purpose of investigating speech acts in the context of second-language learning, perhaps the most important question is whether and to what extent the various aspects of speech acts discussed so far are universal.

Consider first the basic units. Can it be safely asserted that essentially the same classes of speech events (conversations, lectures, discussions, debates, etc.) and the same taxonomy of speech (i.e., representatives, directives, commissives, etc.) hold for all languages and speech communities? Most researchers assume that the answer to this question is yes, but in fact there has been no ethnographic research carried out to confirm or disprove the assumption. It is probably not true that all languages name the same speech acts with illocutionary verbs (does every language recognize a *suggest: insist* distinction?), but again, no research has been reported.

The universality of the strategies for performing speech acts, particularly indirect speech acts, has been discussed in the literature. Gordon and Lakoff say that they have checked with a number of speakers of widely divergent languages and would not be surprised to find that the conversational postulates they propose were universals. Fraser (1978) has recently claimed that the strategies for performing illocutionary acts are essentially the same across languages. Comparing request strategies in fourteen different languages, Fraser found that the same basic strategies were available in each language. If this is correct, then Fraser is correct in claiming that acquiring social competence in a new language does not involve substantially new concepts concerning how language is organized and what types of devices serve what social functions, but only new (social) attitudes about which strategies may be used appropriately in a given context.

Goffman (1976) draws a distinction between "system constraints" (those that follow from the requirements of any communication system), which he suggests are pancultural, and "ritual constraints" (such as constraints regarding how each individual ought to handle himself with respect to others), which can be expected to vary markedly from society to society. System constraints include norms such as those identified by Grice: be relevant, be informative, and so forth. Ochs-Keenan (1976) has attempted to assess the status of some of Grice's maxims cross-culturally and has found that the maxim "Be informative" does not hold in Malagasy society. Interlocutors regularly violate the maxim by providing less information than is required by their conversational partner, even though they have the required information. However, it can be argued that the maxims are universal, but that deviations from the norm force us to attempt to uncover additional maxims, motives, and strategies to account for departures from an "ideal" communication system.

Perhaps the most persuasive (and most detailed) argument for the universality of speech-act strategies has been put forth by Brown and Levinson (1978). They point out that most speech acts are in some way threatening to either the speaker or the hearer, either by imposing on one party's freedom of action, as with acts of requesting (an attempt to restrict the freedom of the hearer), or by damaging the positive self-image of one of the parties, as with criticisms (hearer's face is damaged) and apologies (speaker's face is damaged). Brown and Levinson argue that speakers compute the level of threat involved, considering such factors as social distance, degree of power that one party may have over the other, and the ranking of impositions within a particular culture, and then select a strategy for doing the act. Very threatening actions may not be done at all, and minimally threatening actions are usually done directly and explicitly. It is the great area in between that is most complex. Speakers may select a strategy of "positive politeness," one that minimizes the threatening action by reassuring the hearer that he or she is valued by the speaker, that somehow the speaker wants what the hearer wants, that they are members of the same in-group, and so on. Or a speaker may select a strategy of "negative politeness," redressing the threat to basic claims of territory and self-determination, for example, by apologizing or being indirect and formal. Thus a request for forgiveness might be expressed in a positively polite form as "Gimme a break, Sweetheart," or in a negatively polite form as "I hope you'll be able to excuse my error."

Brown and Levinson describe a great number of positive and negative speech-act strategies and investigate their use in three languages (English, Tamil, and Tzeltal). They report that they find a fine-grained parallelism in the expression of politeness in these unrelated languages, often including the minutiae of linguistic forms. They argue that interactional systematics, the basis for linguistic realizations, are based largely on universal principles.

There is sufficient evidence to argue, however, that speech-act strategies will be found to be universal only if they are phrased in extremely general terms. All languages have some verbs that name performative acts, for example, and some of these may be used to issue directives, but this does not mean that all such request forms in English have literal translations that function the same way in all languages. Consider the distinction between "I request that..." and "I hereby request that...," where the "hereby" not only makes the request yet more explicit but also lends a legal flavor to the sentence. In French a similar distinction may be conveyed through quite different linguistic means, such as the use of an elaborated verb form in preference to a simple one, for example, "Je vous prie" as opposed to "Je vous prie de bien vouloir."

It is possible that "hedges" on illocutionary force may be a universal strategy or negative politeness, but whereas this operation may be carried out by the use of tag questions ("It was amazing, wasn't it?") or by intonation in some languages (including English), in other languages the parallel operation may involve other devices, such as the Japanese particle *ne* (Brown and Levinson 1978: 152).

It appears that other speech-act strategies can also be considered universal only if they are phrased very generally. It is perhaps the case that one can make a request in any language by referring to the hearer's ability to perform the action, but again exact translations of English sentences often fail to carry identical implied force. Searle (1975) points out that although "Can you hand me that book?" can be translated literally into Czech, the resulting sentence will sound extremely odd to a Czech speaker. English "can," "could," and "able" when indicating a request can be translated into Cantonese only as *hoyih*; other modals usually translated into English as "can" refer specifically to physical ability and do not imply directive force. A sentence like "Can you reach the book on the top shelf?" if translated with the modal *naahnggau* ("able") would be answered with "yes" or "no," with no attempt to get the book by the hearer (Marcus, personal communication). Green (1975) observes that conditional forms equivalent to English "would" ("Would you leave it on my desk when you finish, please") cannot carry imperative force in Spanish, Hebrew, or Japanese, although they can in English, German, and Finnish. In English, we can make requests with nonliteral *let's* ("Let's all think before we raise our hands"), but Cole (1975) reports that in both Swahili and Yiddish such constructions are ungrammatical.

Searle has argued that the mechanisms (strategies) for indirect speech are general, not peculiar to this language or that, but within this framework certain standard forms tend to become conventionally established as the standard idiomatic forms. The standard forms for one language may not maintain their indirect speech-act potential when translated into another language, because (a) the translation may not be idiomatic in the second language and (b) even if idiomatic, the resulting forms may not be those that are conventionally selected as devices for indirect speech acts (Searle 1975).

Even if speech-act strategies are to a certain extent universal, therefore, learners of new languages still need to learn several important things. They need to learn the particular conventionalized forms in the new language, particular applications of general principles that vary systematically among cultures and groups (and to a certain extent among individuals). They need to learn the general "ethos" of the new speech community, whether the interactional style in general is stiff and formal or relaxed and open. They need to learn which speech acts are particularly threatening in a particular culture. One culture might place particular emphasis on modesty and circumspection in the expression of speaker beliefs, for example, whereas in another community requests (or criticisms) might be especially threatening. Learners need to learn the social relationships of the community, the networks of relationships and responsibility that obtain, which kinds of acts can be directed toward which persons, and so on (Brown and Levinson 1978). Learners also need to learn some very specific contexts that call for particular speech acts and that vary from society to society. Apte (1974) has identified the contexts that call for "thank you" in South Indian languages (very restricted), as opposed to American English (extensive). Ueda (1974) has discussed refusals in Japanese, the situations that permit saying "no," and the ways to refuse a request when a direct refusal is not possible.

Candlin argues that interethnic and intercultural variation among mother tongues, domains of language use, interlanguage attitudes, and language-learning purposes lead to misunderstanding, and that such misunderstanding can be understood through the study of discourse patterning. He stresses that the performance of speech acts depends on "culturally specific appropriateness criteria" (Candlin 1978). Clyne (1975) discusses communication breakdown (where an intention is misunderstood) and communication conflict (where a misunderstanding leads to friction between speakers) and suggests that both can often be attributed to cross-cultural (interlingual or dialectal), social (sociolectal), or individual (ideolectal) differences in communicative competence rules, for example, different rules for the realization of particular speech acts. This suggests that a fruitful area of research in second language acquisition is the contrastive analysis of norms for the realization of speech events and speech acts in different speech communities, which could usefully complement contrastive analysis, error analysis, performance analysis, and related approaches.

Implications for language-learning research and theory

The preceding account of speech events and speech acts reviews the major contributions to speech-act theory that have been made by linguists, philosophers, ethnomethodologists, and others. We now consider in what ways speech-act theory can contribute to our understanding of second language acquisition. A major contribution of speech-act theory is in its clarification of dimensions of communicative competence. Although the concept of communicative competence is not new, much remains to be done to substantiate the concept empirically, and the study of the role of speech acts in second-language learning could make a useful contribution to our knowledge of how second and foreign languages are acquired.

Until recently, theories of second-language learning have followed, rather narrowly, models developed in linguistic theory. Thus it was widely assumed that transformational-generative grammar could serve both as a general model for language and as an explanatory model for second-language learning. Within much L2 theory and research the primacy of syntax has been taken for granted and the syntactic paradigm has been dominant. Although phonology and other areas have not been ignored, second-language learning has largely been described as a continuum of gradually complexifying syntactic systems. The bulk of the empirical research of recent years has been on such issues as morpheme development, error analysis, and developmental study of L2 syntax, relating these to the concept of proficiency in a second or foreign language. Speech-act theory, on the other hand, defining proficiency with

115

reference to communicative rather than linguistic competence, looks beyond the level of the sentence to the question of what sentences do and how they do it when language is used. It thus broadens the scope of enquiry to include the study of how second-language learners use sentences to perform speech acts and to participate in speech events. In first language acquisition, the acquisition of speech act routines has recently been considered of primary importance.

First-language learning

Halliday (1975), Dore (1975, 1977), and Bruner (1975, 1978) have examined the development of speech acts in young children (under 1 year of age) and concluded that knowledge of communicative function precedes true language. Dore (1975) in particular argues that illocutionary force is a language universal, that the speech act is the basic unit of linguistic communication, and that early language development consists of the child's pragmatic intentions gradually becoming grammaticalized. Bruner (1978) has characterized the empiricist associationist view of language learning as "impossible" and the nativist view as "miraculous" and suggests that a speech-act viewpoint is more explanatory than either. Bruner argues that mother-tongue acquisition is a problem-solving transactional enterprise, involving an active language learner and an equally active language teacher. Bruner stresses the importance of mother–child interaction and finds this related to the progression in the kinds of requests made by children. First requests are directed at nearby objects, usually held by the mother, and the mother's main job seems to be to establish the sincerity of the request. A second type of request is related to shared activity in games, for example, "Mommy read," in the context of reading together. These requests – and the mother's responses – are tied to the development of turn taking, the assignment of roles, and agency. The last type of request to develop, emerging at 15–16 months with Bruner's children, is for supportive action, such as persuading the mother to get a toy telephone from the cupboard so that the child may play with it. Although in both the earliest and the latest requests in the sequence what is desired may be an object, the later request forms are more sophisticated because they involve a goal and a means of getting to it. A similar distinction has been drawn by Halliday between the instrumental ("I want") and the regulatory ("Do as I tell you") functions of early language.

Clark and Clark (1977) report that at the two-word stage children use mainly two types of speech acts, assertions (representatives) and requests (directives). They do not promise things or use declarations; these are not added to their repertoire of speech acts until they are considerably older, but they elaborate the kinds of directives and representatives they make as soon as they begin to produce longer utterances.

Reviewing studies by Halliday (1975), Bates (1976), Dore (1975), and Garvey (1975) on early request forms, Ervin-Tripp concludes:

From a very early age (children) have a rich system of alternations in form that is systematically related to social features. They sensitively identify social contrasts signalled by tag modals, polite forms, address terms, modal embeddings. What they gradually learn to do is conceal their purposes. While they use diverse syntactic forms, they still refer explicitly to their desires and goals, when they are not obvious from the context. So the major differences between adults and young children is not diversity of structure, not diversity of social features – though the rules may increase in number of variables and in complexity with age – but systematic, regular, unmarked requests, which do not refer to what the speaker wants. Wide use of tactful deviousness is a late accomplishment. (1977: 188)

Mitchell-Kernan and Kernan (1977) have looked at the choice of directive type among older children (7–12 years) and found that both requests and refusals are in some cases peculiar to children's culture in the way they are elaborated. Children so often use directives to define and test status relationships and obligations that they react testily to directive forms that, on the surface at least, seem perfectly appropriate. Whereas requests that have little cost are usually honored by adults, Mitchell-Kernan and Kernan found that their children did not honor them and frequently insisted on courtesy phrases (e.g., *pretty please*), and even if these were used did not always comply. The frequent use of challenges ("Who do you think you are?") indicates that the children are constantly on guard to preserve their rights and to defend themselves against challenges to their status.

SECOND-LANGUAGE LEARNING

In reviewing research on second- and foreign-language learning, Swain (1977) proposes a four-part model of second-language learning, isolating four areas of relevant research:

1. *Input factors* refers to input to the learning process or situation, and includes both linguistic and extralinguistic variables.
2. *Learner factors* refers to the contribution of learner variables (age, attitude, motivation, etc.) to the learning process.
3. *Learning factors* refers to strategies and processes used by the learner to learn elements of the target language – generalization, imitation, transfer, analogy, inference, and so forth.
4. *Learned factors* refers to the particular feature of the target language being acquired by the learner (question forms, auxiliaries, negatives, phonology, etc.).

We will consider speech-act theory with reference to two of the factors discussed by Swain, namely, input factors and learning factors, and discuss how speech-act theory contributes to our understanding of the nature of the input to the learning process and to the strategies used by the learner in learning or using a second language.

INPUT

A theory of second language acquisition must take account of the input to the learning process. The study of speech events and speech acts allows for focus on the typical speech settings encountered by second-language learners and the identification of discourse structure and norms for the speech events encountered. This includes opening and closing sequences, turn-taking rules, sequencing rules, presupposition, role marking, as well as speech acts (Coulthard 1977). In the study of language input to second-language learning the structure of speech events within the language-teaching classroom is particularly important. The structure of classroom language can be defined with reference to its discourse characteristics (Holmes 1978). Turn taking is controlled by the teacher in typical classroom settings, and the amount of talking is likewise weighted in the teacher's favor. Classroom talk is largely teacher talk. Delamont, quoted by Holmes, notes that of teacher talk, 50 percent is made up of the speech events of *teaching* or *lecturing* and the other 50 percent includes "explicit disciplinary and management moves and...reactions to pupils' contributions." The speech function of questioning is frequent in classrooms, but it is typically a closed question from the teacher where only one acceptable answer is required, and not an open question where several different answers are possible. Coulthard (1977: 81) reports the observation that teachers typically ask questions not to find out answers, but to find out if students know the answers. Once students have produced the answer they need to know whether it was the right one. The follow-up move, referring back and commenting on the answer, allows for the need.

T: Initiation: What did we call this picture?
P: Response: Piece of paper.
T: Follow-up: A piece of paper. Yes.
T: Initiation: What did we call this?

The speech function of *orders* is likewise frequent in classroom language, with a wide range of linguistic realizations. Learning within a classroom context must therefore be understood in relation to the highly structured and selective type of language that typifies classroom language and teaching situations.

Second-language learners may encounter other situations as input to the learning process that show particular discourse structuring. Candlin et al. (1976) have studied speech events within the context of doctor–patient communications, with a view to identifying the structure of relevant speech events, to clarify the difficulties encountered by foreign doctors working in British hospitals. Such learners have to acquire rules for the speech event of *the consultation*. Speech acts identified as typical within the consultation speech event include greet, elicit, interrogate, question, make sure, extend, action-inform, diagnose-inform, progress-inform, and so forth. "Investigation of a wide range of consultations revealed that casualty consultation discourse is highly structured, in that there are significant probabilities to the occurrence of the above functions and to their distribution" (Candlin 1978: 15).

LEARNING FACTORS

Under this heading Swain lists a number of second-language learning strategies and processes. The following seem to apply to research into the acquisition of speech-act rules in a second or foreign language: (1) inference, (2) transfer, (3) generalization, and (4) transfer of training.

The category communication strategies identified in the L2 literature with reference to the acquisition of syntax would appear to be redundant with reference to speech acts, since all the examples discussed here can be regarded as instances of communication strategies.

1. *Inference.* Inferencing is defined as the process by which the learner derives a hypothesis or conclusion about language based on the evidence presented. It is the means by which the learner forms hypotheses about the target language. Candlin refers to "interpretive strategies," which enable the speaker/hearer to retrieve discourse value from speech situations to arrive at an interpretation whereby the hearer's (reader's) interpretations match those of the speaker (or writer). Candlin emphasizes that discourse value is not a constant but varies according to the type of discourse, the relations between the participants, and the influence of the setting and the topic. Thus, for example, the sentence *Is the cook new?*, said in the kitchen of a restaurant by a waiter on noticing an unfamiliar face in the kitchen, may be interpreted as a yes/no question asking for information. The same question, put by a client in the restaurant to a waiter on receiving a poorly prepared meal, would have the illocutionary force of a complaint.

The nature of inferencing or interpretive strategies in speech-act theory remains problematic even for native speakers. But instances of communication breakdown and misunderstanding among nonfluent language users suggest they frequently operate primarily at the surface-structure level, identifying propositional content where it is marked directly by lexis or grammar, but often missing indirectly marked speech acts and functions. Thus *will* might be understood as a marker of future tense, for example, and modal overtones missed.

In one case, a Japanese woman who had lived in the United States for about a year did not respond to indirect request forms, such as "can you" and "will you," but only to the explicit request marker "please." She later recognized the directive intent of such indirect forms but still misinterpreted them, thinking that such forms could be interpreted (and used) only in sales clerk–customer or other service interactions (Honda, personal communication).

Austin (1962) refers to *uptake*, that is, the interpretation of the illocutionary force of a sentence by the hearer, which may differ from the *intended uptake* of the speaker. The following exchange between a customer in an airline office (a Korean woman) and two sales clerks illustrates the contrast between intended uptake and uptake, and also demonstrates the practical difficulties of determining inferencing strategies. The customer was trying to change flights from one airline to another. Business was slack and a second sales clerk was occasionally joining in the transactional discussion.

Sales Clerk 1: But Korean Airlines won't endorse the ticket, I don't think.
Sales Clerk 1: (*Looking directly at customer*) You can call them and ask.
Customer: OK...would you do that please? Would you phone them and ask?

Sales Clerk 2 meant her remarks as a suggestion to the customer that she phone. The customer either thought that the suggestion was directed at Sales Clerk 1, or misinterpreted the utterance as an offer to make the call or as a general statement of possibility (i.e., as meaning "One could call..."); *or* she chose to interpret the utterance in one of these ways. The casual observer cannot tell in this case. On questioning the clerk as to how she would analyze the exchange she later said, "She's not as dumb as she pretends."

Nonfluent language users would thus appear to be more dependent on contextual or linguistic clues in inferencing. This in turn shapes the discourse directed to them by native speakers. Foreigner talk would appear to contain more explicit performatives than speech directed to fluent language users. Thus a teacher's opening to a joke addressed to a class of L2 learners began "Let me tell you a joke...I'm going to tell you a joke...OK." Such direct marking of the illocutionary value of the speech event would not be necessary with fluent language users, who would be expected to infer the intended uptake from perhaps "Did you hear the one about...?" Candlin notes that for foreign university students to derive the intended uptake from university lectures they need to be aware of the careful and close integration of the visual, paralinguistic element with the spoken word if they are going to understand the constant interplay in lectures between "the *main* and the *subsidiary* planes of discourse – the essential argument and the audience-directed subsidiary comment" (Candlin 1978: 22).

2. *Transfer*. Though the concept of transfer or inference has often been applied to the explanation of L2 performance at the phonological and syntactic level, little attention has been given to the effect of transfer operating at the level of discourse rules or to its effects on speech event and speech-act realizations in second-language performance. There is evidence, however, to suggest that rules governing speech events may differ substantially from one language group to another, thus leading to different rules and norms for turn taking, amount of talking, speech-act realizations, and so forth.

Thus the Anang value speech highly and the young are trained in the arts of speech, while for the Wolof, speech, especially in quantity, is dangerous and demeaning. French children are encouraged to be silent when visitors are present at dinner; Russian children are encouraged to talk. Among the Arucanian there are different expectations of men and women, men being encouraged to talk on all occasions, women to be silent – a new wife is not permitted to speak for several months. (Coulthard 1977: 49)

Particular speech events, such as telephone conversations, have also been compared from a cross-cultural perspective, showing how transference of rules and expectations from one language to another may create confusion or misunderstanding.

In Japanese, callers rather than answerers generally speak first on the telephone. In France, the fact that telephone calls are generally regarded as impositions on answerers may account for the fact that there are restrictions on caller behavior that do not hold in English-speaking countries (Godard 1977). In Egypt, there is an expectation that many calls will result in wrong numbers and callers frequently demand to know the identity of answerers; this seems rude to foreigners resident in Egypt, who often conclude that there are no rules at all for "polite" telephone behavior in the country (Schmidt 1975).

Clyne (1975), in a study of immigrants in Australia, discussed "pragmatic transfer," based on transfer of speech-act rules from one language to another, which can lead to communication breakdown or communication conflict. Transfer may operate with respect to a number of dimensions.

a. *Difference in opening or closing formulas for speech events*. Speech events in a given language may have differing opening or closing formulas that, when transferred to the target language, lead to incongruence. For example, with regard to *meal talk*, French and Malay begin with "bon appetit" and "selamat makan," respectively, which when transferred to English as *good eating* or *good appetite* appear unusual.

When languages have similar formulas, ritualistic or markedness considerations may be at variance. Greetings in many (perhaps all) speech communities may include questions about the addressee's health, for example, "How are you?" In English, Hindi, Spanish, French, and many other languages such questions are largely ritualistic and need not be answered sincerely. In English, "How are you?" is often not answered at all. In Arabic, on the other hand, the question *must* be answered, and in almost all contexts the only appropriate answer is the ritual response formula "ilhamdulillah" ("praise to God"). In Thai, however, "sabaaj dii ryy?" ("How are you?") is a nonritualistic, marked greeting, generally used only if one person has not seen the other for a long time and/or is sincerely concerned about his or her health. The unmarked greeting form in Thai is "Paj naj?" ("Where are you going"). Transfer of unmarked formulas could well lead to English speakers judging Thais to be far too curious about the other's whereabouts, whereas Thais may wonder why English speakers are so concerned about health problems (J. Fieg, personal communication).

b. *Formulas used to realize a speech act have different meanings in two languages.* A common transferable formula may exist, but with quite different uptake in the native compared with the target language. An offer of a cigarette, for example, is declined in German or Indonesian with the equivalent of *thank you*, but accepted with *thank you* in English. Indonesians frequently cause confusion by declining offers with *thank you*. Their interlocuters, if native speakers of English, have been heard to respond with "Do you mean *thank you* or *no, thank you?*" Likewise a native speaker of English who responds to an offer of something when speaking Indonesian, with the Indonesian equivalent of *thank you*, may be taken as having declined.

Silence is particularly ambiguous and difficult to interpret cross-culturally. Silence after a request may be taken as either assent or refusal in many cultures, but the non-native speaker will have great difficulty deciding which meaning is meant in unfamiliar contexts.

Formulas that are realizations of the same communicative or politeness strategy but that are only parallel and not identical in form and use may cause particular difficulty. A general strategy of negative politeness is to attempt to minimize the imposition on the hearer. In English, this can be done by using such expressions as "just" or "a little" (e.g., "I just want to ask you a little favor") or euphemisms, such as "borrow" for "take" ("Can I borrow a cigarette?") or "a second" or "a minute" for "a few minutes" (e.g., "I'll be with you in just a second"). Exactly the same strategy and similar (but not identical) linguistic realizations are involved in the Arab's or Persian's or Indian's or Mexican's use of a sentence like "This will be ready tomorrow," meaning "in a few days" (Brown and Levinson 1978). However, the native speaker of English generally will take "tomorrow" only in its literal sense, will be angry when the goods are not provided on time, and will be tempted to make extreme generalizations about the character and sense of time of the people in the new culture.

c. *Different social conventions associated with realizations of speech acts.* Here a number of different dimensions may be subject to transfer. We need to consider at least the following:

Appropriateness of topic. Here we are concerned with what, for example, one can request in one language compared with another. Which requests can safely be declined? What can be denied or disagreed with and how safely can one transfer such choices across languages? What topics can one ask about on a first encounter with a stranger of equal status? of higher status? of lower status? of the same sex? of a different sex? Thus common questions from Asians on first encounters are *Are you married? How old are you? What is your salary?* The Arabic question that most annoys non-Arabs is *How much did it cost?* Such questions violate culturally specific speech-act conventions in English.

Degrees of directness of realization of a speech act. A particular speech act, such as *refusal*, may be expressed differently in two languages. Geertz (1960), for example, discusses how *refusal* is communicated indirectly in Javanese. He describes a typical situation that his language teachers would use in the model conversations they used to teach him Javanese.

Two men are speaking. One wants something from the other (a loan, a service, his company in going somewhere) and both know it. The petitioner does not want to put his petition directly for fear of angering the petitioned; and the petitioned does not want to state his refusal directly for fear of frustrating the petitioner too severely. Both are very concerned with the other's emotional reactions because ultimately they will affect their own. As a result they go through a long series of formal speech patterns, courtesy forms, complex indirections, and mutual protestations of purity of motive, arriving only slowly at the point of the conversation so that no one is taken by surprise.

Clyne discusses culturally specific routines for the realization of such speech acts as *persuading* and *apologizing*. "Persuasion may be done through speech acts like the promise of a bribe, a threat of complaint to a higher official, flattery, or self-eulogy, or by overstating the case" (Clyne 1975: 4). Transference of routines from one culture to the other may lead to the interpretation that the speaker is aggressive, impolite, uncouth, and so forth.

3. *Generalization.* This term includes "regularization," "overgeneralization," analogy, and related concepts referred to in the literature. In the second-language learning literature it refers to the extension of something known in the L2 to a new context. With reference to speech-act rules we will apply the term to the extension of speech-act and speech-event rules to inappropriate contexts.

a. *Opening or closing sentences for speech events.* Consider the following exchange, made by a non-native speaker to an office colleague on encountering him in the corridor.

Non-native speaker: How do you do?
Native speaker: Oh hi.

Here the phrase *How do you do* has been extended beyond its boundaries in English – a greeting said on a first encounter in a formal-semiformal situation – to become a generalized greeting said on encountering friends. The appropriate greeting is of course *How are you* or some such phrase.

1st encounter   *Subsequent encounter*
How do you do.   How are you?
                     Hi, etc.

Leave-taking formulas may also be generalized to speech events where they are not appropriate. The following exchange is between an office boy delivering a consignment of books to an office and a receptionist.

Office boy: Where shall I put these books please?
Addressee: Put them on the table.
Office boy: (*some minutes later*) I'll be making a move now.

b. *Speech-act routine generalized to inappropriate context.* Some errors that on first sight would be attributed to stylistic inappropriateness or mistakes of lexis may turn out to be instances of a routine, appropriate to a particular speech act, generalized to a different type of speech act where it is no longer appropriate. A yes/no question, for example, which functions as a request for information, can be answered with yes/no plus verb repetition.

Do you have a car? Yes, I do.

A request, however, cannot be answered in the same way.

Can you pass me the milk? Yes, I can.

Borkin and Reinhart (1978: 58) discuss second-language learners' difficulties with the phrases *excuse me* and *I'm sorry*. A typical mistake is to use these for inappropriate speech acts, as in the following example where the non-native speaker declines an invitation to the movies.

Excuse me. I'd like to go but I don't have time.

Homer, a 5-year-old Iranian child, generalized the English formula "What's this?" to numerous contexts beyond simple NP identification (Wagner-Gough and Hatch 1975).

1. Identification
   a. What this is Elmer. (= This is Elmer.)
   b. What this is? (= What is this?)
2. Advice or help
   a. What this is? (= What should I do now?)
3. a. What is it tunnel. (= Stop pushing sand in my tunnel.)
   b. What this is Homer. (= I'm Homer and you can't tell me what to do.)
   c. What is this this it. (= Give me that truck.)

Of course, "What's this?" is multifunctional in adult native English (compare "What's this" said scornfully, curiously, hintingly, etc.), so that some of Homer's generalizations may be functionally appropriate and others not; it is difficult to evaluate functional appropriateness in this case when grammatical relationships remain unclear.

4. *Transfer of training.* This category refers to features of the learner's interlanguage that are traceable to teaching procedures used or to the particular textbook or teaching materials from which the learner has studied a language. Here are two examples of what was interpreted as inappropriate directives and that are probably traceable to transfer of training. They were noted by the spouse of a non-native speaker (NNS).

Example 1. Mother (a non-native speaker) to her son.
    So after supper you will do your homework.
Example 2. The wife to her husband.
    Tomorrow we will go to see the movie, all right?

Even given that husbands and wives who speak the same language are often at odds over the choice of directive forms used in the family, something more appears to be going on here. The first sentence, addressed to the NNS's son, would be perfectly appropriate if homework were an issue in the family. However, it is not, and the NNS reports that she meant to *suggest* and did not intend to be or sound imperious. The native-speaking spouse suggested that in both these examples *can*, or even better, *c'n*, would have been a better choice of modal to convey the reported intentions of the speaker. But this NNS never uses *can* when reference is to future time, even though this is possible in the native language. She was taught that it is extremely important to indicate time reference in English, and she was taught (contrary to fact) that uncontracted forms are always more polite and proper than contracted forms. In general this speaker pays careful attention to literal meanings. The relationship between her forms and her social meanings could be defined in terms of conversational postulates, though the details of the rules for use of these postulates would differ somewhat from those of a native speaker.

Transfer of training may interact with the other learning factors, such as transfer and generalization, as well as attitudes toward languages, leading to inappropriate language. In Japanese, for example, a great deal rests on control of a highly complex system of honorifics. When Japanese learn English, they find nothing very similar, nothing that can be directly transferred. In addition, they generally believe and are probably taught (in accordance with the prevailing stereotype) that whereas Japanese is a very "polite" language, English is "logical," "direct," and not very polite. Japanese learners of English may therefore be insensitive to the nuances of English politeness, which are not concentrated in one sub-system of the language.

Implications for research and teaching

The review presented here raises a number of questions that require empirical investigation and further study before conclusive statements can be made. We have focused primarily on proficiency in the realization and interpretation of speech acts, rather than the acquisition of speech-act rules. The acquisition of pragmatic or communicative competence is an emerging interest in language acquisition studies. Pragmatic rather than grammatical constraints are seen as crucial in accounting for both the structuring of child language utterances and interlanguages, in the work of Peters, Wagner-Gough, Hatch, and others. Peters (1977) has distinguished two styles of first-language acquisition: an analytic style, one word at a time, and a "gestalt" style, an attempt to use whole utterances in socially appropriate situations. Many investigators of sec-ond-language learning (e.g., Wagner-Gough and Hatch 1975) have re-ported that second-language learners are apt to use a gestalt style even more than first-language learners, using prefabricated routines and pat-terns (which may include speech-act formulas) in an attempt to com-municate in a socially appropriate way beyond their linguistic competence. One issue of current concern is the degree to which such formulaic language is crucial to the overall development of language. Fillmore (1976) argues that the use of such formulaic speech, motivated by the learner's need to establish social contact, gradually evolves into creative language. Krashen and Scarcella (1978), on the other hand, maintain that routines and patterns play only a minor role in second language acquisition, with the creative construction process evolving in an essen-tially independent manner. Study of the acquisition of speech acts by non-native speakers should enable us to clarify these and other issues. Possible issues for further research are the following:

1. Descriptive studies of the types of speech acts encountered in specific settings for second-language use and learning, according to such factors as age of speakers (e.g., adult–child; child–child) and roles (e.g., teacher–student;

friend–friend; parent–child) – in particular settings (classroom; work domain) and for specific speech events (e.g., interviews; conversations).

2. Studies relating stages of grammatical development to speech-act realizations in interlanguages of different types of learners.
3. Studies of acquisition of rules for the realization and interpretation of speech acts over time among interlanguage users.
4. Cross-linguistic comparisons aimed at determining whether different languages make use of the same classes of speech acts and similar strategies for realizing and interpreting speech acts.
5. Studies of the effects of speech-act realization on the discourse patterning and conversational structure of non-native language users in different types of discourse.
6. Study of pragmatic errors in non-native discourse, for example, the failure to code or interpret speech acts appropriately or to recognize or assign appropriate illocutionary force to utterances of native speakers.
7. Studies of the attitudes of native speakers to violation of native-speaker rules for speech-act realization, and the contribution of such violation to communication conflict or breakdown.
8. Studies relating strategies for the performance and acquisition of speech-act rules to language-learning processes in general, for example, to what degree do such factors as transfer, inferencing, and overgeneralization also apply to pragmatic dimensions of language learning?

The relevance of speech-act theory and research to language teaching is through its contribution to the theory of communicative language teaching. Writers on communicative syllabus design, such as Munby and Wilkins, make use of speech-act and speech-event theory in their accounts of notional and communicative syllabuses for language teaching, as have various other writers on communicative teaching (Paulston 1974, P. Allen 1977, Stratton 1977, Holmes and Brown 1977, Widdowson 1978). The central issue is to what degree successful second-language learning can be identified with acquiring rules for speech-act realization and interpretation. An emphasis on strategies for speech-act realization as a central goal for intermediate and advanced language teaching would lead to a focus on learning as a *process* rather than on what is learned as a product. Another basic issue concerns translating the concepts of speech-act theory and discourse analysis into units that can be realized within a language teaching program, that is, that can be operationalized for teaching purposes. Candlin (1978) warns: "We know enough, however, to realize methodologically that we must avoid latter day 'structuralism' of concepts and site utterances firmly within connected discourse. Furthermore ways of teaching should shift from teacher-telling to learner interpreting within a syllabus whose prime goal is the development of strategies for discourse processing, rather than as an assembly of items." Candlin's work on speech events within doctor-patient communications begins from "detailed functional description of native speakers' interaction, and attempts not simply to teach single functions but to show doctors how to open and close interviews, how to participate in other types of exchange, how to build exchanges into longer sequences, how to manipulate the turn-taking system" (Coulthard 1977: 146). The progression from grammatical to communicative competence within a formal language teaching program is thus a movement toward the organization of learning and teaching in terms of creating contexts for the realization and interpretation of speech acts within a framework of discourse rules. Questions that require further consideration from this perspective include:

1. To what degree should realization and interpretation strategies for speech acts be taught explicitly in a language teaching program?
2. How useful are contrastive statements of such coding procedures for learners whose mother tongues adopt different coding strategies?
3. What speech acts are basic and can speech acts and discourse rules be ordered for the purpose of teaching?
4. Are techniques for the teaching of other areas of the target language (dialogues, drills, etc.) also appropriate for teaching discourse rules, or are speech-act rules acquired as a byproduct of communication?
5. How do we choose, for the purpose of teaching, the forms for the realization of speech acts?
6. To what degree should the emphasis on ability to perform and interpret speech acts take priority over the ability to code sentences grammatically within a teaching program?

9 Cross-cultural aspects of conversational competence

Jack C. Richards and Mayuri Sukwiwat

Our understanding of the nature of second- and foreign-language learning has greatly expanded in recent years as a consequence of research into many dimensions of language and behavior that were previously unexplored. Studies of the acquisition of syntax, for example, have begun to incorporate such concepts as markedness theory, information structure, discourse function, variation theory, linguistic universals, and richer learning theories that make use of models of cognitive processing. This has given a new impetus to the study of language transfer and has generated new hypotheses that are currently being developed by researchers in second language acquisition.

A further input to our understanding of second-language learning has been provided by studies of aspects of learning that relate to communicative or sociolinguistic competence. These have drawn on research and theory in sociology, pragmatics, and discourse analysis in attempts to describe how language learners develop the ability to use language for social interaction. For the speaker of a foreign language, any conversational exchange with a native speaker of the target language is a form of cross-cultural encounter. This makes the study of non-native conversational discourse rich territory for the exploration of how culturally specific assumptions and strategies for conversation surface in cross-cultural encounters. In this chapter we consider the effects of transfer of native-language conversational conventions into target-language conversational discourse. To do this we will examine several aspects of conversational competence and how these may be affected by transfer of native language conversational norms.

Conventional usage in conversation

In studying conversational discourse, a distinction can be made between grammatical competence and conversational competence. Grammatical competence describes a speaker's knowledge of the underlying systems of vocabulary, morphology, and syntax that are required to construct grammatical sentences in a language. The sentence is the unit of description for grammatical competence. Conversational competence, however, is defined not with reference to the sentence, but to the utter-

129

ance. This refers to the speaker's knowledge of how speech acts are used in social situations. There are many sentences in a language that are not used as utterances. For example,

It's half after two.
It's a third after two.
It's two fives after two.

are all sentences in English, but they are not conventional ways of telling time in English. They have no status as utterances. The set of grammatical sentences that are utterances in a language is much smaller than the set of sentences in the language. For any speech act, a conventional set of ways of coding it exists. Thus the utterances that could be used to perform the speech act of "requesting a cigarette from someone" includes A but excludes B:

A	B
Got a cigarette?	The speaker requests a cigarette.
Could I have a cigarette?	A cigarette is requested by me.
I'd love a cigarette.	That which I request from you is a cigarette.
Gimme a cigarette.	

In studying how utterances are used, we observe that many have a special status in conversation. They recur, are predictable, and are associated with particular social situations and with particular types of interactions. Such utterances may be referred to as *conversational routines* (Coulmas 1981). Consider the following examples:

Have a seat.	Seen any good films lately?
Check please.	What did you think of the film?
Nice to meet you.	Could you speak up a little?
How are you?	You're looking very well.
May I know who is calling?	No harm done.
I'll be with you in a minute.	Don't worry about it.
Come again soon.	We must get together again sometime.
See you later.	Have some more.
As a matter of fact...	Are you following me?
Let me see what I can do.	Would you mind repeating that?
Sorry I'm late.	What a shame!
What a nice day!	In a case like this...
Yes please.	As far as I can tell...
You must be starving!	Just between you and me...

Routines of the sort identified here include several different types of conventional utterances. Some are situational formulas, such as *Check please*, said in a restaurant when requesting a bill. Some accompany particular speech acts, such as *Don't mention it*, as a way of acknowledging thanks. Some signal directions within discourse, marking speaker attitudes toward what has been said or what is to be said, such as *as a matter of fact* (Keller 1981).

Many social events require the use of conversational routines, as do the majority of speech acts. Associated with the everyday round of activities that constitute the lives of all of us is the use of language in predictable ways. Conversational routines help define speech situations, and their appropriate use is a vital component of social competence in a language. Pawley and Syder point out that the ability to use routines contributes to the sense of naturalness and nativeness about a person's speech (Pawley and Syder 1983). Speakers of a language appear to know hundreds of them and the situations when their use is required. They are not generated in the same way as novel utterances, but appear to be preprogrammed in a way in which novel utterances are not.

In second-language learning, routines are often acquired before their function is fully understood. They are picked up as "canned utterances," and their use may lead to an impression of fluency that the learner does not really have. A stock of routines may even constitute a survival strategy for learners, who can maneuver their way across the surface of many transactions with the occasional use of routines. Successful mastery of routines, however, poses special problems, since there may be wide differences between the form and function of routines in the mother tongue and target language.

Conversational routines and language transfer

The learning of conversational routines in a second language is influenced by a number of dimensions of L1–L2 noncorrespondence (cf. Coulmas 1979).

Differences in social situations

Cultures define social situations differently. Although there are many social situations that are common across cultures, such as meals, weddings, and funerals, there are others for which no direct equivalence exists in the other culture, such as "at the pub" in Britain, attending a Buddhist ordination ceremony for a young man in Thailand, or visiting elders and family members on Chinese New Year in Chinese societies. Presumably, routines are associated with these and many other culturally specific events that are particular and unique to the culture in which they occur.

Same situation: different routines

Even where social situations are similar in two cultures, the routines associated with them may differ. The way a routine that accompanies a speech act is acknowledged may also vary. In English a compliment may be acknowledged with thanks:

A: That was a lovely meal.
B: Thank you, I'm glad you liked it.

However, in Thai culture the hostess might not respond verbally to the compliment, since this may not sound suitably humble. Apologies rather than thanks are appropriate replies to compliments in other cultures.

A: What a nice dress!
B: Oh, it's just an old thing I've had for years.

Different routines used in responding to a speech act may reflect a choice of a different member of a set of possible responses. For example, in offering an apology the speaker may

1. make an expression of apology
2. explain or account for his or her behavior
3. acknowledge responsibility
4. make an offer of repair
5. make a promise of forbearance

(Olshtain and Cohen 1983)

However, the selection of which option to express (through routines, in many cases) may vary across cultures. In one language, speakers may typically make an expression of apology, and in another they may simply explain or account for their behavior. Olshtain observes that Hebrew speakers using English may sound less apologetic than they intend, since they typically "provide an excuse without making formal use of the performative verb" (Olshtain and Cohen 1983).

Same routine: different function

Two languages may share a similar routine but use it differently. In English *thank you* may be used to express gratitude, but in Japanese the equivalent routine may not sound sincere enough, leaving the speaker with the urge to add *I'm sorry*.

When a Japanese wants to express sincere gratitude, he feels urged to say "I am sorry," since "thank you" does not sound sincere enough. This is one of the typical mistakes Japanese make in their interactions with English speakers, the latter being likely to say "Why sorry?" (Sugiyama, in Coulmas 1979)

Routines with different functions in one language may be translated by a single routine in another. For example, the English routines *You're welcome, Don't mention it, Not at all, It doesn't matter,* and *Never mind* may all be translated by the Thai routine *maj pen raj*. In English, *Never mind* and *It doesn't matter* can be used to acknowledge an apology and are used by the person addressed to minimize the seriousness of the offense. The expressions *You're welcome, Don't mention it*, and so on, are used to acknowledge thanks. The Thai routine, however, is used as a response both to gratitude and to apologies. Thais using the English routines interchangeably hence produce pragmatic errors, such as the following:

Boss: Thanks a lot. That was a great help.
Secretary: Never mind.

Or, after a guest has knocked over a glass of wine:

Hostess: Oh dear!
Guest: Never mind. Let me clean it up.

Correct routine: wrong situation

The non-native speaker may extend routines to situations where they are not appropriate, such as using a formula that is restricted to a certain social or age group, in an inappropriate situation. For example, *Nice to meet you* would be an inappropriate way for an adult to respond on being introduced to a young child. The following examples are deviant for similar reasons:

1. A: Would you like to see a movie?
   B: *Excuse me*, but I'm not free.
2. A: Like something to eat?
   B: *To my mind*, I'll have a cup of coffee.
3. A: Do you like the steak?
   B: *Without a doubt*, it's excellent.
4. A: Terry's father has passed away.
   B: *What a nuisance.*

Different sincerity conditions for a routine

The conditions necessary for the correct performance of a speech act may differ across cultures, leading to non-transferability of routines. Japanese and French, for example, both allow for the use of a routine before eating: *bon apétit* and *ita dakimasu*; but the Japanese formula cannot be used by the one who provides the meal (Coulmas 1979).

133

Other problems

The fact that the meanings of many routines are idiomatic, and hence not interpretable from knowing the meanings of their constituent lexical items, poses many problems for second- and foreign-language learners. The relation between form and function in routines like the following can be learned only from repeated observation of the utterance in context:

Let me see what I can do.	(used as a precloser)
You bet!	(used to mark agreement or confirmation)
Oh you shouldn't have!	(used as an exclamation of appreciation)

Routines that mark directions within discourse, sometimes known as gambits, are particularly difficult to comprehend. Consider how the following might be explained or translated, for example:

mind you though...	keep me posted...
but then again...	actually...
as far as I'm concerned...	the funny thing is...
now that you mention it...	by the way...
and another thing...	the thing is...
in the long run...	just a small point...
let's face it...	not on your life...
when it comes to that...	

Attempts to arrive at the meanings of these and other verbal routines by decomposing them in the way nonidiomatic utterances are interpreted often lead to frustration for the language learner.

Interactional dimensions of conversation

The observations made so far concern the form of the language of conversational interaction. We have seen that conventional utterances occur with particular social events and discourse functions. In what follows we consider the participants in the speech event itself. Our focus here is (a) how conversational discourse reflects relationships and interaction between participants, marking dimensions of social distance, status, and politeness, and (b) the effects that different linguistic conventions for marking such dimensions have on the interlanguage of second-language learners.

Verbal repertoires

Conversational competence in a language involves the use of different speech styles according to whom the speaker is addressing and the circumstances under which the act of communication is taking place. The range of linguistic varieties a speaker has at his or her disposal may be referred to as a verbal repertoire (Platt and Platt 1975: 35). The concept of verbal repertoire includes (a) how a speaker varies the form in which a speech act is coded and (b) the choice of particular strategies of interaction. Jacobson (1976) suggests that English allows for at least five styles of speaking:

1. peer's style
2. formal style
3. style appropriate for small children or when addressing them, that is, an adult's style comprehensible to small children (not necessarily baby talk)
4. informal style appropriate when talking to a close member of one's family
5. informal style appropriate when talking to an adult who is not a member of the family

Brown and Levinson have shown that pragmatic, semantic, lexical, syntactic, and interactional tactics are involved in selecting an appropriate style of speaking. A switch in style may involve more than simply the choice between *Could you possibly lend me a cigarette?* and *Got a cigarette?* It may involve noticing or attending to the hearer's interests, wants, and needs, exaggerating interest, approval, or sympathy with the hearer, using in-group identity markers, and so on (Brown and Levinson 1978). In observing the acquisition of verbal repertoires by foreign-language learners, several different dimensions of noncorrespondence between the first and second language are possible, raising interesting problems in the study of language transfer and interlanguage processes.

Different systems of marking

Whereas all languages contain systems of repertoires or speech styles, the ways in which such systems are manifest in particular languages differ considerably. What is marked in the lexicon or morphology of one language may be communicated by stress or intonation in another. Suasion, for example, may be expressed by several devices in English, including the emphatic *do*.

Do come and visit us.

In Thai, suasion may be marked by word tone and by repeating the main verb and the particle.

maa jîam raw ná. maa ná.
(Come visit us ná. Come ná.)

To be more emphatic, the vowel of the particle can be lengthened.

maa nâa
(Come + particle with long vowel.)

135

Respect or politeness may also be marked very differently in two languages. In English, for example, respect may be marked by clausal constructions:

I wonder if I might ask if. . .
Would it be possible for you to. . .

In Indian languages, however, such phrases as *Could I have* and *I would like*. . . "imply social inequality and tend to be avoided in ordinary speech. Respect is conveyed through special honorific particles or through professional or other titles, not through verb constructions" (Gumperz and Roberts 1978: 102). Speakers of Asian languages (e.g., Thai, Javanese, and Hindi) may initially be puzzled by the lack of any equivalence between the systems used for making style differences in English and their mother tongue. Forms used to mark politeness in Thai (the particles), for example, occur in sentence-final position; but hedging devices, such as *I wonder if I could*, have the status of routines in English and occur in sentence-initial position. Thais are used to varying sentence-final particles according to the status, age, and sex of their interlocutor, and will initially search in vain for forms with a similar function in English. Later, on associating this function in English with the modals, they may overuse them:

Would you mind if I would like to smoke?

Different systems of levels

We have seen that at least five levels of speech are distinguishable in English, and presumably similar differences can be marked linguistically in all languages. The perceived number of levels is less important than the relative distance between them. In languages like Thai and Javanese, there is a greater degree of social distance implied in the difference between the most informal and the most formal level than in the corresponding contrast implied in English, and the levels themselves are more rigidly differentiated through variation in the pronominal, verbal, and honorific systems. Geertz provides an illuminating account of how these levels operate in Javanese (Geertz 1960). There are many similarities in Thai. For example, the word *eat* in Thai has many different variants, according to the interactional style. The following are some of the more commonly used ones.

1. royal language (*sawěey*) used with members of the royal family
2. deferential (*rèppràthaan*) used with superiors; marks social distance and formality
3. neutral (*kin*) used between equals or when addressing inferiors
4. vulgar (*dèek*) considered "vulgar" among the educated; may be used among males as marker of intimacy

Changes in voice quality, rate of delivery, and intonation also accompany different styles in Thai. When speaking to an elder or superior, uncontracted forms are more frequent, the voice is lowered, and a slower style of speaking is used. An Asian learner used to such a system may not feel that English allows for a sufficiently "high" form. This may lead to an overuse of honorifics or titles such as *sir* (used when addressing both males and females), to more frequent use of apologies, and in written English to a preference for a florid prose style with ornate vocabulary. The significance of contrasts between the systems of speech levels used in English and many Asian languages is related to differences in how much social power is attributed to particular social roles in different societies.

Differences in the power paradigm

The amount of social power attributed to particular social roles in a culture may be referred to as the power paradigm. One of the goals of conversation is to determine the relative power of speaker and hearer. If the speaker and hearer are judged to be of equal power, a casual speech style is appropriate that stresses affiliation and solidarity (Good 1979). If the participants are not of equal power, a more formal speech style is appropriate, one that marks the dominance of the speaker over the hearer. However, what might be a suitable context for formal style in one language may be a situation where casual style is thought to be appropriate in another. This is because different cultures attribute different power values to particular social roles.

In Japanese and Thai societies, for example, a greater degree of power accrues from age and occupation than it does in American society. This means that in Japanese and Thai conversational interaction, for the dyads older person/younger person, professor/student, or doctor/clerk, the first member of each pair holds a relatively greater degree of power than he or she would hold in American society. In Japanese and Thai, a formal style would be expected in encounters between such pairs, whereas in American society a less formal style could be used. American students, for example, sometimes call professors by their first names, a situation which would be unheard of in Japan or Thailand.

Thai society is an example of a culture where hierarchical dimensions are sharply marked. Every individual represents a position vis-à-vis others in the society, and is identified and addressed as such. As Mulder observes, in Thailand "the presentation of one's social self tends to include the whole set of one's social paraphernalia" (Mulder 1979: 68). Address terms in Thai thus name occupations, such as *acaan* (teacher), *khun mɔɔ* (honorific term + doctor), *thâan phûu amnuajkaan* (honorific term + Director), *thâan nai phon* (honorific term + General), and so on. Age may also be part of the address system in Thai. An older brother or sister is addressed as *phîi* (older brother or sister), and *nɔ́ɔŋ* is the term of address for a younger brother or sister. In face-to-face inter-actions, address terms (honorifics + position/occupation) are usually used instead of personal names, especially when the speaker is younger and lower in social position than the hearer. Although Thais use first names, this does not express solidarity in the same way as it does for Americans.

Different social obligations may also result from different perceptions of the power paradigm. A Japanese office worker who is invited by his or her employer for a drink or a meal is, for all practical purposes, quite unable to decline the request (Ueda 1974). An American employee in a similar situation would feel free to offer an excuse if he or she wished to decline the invitation.

Politeness and face

Appropriate styles of speaking according to the power paradigm of the interaction indicate the degree of perceived affiliation or distance be-tween speaker and hearer. Successful use of these strategies creates an atmosphere of politeness that enables social transactions to proceed without threat to the face of speaker or hearer. In Brown and Levinson (1978) a convincing case for the role of politeness strategies as face-saving devices is outlined (see Chapter 8). Brown and Levinson's thesis is that speakers estimate the "cost" of a particular speech act in terms of its relative threat to speaker, hearer, or both. To do this, speakers make use of their perceptions of the degree of social distance between speaker and hearer, the degree of dominance or affiliation, and the relative status of a particular type of act within a given culture. Then they choose the appropriate conversational style.

But because of cross-cultural differences in the perception of the power paradigm in particular situations, the same transactions may involve far greater "face costs" in one culture than in another (Imai 1981). In Thai, the concept of face is referred to by the term "kreeŋcaj," which means taking the other person's face needs and feelings into account so that no threat is involved either to speaker or to hearer. This leads to indirect strategies for the performance of certain types of speech acts in situations where English speakers would not necessarily see the need for indirect-ness, since they perceive no threat to face. Thus in the case where A wants a favor from B, the preferred strategy for a Thai is to hint and talk around the topic. An example was provided by an American teacher recently arrived in Thailand, who went on a boat cruise with a group that included the governor of the province. The governor seated himself on comfortable cushion seats provided on the boat deck, and other Thais present did likewise. The foreigner as an act of courtesy seated herself on a less comfortable wooden chair. Several Thais present repeatedly invited her to sit on the more comfortable cushions on the deck, but she politely declined. Much later she realized the reason for their persistent invitations and hints. From her position on the chair, the foreigner was in a higher position than the governor – a cardinal sin in Thailand. The embarrassed Thais tried hints and suggestions, but would not raise the issue directly. The American missed the illocutionary force of their invitations.

In Thai society, a key component of the ethos of social behavior is the preservation of social harmony among individuals. This, of course, is probably a universal; however, it is in the interpretation of how language can be used to maintain it that we see cross-language variation and interference. Thais are taught to avoid overt acts of disapproval, criticism, displeasure, resentment, anger, and the like. In a traditional Thai family, Thais are taught to mask their negative emotions. Many Western cultures on the other hand value individualism. A child or adult who displays views and opinions that are at variance with commonly held beliefs is seen as having an independent mind. From an early age American children, it seems, are encouraged to express their opinions, even when these are at variance with those of their parents, siblings, teachers, and so forth. Disagreement is regarded as an essential element in situations where information and attitudes are exchanged or discussed, such as at meetings or conferences. Thais, however, view disagreement with another as a personal matter. It is not something to be displayed in public. Frank criticism or expression of disapproval is not typically expressed in such situations as meetings or conferences, where people of different rank and status are interacting. Thais are often surprised when they see Americans vigorously disagreeing or questioning each other's opinions in a class or conference, for example, then cordially chatting or sharing a drink outside the meeting room.

The tendency for Thais, like other Asians, to downplay disagreement can be seen manifested particularly in international conferences, meetings, and seminars. Many Thais will not express disagreement unless absolutely certain that they are correct with respect to the point in question.

Similar observations have been made of the Japanese. In Japanese society, group membership and solidarity is regarded as more important than individual identity, whereas the opposite may be true for American culture. The Japanese learns to value conformity to the group. "Real friendship means total acceptance by the group, and they reject the [American] concept of what friendship involves with its backslapping heartiness, baring of one's inmost soul, and indulgence in heated arguments about disputation subjects" (Roggendorff 1980). Japanese and

Americans thus differ in what they feel is appropriate to reveal about themselves in interpersonal encounters. Americans are consequently much more prone to disclose personal or inner private experience, topics that would be avoided in similar situations by Japanese. Japanese avoid conversational topics that might lead to disagreement, or witty verbal display, for fear of disturbing the harmony of the group.

Presentation of self

One of the functions of conversation is to keep the channels of communication open and to establish a suitable atmosphere of rapport. Goffman has argued that "in any action, each actor provides a field of action for the other actors, and the reciprocity thus established allows the participants to exercise their interpersonal skills in formulating the situation, presenting and enacting a self or identity, and using strategies to accomplish other interactional ends" (cited in Watson 1974). "Enactment of self" means the view of the self or inner being that one communicates. How is this expressed?

The impression we convey of ourselves depends on what we talk about, how much talking we do, how much power or dominance we assert, attitudes we communicate toward such things as our past accomplishments and future plans, and the topics we select to discuss (Scollon and Scollon 1981). Cultures vary as to whether the favored style for interpersonal communication is one in which speakers reveal very little of themselves (their beliefs, wishes, opinions, likes, dislikes, etc. – things that may not be shared with others) and cultures in which there is generally a willingness to reveal details of one's inner self on interacting with others. Barnlund investigated the concepts of public and private self and their effect on contrastive communicative styles among Japanese and Americans (Barnlund 1975). In comparing communicative styles between Japanese and Americans, he found that because Japanese reveal only a small amount of their inner experience in conversation:

a. They interact more selectively and with fewer persons;
b. they prefer regulated to spontaneous forms of communication;
c. with respect to topics they discuss, they communicate verbally on a more superficial level;
d. they show a reluctance for verbal intimacy;
e. they resort to defensive reactions sooner and in a greater number of topical areas;
f. because they explore inner reactions less often and at a more superficial level, they must be less known to themselves.

What is postulated, thus, is a difference not of kind but of degree between the psychic structure and communicative behavior of Japanese and Americans, a difference that is significant rather than trivial. This difference, reflecting cultural norms and values, causes members of these two cultures to talk differently, about different topics, in different ways, to different people, with different consequences. (Barnlund 1975: 433)

Like Japanese culture, Thai society favors more regulated forms of communication, in which involvement is restricted and there is only limited disclosure of self. There are thus aspects of self that are not considered relevant to disclose in Thai social situations. This is well illustrated by different norms in American and Thai culture concerning introductions. In American culture, introductions are much more important than they are in Thai culture. When a third person enters a room, office, car, and is unknown to others present, the usual custom for Americans would be to introduce themselves. An introduction serves as a conversational opener. In Thai culture, an introduction is not needed as an opener in such circumstances. If a Thai enters a room to talk to one person in the room, for example, there is no need perceived to introduce the visitor to everyone else present, nor is such an introduction a prerequisite for the person to join in conversation with others present. This fact often perplexes Americans in Thailand. One American who had been working on a rural development project for a year learned that his Thai counterpart was married and his wife happened to work in an adjoining office. The Thai had seen no need to present her. Under similar circumstances, however, an American would feel it normal to want to introduce his wife to everyone in the office.

Thus if we compare two cultures, we may find what is regarded as part of the private self in one may be part of the public self in another. If we compare the topics in the following list, we may find differences in how they are assigned to the domain of public self versus private self, and consequently the likelihood that they will be discussed in particular types of encounters. Some will be regarded as unsuitable topics for public discussion in one culture, but not necessarily in another.

one's family and children
hobbies and spare time interests
political beliefs
religious beliefs
personal finances
personal possessions
career plans
ambitions

Thais, for example, would normally refrain from praising family members in public. There is a Thai poem that gives directions on whom to praise or not to praise.

If your teacher is good, tell him so.
If your servant does an excellent job,

tell him after the job is done.
If your friend is good to you,
praise him behind his back.
But never praise your children or your wife.

Americans, by contrast, regard family members as natural topics for discussion with friends and acquaintances. American politicians praise their wives for helping them win elections. In Thai culture, one learns about the qualities of a husband or wife only from booklets printed in memory of the departed souls distributed at a funeral.

Conclusion

Theories of how we teach conversation reflect our views of what conversation is. Conversation is often defined very narrowly as the oral exchange of information. EFL/ESL materials often focus on conversation as the finished product of the act of communication, rather than on the processes that underlie conversational discourse. We see several areas of application for the view of conversation outlined in this chapter.

The observations we have presented derive from published accounts and ethnographic studies of an exploratory nature, but there are many areas of conversational discourse that remain relatively unexplored. For example, the investigation of the scope of conversational routines is still in its infancy. The only major empirical study available is that of Keller, who focused on only a subset of conversational routines. There is scope for much broader-based data collection, directed both to L1 norms and cross-language comparisons.

Information about the potential for transfer of L1 conversation norms into L2 conversational discourse is another under-utilized area. This information should be used in the training of native-speaking teachers of English, many of whom assume that what is true for English is a norm for all other languages. Teachers in training need to be alerted to the fact that the solutions adopted in English conversational discourse are by no means universal. Awareness of how they contrast with conversational styles in other languages will lead to a greater sensitivity to what is involved in cross-cultural communication.

And, finally, it is important to be aware that the concept of English as an International Language currently being discussed in several quarters (L. E. Smith 1981) suggests that native-speaking norms are not necessarily the only acceptable ones for use in many contexts where English is spoken. We hope we have outlined some dimensions of what could be included in a communicative grammar of international English.

Such a grammar would include a description of rules of speaking that operate in different contexts where English is used and would be sensitive to underlying culture-bound assumptions about language and communication.

10 The status of grammar in the language curriculum

Grammar has traditionally had a central role in language teaching. Particular theories of grammar and theories of learning associated with them have provided justifications for syllabuses and methodology in language teaching for thousands of years. Despite the impact communicative approaches have had on methodology in recent years, the bulk of the world's second- and foreign-language learners continue to learn from materials in which the principles of organization and presentation are grammatically based. In this chapter we review the status of grammar in language teaching and consider how knowledge of and skill in grammar contribute to language proficiency. In the first part of the chapter we consider grammar from the perspective of language proficiency. In the second part we examine the relationship of grammar to proficiency in the light of second language acquisition research. In the last section we consider consequences for language-curriculum development.

What does it mean to know a language?

The factors involved in knowing a language include grammatical competence, communicative competence, and language proficiency. Our view of the status of grammar in language teaching will reflect our understanding of the role of grammar in language use. This in turn will depend upon whether we adopt a linguistic, sociolinguistic, or psycholinguistic perspective on language.

Grammatical competence

The linguistic perspective, seen in the concept of grammatical competence, was proposed by Chomsky in his writings in the 1950s and 1960s. At that time, knowing a language was equated with knowing the grammar of that language. Grammatical competence was the knowledge underlying our ability to produce and understand sentences in a language. We call upon our grammatical competence to express meanings in ways that are native-like in the target language. At times, we may be prevented from applying our grammatical competence, through fatigue, distractions, or other aspects of "performance." The theory of transformational

144

grammar captured our ability to realize propositions in sentence structure through rules for the construction of words, phrases, and clauses; through the choice of grammatical categories, such as subject, predicate, and complement; and through grammatical processes, such as ellipsis, pronominalization, reordering, and transformation.

Communicative competence

The sociolinguistic perspective is seen in the concept of communicative competence (Hymes 1972). Hymes pointed out that in addition to our knowledge of rules of grammar, knowing a language entails being able to use it for social and communicative interaction, that is, "knowing when it is appropriate to open a conversation and how, what topics are appropriate to particular speech events, which forms of address are to be used, to whom and in which situations, and how such speech acts as greetings, compliments, apologies, invitations and complements are to be given, interpreted and responded to" (Wolfson 1983: 61). Hymes used the term *communicative competence* to refer to knowledge both of rules of grammar, vocabulary, and semantics, and rules of speaking – the patterns of sociolinguistic behavior of the speech community. Neither the concept of grammatical competence or communicative competence, however, describes how such "competence" is used in actual communication. Rather, a psycholinguistic or performance-oriented perspective is needed; and this we can gain by considering the concept of language proficiency.

Language proficiency

The notion of language proficiency is fundamental in language program design, language teaching, and language testing. It refers to the degree of skill with which a second or foreign language is used in carrying out different communicative tasks in the target language. Farhady comments,

Language proficiency is one of the most poorly defined concepts in the field of language testing. Nevertheless, in spite of differing theoretical views as to its definition, a general issue on which many scholars seem to agree is that that the focus of proficiency tests is on the student's ability to use language. (1982: 44)

J. L. Clark suggests that proficiency is the learner's ability

to use language for real-life purposes without regard to the manner in which that competence was acquired. Thus, in proficiency testing, the frame of reference...shifts from the classroom to the actual situation in which the language is used. (1972: 5)

The concept of language proficiency differs from the concepts of grammatical or communicative competence in several important ways.

1. It is defined not with reference to knowledge, or competence, but with reference to performance, that is, to how language is used.
2. It is defined with reference to specific situations, purposes, tasks, and communicative activities, such as using conversation for face-to-face social interaction, listening to a lecture, or reading a college textbook.
3. It refers to a level of skill at carrying out a task, that is, to the notion of effectiveness. Thus it has associated with it the concept of a criterion that can be used to evaluate the degree of skill with which a task is performed.
4. It refers to the ability to call upon a variety of component subskills (i.e., to select different aspects of grammatical and communicative competence) in order to perform different kinds of tasks at different levels of effectiveness. (Cf. Canale 1983, who distinguishes between grammatical competence, sociolinguistic competence, discourse competence, and strategic competence, all of which constitute communicative competence.)

To determine the status of grammar within the language curriculum it is necessary to consider how grammatical knowledge contributes to language proficiency. Work in language-proficiency testing provides useful insights in this area.

In the Foreign Service Institute (FSI) oral proficiency scale, which has been in widespread use in American government agencies as an instrument for assessing the oral proficiency of government employees, three component skills are assessed in determining a person's level of language proficiency. These are referred to as functions (functional ability), content (topics expressed and understood as well as vocabulary knowledge), and accuracy (grammar and pronunciation). However, those who work with the FSI scale have emphasized that the contribution of different component skills varies according to the learner's level of proficiency (Higgs and Clifford 1982).

The Foreign Service Institute Oral Interview Test of speaking proficiency, for example, takes five factors into account when determining a person's speaking proficiency: accent, comprehension, fluency, grammar, and vocabulary. Adams (1980) demonstrates the difference between proficiency levels in terms of the most discriminating factors in the FSI Oral Interview Test that contribute to average performance at each level (Table 1). But the factors that contribute most to a given level on the FSI scale vary. In the factor analysis carried out on the data, "each previously selected factor is reviewed at every step to see if the information it provided as a single factor is now contained in a combination of factors. If a factor turns out to be redundant, it is removed from the list of significant factors" (Adams 1980: 3). This explains why all five factors are not present at every level. (See Adams for fuller details.)

TABLE 1. THE MOST DISCRIMINATING FACTORS IN THE FSI ORAL INTERVIEW TEST

Level	Factors in descending order of significance
0+−1	Vocabulary
1–1+	Fluency Comprehension Grammar Vocabulary
1+−2	Comprehension Grammar Accent Fluency
2–2+	Fluency Comprehension Accent Vocabulary
2+−3	Grammar Accent Vocabulary Comprehension
3–3+	Comprehension Fluency Grammar
3+−4	Vocabulary Accent Grammar
4–4+	Grammar Vocabulary

Source: Adams (1980).

Within a given proficiency level, tasks may also vary according to the type of subskills they involve. For some tasks the need for phonological and grammatical accuracy may be high (e.g., explaining to someone how a piece of equipment works), and in others it may be relatively low (e.g., shopping in a supermarket; ordering a meal in a fast food store). The same task may be performed at different criterion levels. For example, a speaking task like giving directions may be performed with a primary focus on content: ("You go – this street – King Street – two block –

you turning – Bright Street") or with a focus both on content and accuracy ("First you follow King Street for two blocks. Then you turn onto Bright Street."). The way a task is accomplished will also vary according to the audience. Thus we might recount an incident like a traffic accident in one way when speaking to a policeman and in another way when to a friend.

Language-testing research – particularly research in language proficiency testing – has contributed a great deal to our understanding of the role of grammar within language proficiency. Grammar is seen not as the central organizing principle of communication, but rather as an important component of communication. Its importance, however, varies according to the type of communicative task the learner is performing and according to the learner's level of proficiency. It is not simply a case of "more grammar = more proficient"; grammar skills interact with other language skills and together determine what learners can do at any given level of proficiency and how well they can do it.

Next we look at another source of information on the nature of language proficiency and the role of grammatical skills within it, namely, second language acquisition research.

Second language acquisition and language proficiency

During the last ten years, a considerable amount of research has been conducted into different aspects of second language acquisition (SLA) (see Chapter 5). Although much of this work has not investigated directly the development of language proficiency, much can be inferred about it from the results of the studies. Three issues arising out of this research seem particularly relevant in the context of the present discussion: the invariant order of grammatical development, delayed grammatical development, and variable use of rules.

Invariant order of development

One of the first important findings of SLA research was the discovery that L2 learners pass through clearly identifiable stages as they acquire the grammar of the target language (see Chapter 5). Although there is debate about some aspects of the invariant-order hypothesis (e.g., concerning the nature of individual variation in development; the effect of a naturalistic versus formal context on developmental order; the influence of the mother tongue; and the effects of input features – cf. Wode 1982, Pica 1983, Pienemann 1984), there is now a substantial body of evidence to suggest that second-language learners do indeed pass through stages in the acquisition of grammatical features and that these developmental stages are similar for learners of various language backgrounds. These developmental orders are typically taken as evidence to support the claim that second-language learning is a "creative construction process," in which learners construct their own interlanguage systems. "The observed morpheme order is the result of the underlying process of acquisition" (Krashen 1982: 61). The fact of an invariant or naturalistic order for the development of grammatical morphemes (if indeed it is a fact), however, is in itself of little significance, unless it can be related to a theory of the development of language proficiency. Givon's account of the differences between pragmatic and syntactic modes of communication can be used to relate the empirical findings of the morpheme studies to a proficiency-oriented view of second language acquisition (Givon 1979). (Givon makes no such connection himself; this is my own interpretation.)

Using data taken from studies of differences between child and adult, pidgin and creole, and informal (unplanned) and formal (planned) speech, Givon argues that in learning a language we acquire two modes of communication. One, termed the *pragmatic mode*, is a system of communication in which functions, topics, vocabulary, and word order are the primary organizing mechanisms. This is seen in child language, in pidgins, and in unplanned informal speech. The other, which Givon terms the *syntactic mode*, is characteristic of adult language, creoles, and formal speech. Givon (1979) illustrates some of the differences between these two modes of communication:

Pragmatic mode	*Syntactic mode*
a. Topic-comment structure	Subject-predicate structure
b. Loose conjunction	Tight subordination
c. Slow rate of delivery (under several intonation contours)	Fast rate of delivery (under a single intonational contour)
d. Word order is governed mostly by one pragmatic principle; old information goes first, new information follows	Word order is used to signal semantic case functions (though it may also be used to indicate pragmatic–topicality relations)
e. Roughly 1-to-1 ratio of verbs to nouns in discourse, with the verbs being semantically simple	A larger ratio of nouns over verbs in discourse, with the verbs being semantically complex
f. No use of grammatical morphology	Elaborate use of grammatical morphology
g. Prominent intonation/stress marks the focus of new information; topic intonation is less prominent	Very much the same, but perhaps not exhibiting as high a functional load, and at least in some languages totally absent

Givon argues that syntax arises out of the pragmatic mode. As language learning proceeds, loose pragmatic structure develops into tighter syntactic structure, with morphology and syntax developing into better code-emerging semantic and pragmatic distinctions. Reliance on a primarily pragmatic mode of communication is proposed as the normal initial stage in language acquisition. From this perspective, the natural order for the development of English morphology seen in SLA studies can be interpreted as a reflection of the movement from the pragmatic to the syntactic mode (see particularly Givon's level f in the preceding list). The naturalistic emergence of grammatical competence that the morpheme studies demonstrate can thus be interpreted as evidence of a gradual refining of the learner's capacities to package communicative meanings and intentions.

The significance of Givon's work has been acknowledged by several SLA researchers, and a number of studies have been undertaken to test whether Givon's claims hold true for second language acquisition (Schumann 1981, Sato 1983). It may well be that the particular features Givon attributes to the pragmatic and syntactic modes will have to be modified, but the basic claim of the theory appears to remain valid. Language proficiency is hence seen to involve two basic modes of development, although, as other SLA studies have demonstrated, the two do not necessarily develop at the same rate.

Delayed grammatical development

Although second-language learners may evidence an invariant order for the acquisition of certain grammatical features of the target language, for many language learners such acquisition does not lead to gradual mastery of all of the features of the target language. These learners, despite prolonged contact with and use of English, fail to go beyond an initial level of proficiency in many areas of grammar, despite developing greater control in other areas of communicative competence. Schmidt (1983a, 1983b), for example, presents a case study of an adult ESL learner in an English-speaking community who uses English extensively for social and professional purposes, yet displays remarkably little progress over a five-year period of observation in acquiring nine grammatical morphemes (Table 2). Higgs and Clifford (1982) document a similar phenomenon in describing the typical performance of students taking intensive foreign-language courses at the Defense Language Institute. Many students in such programs are unable to progress beyond a rating of 2 or 2 + on the FSI scale (the "terminal 2 syndrome," as the authors describe it) and lack sufficient control of the grammatical component of language proficiency to obtain a higher rating, despite intensive instruction. They may have a reasonable control of topics and vocabulary

TABLE 2. ORDER OF ACCURACY FOR NINE GRAMMATICAL MORPHEMES IN OBLIGATORY CONTEXTS (IN %)

	July 1978	*Nov. 1980*	*June 1983*
Copula *be*	95	94	84
Progressive -*ing*	92	90	90
Auxiliary *be*	91	89	85
Past irregular	25	55	51
Plural	5	32	21
3rd singular -*s*	0	21	24
Article	0	6	2
Possessive -*s*	0	8	10
Past regular	0	0	0

Source: Schmidt (1983b).

(indeed, they may be rated 3 + or 4 on these dimensions), but they are weak on grammatical accuracy.

This pattern of high vocabulary and low grammar is a classic profile for a terminal 2/2 +. In fact, the terminal [2/2 + profile]...is encountered all too frequently in government screening programs. It is important to note that the grammar weaknesses that are typically found in this profile are not *missing* grammatical patterns which the student could learn or acquire later on, but are *fossilized* incorrect patterns. Experience has shown again and again that such patterns are not remediable, even in intensive language training programs or additional in-country living experience. (Higgs and Clifford 1982: 67)

Schumann (1978) provides further data on a subject who failed to make progress in grammar. Schumann studied six learners over a ten-month period and found that one learner

showed very little linguistic development during the course of the study. Four stages were found in the acquisition of the English negative, no V, don't V, aux-neg, analyzed don't; throughout the study Alberto remained in the first stage. Two stages were found in the acquisition of English Wh-questions; throughout the study Alberto remained in the first period of the first stage. (Schumann 1978: 65)

In the light of the distinction between pragmatic and syntactic modes of communication, cases like these may be interpreted as situations where learners develop proficiency in the pragmatic mode at the expense of the syntactic mode of communication. Schumann (1978) offers a sociopsychological explanation to account for nonacquisition of the syntactic mode, in terms of his acculturation theory. Schumann attributes his subject's lack of grammatical development to social and psycholog-

151

ical distance from the speakers of the target language and to the fact that pidginized speech appears to be sufficient for his restricted communicative needs. Schmidt's study, however, does not support Schumann's acculturation theory, since his subject was well acculturated. Despite extensive use of English for social and personal purposes, the subject's grammatical development remained very limited. Higgs and Clifford propose that the reasons for the terminal-2 syndrome encountered in many U.S. government language programs is that in many foreign-language programs, where there is an initial emphasis on communication, and in particular comprehensible communication, learners' production or output demands in the target language may soon outstrip their grammatical competence. The results are learners who are successful but grammatically inaccurate communicators. There may be too few demands within the curriculum for use of the syntactic mode. In addition, there is often not enough focus on grammatical accuracy in such programs.

Schmidt's study is a test case for a different form of validation of Givon's theory, however, since Schmidt's subject used English exclusively for speaking and listening; he had virtually no contact with written modes of communication. (Again, in what follows I am interpreting Givon in the light of my own discussion of proficiency.) Now it could well be the case that acquisition of the syntactic modes is dependent upon use of other-than-oral modes of communication. Many of the linguistic features of the syntactic mode cited by Givon (e.g., passivization, use of relative clauses, subordination in the verb phrase, use of complex verbs, complex genitive constructions) are features more characteristic of or more frequent in written rather than spoken discourse. Hence it could be said that lack of contact with the written mode (either in reading or writing) will lead to retarded development along the syntactic parameter. The converse is presumably also possible, where a learner exposed primarily to the syntactic mode may evidence considerable development along the syntactic parameter but be severely restricted in use of the pragmatic mode, that is, be unable to maintain conversational discourse.

Another important issue arises from cases of retarded grammatical development such as those studied by Schmidt and Schumann. Such cases demonstrate that the degree of development or nondevelopment along a grammatical continuum cannot be taken as evidence of a level of language proficiency. As Schmidt has shown, a learner may have attained a considerable degree of communicative or pragmatic proficiency despite lack of progress in the grammatical domain. An index of grammatical development is not therefore necessarily an index of language proficiency (despite the attempt by some SLA researchers to see these as one and the same thing – cf. Larsen-Freeman 1978). Although language proficiency at its highest levels includes control of morphology and syntax, other components of proficiency may develop relatively independently in certain circumstances; this means that nothing can necessarily be inferred about one (e.g., the pragmatic mode) from the state of development or retardation of the other (e.g., the syntactic).

Variable use of rules

Another phenomenon documented in studies of second- and foreign-language learning is variability in the use or application of rules that learners apparently "know." An individual may demonstrate accurate use of a particular feature of grammar or phonology in one situation (e.g., telling a story) but not in another (e.g., informal conversation). Dickerson and Dickerson (1977) and others (Tarone 1983, Sato 1983) have shown that this type of variation is systematic; the use of target-language features varies systematically according to the situation or context for its use. LoCoco (1976) compared the performance of learners in three different situations and found significant differences in the number of grammatical errors occurring in each situation and also in the degree to which transfer and overgeneralization errors occurred. As Tarone observes, "the linguistic and phonological characteristics of Interlanguage change as the situation changes" (Tarone 1979: 183).

There are several explanations available for the variability evidenced in the second-language learner's interlanguage phonology and syntax. Tarone (1979; personal communication) and others (Dickerson 1975, Sato 1983) have illustrated the effect of task on the use of interlanguage rules. Performance on different kinds of tasks (e.g., reading aloud from a word list, telling a story, free conversation, an interview, a written grammar test, an oral grammar test) may vary. This is because the amount of attention to phonological and grammatical accuracy, that is, to language form, differs across task conditions. (Tarone, personal communication, emphasizes that this is not the only variable, however.) Some tasks require little attention to language form (e.g., informal conversation), whereas others require a great deal (e.g., a writing task); this affects the kind of target language forms used as well as the degree to which certain forms are used. This is also predicted by Givon's theory, since the difference between formal (i.e., planned) and casual (i.e., unplanned) speech is another example of the difference between pragmatic and syntactic modes of communication, both of which have their own distinctive grammatical and phonological characteristics.

Krashen's "monitor theory" (Krashen 1981, 1982) attributes variation in task performance to the differing conditions that exist for applying (or not applying) the "monitor." Tasks vary according to the presence or absence of features necessary for the application of the monitor (e.g., the amount of time available, or the degree to which a focus on accuracy is present; see Gregg 1984). McLaughlin's discussion of differences between controlled and automatic processing is an additional dimension (see Chapter 5; McLaughlin et al. 1983).

Research on variation in interlanguage syntax and the effects of task on use of component subskills thus complements the definition of proficiency given in the beginning of this chapter and provides further evidence of how different components of proficiency assume different degrees of significance according to the nature of a communicative task.

Curriculum implications

We have seen that both the literature on language proficiency testing as well as research on second language acquisition support the notion that grammar is a necessary but not sufficient component of language proficiency. The proper context for discussing the role of grammatical and other skills in the curriculum is hence through reference to a theory of language proficiency. This is what we have attempted to present in this chapter. A theory of grammar, or of grammatical development, cannot provide a starting point for a proficiency-oriented curriculum, though such a curriculum must acknowledge the role of grammatical skills within different kinds and levels of proficiency. In developing a proficiency-oriented curriculum, therefore, our goal is to develop a program in which grammatical skills are viewed as components of specific kinds of proficiency. Guidelines for the development of curriculum models are currently being developed in large-scale language programs.

One example of this approach can be seen in the American Council on the Teaching of Foreign Languages (ACTFL) Proficiency Guidelines. These guidelines specify nine levels of language proficiency and include speaking, listening, reading, writing, and cultural components (Higgs 1984). They are intended to be used as general guidelines in the development of foreign-language programs in the United States. Within each proficiency level, expected performance outcomes are specified in terms of subskills related to functions, content, and accuracy. A similar approach has been adopted in the design of on-arrival programs for immigrants in Australia. Ingram comments,

In order to ensure that a language program is coherent and systematically moves learners along the path towards that level of proficiency they require, some overall perspective of the developmental path is required. This need resulted...in the development of the Australian Second Language Proficiency Ratings (ASLRP). The ASLRP defines levels of second language proficiency at nine (potentially twelve) points along the path from zero to native-like proficiency. The definitions provide detailed descriptions of language behaviour in all four macroskills and allows the syllabus developer to perceive how a course at any level fits into the total pattern of proficiency development. (Ingram 1982: 66)

For each type of communicative task the learner is expected to accomplish (e.g., listening, speaking, reading, writing) the proficiency descriptions should describe the criterion that must be attained. As Higgs and Clifford point out in defending such a proposal,

If the goal of the curriculum is to produce Level 3 speakers of a language, then the concentration on language subskills in the curriculum should be representative of their relative importance in performing Level 3 Tasks. Grammar skills would be an important part of the curriculum. If the goal is to produce students with Level 1 survival skills, then the optimum curriculum mix would be entirely different, with a primary emphasis on the teaching and practice of vocabulary. (Higgs and Clifford 1982: 73)

Higgs and Clifford represent the (hypothetical) relative contribution of different subskills, including grammar skills, at different levels of proficiency, in Figure 1.

However, proficiency levels intended for use in curriculum planning will differ somewhat from those intended for use in language-proficiency assessment, since the latter are typically defined negatively, in terms of deficiencies in performance. The proficiency guidelines used in curriculum planning need to be defined positively, in terms of specific but restricted levels of skill. This is not always the case with the ACTFL Proficiency Guidelines. Proficiency levels in language-program development do more than simply specify communicative goals within the curriculum; they also specify the degree of effectiveness with which communication is carried out.

The use of graded objectives in curriculum development currently being implemented in several countries represents an alternative approach to relating grammatical and other skills to levels of performance on specific tasks (Buckby 1981, Page et al. 1982). These are typically defined according to the type of tasks that a second- or foreign-language learner at a particular level of proficiency can be expected to carry out. Proficiency guidelines and graded objectives are different in conception from what are commonly understood as curriculum objectives. This is because they can be derived empirically – that is, drawn from studies of learner performance at different levels of achievement (cf. Brindley 1982). In this way, they are not merely the planner's or applied linguist's views of how target-language performance is established.

How is grammar affected by the shift from "competence" to "performance" as the guiding principle of language-curriculum development? Higgs and Clifford (1982) claim that grammatical accuracy is a fundamental component of lower levels of proficiency for many commu-

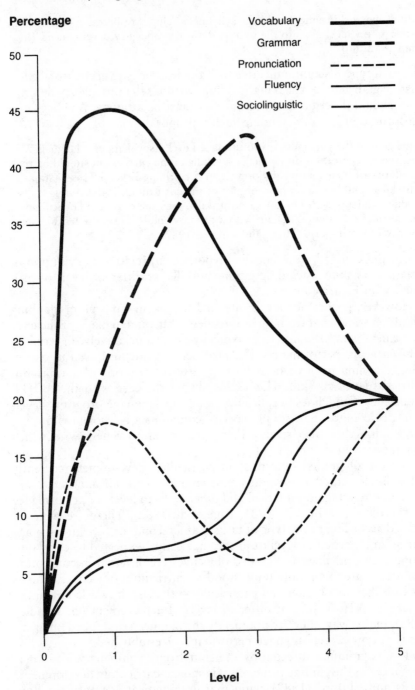

Figure 1. Hypothesized relative contribution of different components of proficiency according to level. (Adapted from Higgs and Clifford 1982.)

nicative tasks. If accuracy is delayed to promote comprehensible output, they say, learners may not be able to move beyond the level of proficiency currently represented by level 2 on the FSL scale. The pragmatic mode will develop at the expense of the syntactic mode. This is not to advocate a return to grammatical syllabuses or grammar drills, because a focus on grammar in itself is not a valid approach to the development of language proficiency. Instead, tasks and activities selected for use at different levels of proficiency should reflect the degree of importance attributed to grammatical accuracy at that level. Furthermore, by focusing on grammatical accuracy we can engage the learner in pedagogic tasks and learning experiences that allow for the development of monitoring, revision, or editing capacities, that is, making grammatical accuracy a part of the communicative process, rather than focusing on the study of grammar for its own sake. Grammatical skills are thus seen as a component of language proficiency rather than as an end in themselves. In conclusion, although grammar must always play a central role in language teaching, its importance can be derived from and related to the proficiencies we plan as the outcomes of language curriculum.

11 Introducing the progressive

Producing a sentence is a task of great complexity. Although we usually say what we want without too much difficulty, the ease with which we use sentences in conversation or writing does not reflect the mental planning and organization that goes into them. This chapter attempts to unravel details of one small part of the system of mental organization that goes into the production of a sentence. It focuses on the *progressive*, a part of the aspectual system of English. I describe here the semantic system that the progressive aspect represents in English, and discuss implications of this analysis for the teaching of the progressive to students of English as a second language.

The progressive may seem to be a relatively trivial part of English grammar, yet the semantic distinction that it represents is one with far-reaching effects. Every sentence in English must have both tense and aspect. It must be in either the past or the nonpast; it must have progressive, nonprogressive, perfect, or nonperfect aspect. Successful mastery of the progressive is hence an urgent goal for language learners. But what is the nature of the grammatical system it represents and what learning difficulties does it pose for students of English as a second language?

Let us consider the sequence of actions in Figure 1 and how they may be described. There are many sentences to describe this set of pictures, but we will consider only four groups:

1. The man gets up. He walks to the door. He opens it.
2. The man got up. He walked to the door. He opened it.
3. The man is getting up. He is walking to the door. He is opening it.
4. The man has gotten up. He has walked to the door. He has opened it.

The differences among these four options for describing the same events concern differences in the choice of tense (*gets up* versus *got up*) and aspect (*is getting up* versus *has gotten*). Tense refers to a set of grammatical markings that are used to relate the time of the events described in a sentence to the time of the utterance itself. There are two tenses in English: present and past. Present tense associates the time of the event to the present moment in time. "The state of the event has *psychological* being at the present moment" (Leech 1971: 1). Past tense associates the time of the event with a time before the present moment. Tense is thus

158

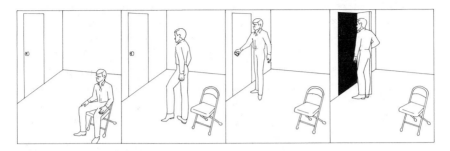

Figure 1

deictic; that is, it points either toward time now or time then. But what is aspect?

As the tense system gives information about the time of the event, the aspect system gives information about the kind of event the verb refers to. We may communicate through aspect such distinctions as whether an event is changing, repeated, habitual, complete, and so forth. English has two aspects, perfect and progressive. I have described the function of the perfect in Chapter 12. Here we will consider only the progressive. The choice of progressive aspect (the form with *be + ing*) or nonprogressive aspect (known as the simple form) is based on a distinction between different types of situations to which verbs refer.

In describing the semantic distinction that governs the choice of simple versus progressive, linguists have made use of two-part divisions (e.g., between *dynamic* verbs and *stative* verbs, as in Quirk et al. 1972), three-part divisions (e.g., between *states, processes,* and *actions* as in Chafe 1970), and four-part divisions (e.g., between *accomplishments, events, activities,* and *states* as in Vendler 1967 and Scovel 1971a). For present purposes, I wish to make a two-part division between a stative situation and a dynamic situation. A sentence referring to a stative situation is one that describes the quality or property of something, for example: *The book is red; I know the answer; I wish I could speak French; This car holds six people.* Such verbs are stative verbs. Quirk et al. divide stative verbs into two classes: verbs of inert perception and cognition (e.g., *believe, feel, know, like, prefer, see, think,* etc.) and relational verbs (e.g., *be, contain, have, owe, require, seem,* etc.). A state, as these verbs illustrate, is something that is thought of as remaining constant from one moment to the next. A dynamic situation on the other hand is one that may involve change and development, or that may have a beginning, a middle, and an end. A verb that refers to a dynamic situation is a dynamic verb. Quirk et al. illustrate five different classes of dynamic verbs: activity verbs (*ask, drink, eat, listen, read, work, write,* etc.),

159

process verbs (*change, grow, widen,* etc.), verbs of bodily sensation (*ache, feel, hurt,* etc.), transitional event verbs (*arrive, died, leave, lose,* etc.), and momentary verbs (*hit, jump, knock, tap,* etc.) (Quirk et al. 1972: 95–96).

The choice between simple or progressive form depends on whether the verb refers to a dynamic or stative situation. Dynamic verbs can be used either in the progressive form or the simple form. Stative verbs generally occur only in the simple form.[1] What governs this distinction? Let us consider the simple form first.

The simple form has several nuances in discourse, depending on the type of verb with which it occurs (e.g., activity, process, momentary, etc.). Generally, it depicts an event as a whole, as complete, as seen unfolding from beginning to end, or as unchanging, and this can be regarded as the basic grammatical meaning of the form.

In the previous illustrations, for example, if we choose to describe the actions as complete, then we use the simple form (i.e., the nonprogressive aspect), using present tense if we wish to describe the actions as taking place now, or the past tense if we wish to describe the actions as taking place at an earlier time. This explains the choice of either *The man gets up* (simple form, present tense) or *The man got up* (simple form, past tense). In both cases the action of getting up is depicted as a complete action. *Get up* is a dynamic verb, but stative verbs are also depicted as unchanging, describing states or properties that are thought of as constant from one moment to the next, rather than as unfolding or developing. For example: *I like coffee; Gold is expensive; This car has four seats.* The use of the simple form with some dynamic verbs (verbs of bodily sensation) turns them effectively into stative verbs: *I feel sick.* The progressive occurs with dynamic verbs (or with verbs that are used as dynamic verbs) and depicts events as incomplete, as changing or developing.

Returning to Figure 1, we use the progressive if we choose to describe the actions as incomplete, using present tense again if we choose to regard the actions as taking place now. Hence, *the man is getting up.* (We will not discuss the additional aspectual meaning communicated through the perfect aspect, but see Chapter 12.)

Actions described by dynamic verbs can thus be viewed as either *complete* or *incomplete* through the choice of simple form or progressive

---

1 It would be more accurate to speak of verbs being used dynamically or statively, rather than dynamic or stative verbs, since many verbs have both dynamic and stative uses. The context is crucial in determining whether the use is stative or dynamic. Compare:

Stative use	Dynamic use
He has two brothers.	She is having a good time.
This cost 50 cents.	My groceries are costing me more and more.

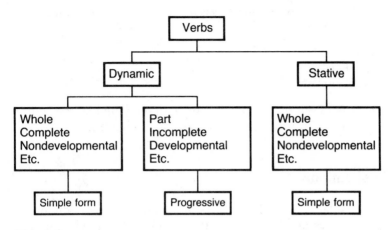

Figure 2

aspect. The choice of the progressive is not governed by a time perspective but by our view of the duration and degree of completion of
the action. The same action can therefore often be described in either
the simple or the progressive form. For example, I can describe the action
of picking up my pen from the table in several ways. I can use the present
tense and the simple form: *Watch. I pick up the pen.* Here the action
is viewed as complete. I can also describe the same action in the past
tense: *What did I do? I picked up the pen.* And if I wish to describe the
action as partially complete, I can use the progressive aspect: *Watch. I
am picking up the pen.*

The choice of the progressive is not governed by whether an action
is taking place now or not, and this is why the progressive is not a tense.
The crucial factor is whether the action is regarded as complete or
incomplete. An incomplete action can thus be located in any time period:

I was reading that book yesterday.
I am reading a fascinating book, but I can't remember where I put it.
I'm reading this book tonight.

(See Quirk et al. 1972 for further discussion of additional nuances conveyed by dynamic verbs in the progressive, according to the different
classes of dynamic verb involved.)

Dynamic verbs thus take the simple form if they are depicted as complete, as a whole, or as unchanging, and the progressive if they are
depicted as incomplete, changing, developing, and so forth. But do we
have the same choice with stative verbs?

A state is regarded as complete and unchanging, and for this reason,
states cannot be described using the progressive aspect. They must be

161

described in the simple form, since this is the form that depicts something complete.

She *has* a cold.
Do you *believe* in UFOs?
This *costs* twelve dollars.

The difference between the semantic distinction conveyed by the choice of simple or progressive can be summarized as in Figure 2.

Dynamic situations

Let us now consider in more detail how this system operates in discourse to produce a wide range of nuances that can all be related to this simple semantic contrast.[2]

Past versus past progressive

The contrast between completed actions (simple form) and incomplete actions (progressive) is illustrated by comparing the simple past with the past progressive.

1. I *painted* the cupboard.   I *was painting* the cupboard when I fell.
2. I *cleaned* the kitchen this morning.   I *was painting* the kitchen this morning.
3. I *learned* French in Montreal.   I *was studying* French in Montreal.

In (1) a completed event contrasts with an event that is not completed because it is interrupted by another action. In (2) an action depicted as having duration and having been completed within a time period (this morning) is compared with an action that is not completed within a time period but is depicted as having been in progress during the time period. In (3), similarly, an action depicted as finished is compared with one depicted as not totally accomplished. This is supported by the lexical change from *learned* to *study* (rather than *I was learning French in Montreal*).

2 It should be noted that, whereas the aspectual meaning of the progressive–simple distinction is based on the whole–part distinction, the perfect adds another aspectual dimension that can operate together with the simple–progressive distinction, namely, that between an event depicted in relation to the time of an utterance (present versus past) and an event depicted in relation to an earlier situation or point in time (past/present versus perfect). Compare *What did you do? What have you done? I saw it. I have seen it.* (See Comrie 1976.)

Simple form versus present progressive

The contrast between completed actions (simple form) and incomplete actions (progressive) may also be seen in the contrast between present tense and progressive aspect. We may compare:

4. I tell you you are wrong.   I am telling you you are wrong.
5. Reagan wins.   Reagan is winning.
   (Headline in newspaper.)
6. Here they come!   They are coming.
7. I get up at six.   Nowadays, I am getting up at six.
8. Now we add the eggs to the mixture.   Now she is adding the eggs to the mixture.

These sentences illustrate several subtle effects of the contrast between complete and incomplete actions. In (4) we have an example of verbs of communication, such as *warn, write, advise*. When these are used in the simple form, they depict the act of communication as complete; hence this is an appropriate form for threats, warnings, and so on. It is as if nothing further is going to be said. This form is also used for speech acts that bring about a change in the state of affairs in the real world, for example, *I declare you husband and wife. I name this ship the Royal Star*. The progressive is used with verbs of communication when the act of communication is not regarded as complete. Something further may have to be said, for example, *What I am trying to say is. . ., Are you really saying that you believe she stole the money?* In (5), Reagan's success is seen as final and beyond dispute. In *Reagan is winning* the results are seen as tentative and subject to change or confirmation. In (6), *Here they come!*, said just as we see our guests get out of a taxi, focuses on their arrival as a completed act. In *They are coming*, their arrival is seen as in progress, with further stages still to be completed. In (7), we have the habitual present, which is sometimes mistakenly explained as the basic meaning of the simple form. What it does in fact do is depict a single action (my getting up) as being typical of my daily behavior, which is thus seen as regular and unchanging. This is why the simple form is used. But in "Nowadays, I am getting up at six" we depict what is true only for the present and say nothing about past or future behavior. In (8), we have an action that has been isolated from a series of actions that make up a recipe. Recipes – like plans, directions, ceremonies – are complete or unchanging in as much as the different acts that make up the event have a fixed place or follow a predictable sequence. However, if we are not aware of such a sequence, we may describe each action as an independent event rather than as part of a sequence and thus use the progressive: *Now she is adding the eggs to the mixture*. A magician, for example, knowing exactly what trick comes next, can give a running commentary in the simple form: *Watch what I do. I take this box and put the rabbit in it. Now I cover it with this cloth.* A child in the audience watching the magician, however, does not know what will happen next. For the child, as naive spectator, each action unfolds independently and unpredictably, hence the progressive could be used. *Look, mommy. Now the magician is putting the rabbit into the box.*

Stative situations

We saw earlier that stative verbs are used in the simple form, because a state is complete and cannot be depicted as changing or developing.

I know the answer.	*and not*	I am knowing the answer.
She has three brothers.		She is having three brothers.

There is a clash between the semantic concept of a state and the feeling of temporariness conveyed by the progressive aspect, and this is why verbs like *know, want, believe* are said to avoid the progressive.

Some verbs, however, are used to describe both stative situations and dynamic situations or actions. When used in the simple form, they describe stative situations; when used in the progressive, they describe dynamic situations. For example:

9. We live here.	We are living here.
10. He sings well.	He is singing well tonight.
11. I feel ill.	I am feeling ill.
12. The hem on this dress shows.	Your slip is showing.
13. I think it is true.	I'm thinking about it.
14. I wonder if you can help me.	I was wondering if you could help me.

In (9) *live*, as a state, is contrasted with a temporary activity for which *stay* could also be used, for example, *We are staying here.* In (10), a permanent capacity or attribute is compared with performance on a single occasion. The contrast between permanence and impermanence is another manifestation of the basic semantic contrast between complete and incomplete that underlies the simple/progressive distinction. In (11), we have a verb of bodily sensation, *feel*. This class of verbs, which includes verbs like *ache* and *hurt*, allows us the option of depicting a bodily condition as either a state, in which case we use the simple form, or a temporary condition, in which case we use the progressive (see Scovel 1971b). In (12), we have a permanent characteristic of something being compared with a temporary aspect of the situation. A woman may thus adjust her dress so that her slip does not show, but she cannot remedy a visible hem so easily. In (13), we compare a state of mind with a temporary mental activity. In (14) a state, *wonder*, is compared with something temporary, *was wondering*. The latter is subject to change, less committed, and therefore thought to be more polite.

Various other uses of the progressive have been commented on by grammarians (see Palmer 1965, Hirtle 1967, Leech 1971, Scovel 1971a, Comrie 1976), in particular, its use to describe persistent activity and future events.

Persistent activity

Sometimes the use of the progressive suggests a repeated and generally irritating or regretted activity: *You're always arriving late, I'm always borrowing your cigarettes*. This usage normally requires an adverb. Perhaps the reason for the progressive here is that it leaves open the possibility of future change or improvement, a nuance that is not present when the simple form is used: *You always arrive late*. Here the characteristic behavior is depicted as unchangeable.

Future events

English has no future tense. It makes use of a variety of verb forms, including the progressive, to depict future events. The progressive is used for future events that are under human control and/or under the control of the subject and is typically used to describe plans, arrangements, intentions, and so forth. These can be regarded as having begun in the sense that a decision has been made, but they are incomplete because their realization takes place at a future time: *I'm leaving at six o'clock, We are having a test tomorrow*. Sentences that do not refer to events that involve human planning, decision making, and so on, cannot be described as future events using the progressive: *The sun is rising earlier in the summer*.

How does using the progressive for future events differ from using the simple form for future events? The use of the simple form suggests that the events are out of the control of the subject of the sentence. They are hence seen as fixed plans, and the possibility of change is not foreseen: *We leave at 7 p.m. and arrive at New York at 11. The film starts at 7:30*. Future events depicted through this verb form are likewise limited to events that are subject to human planning. Hence, we cannot have: *It rains tomorrow*.

Implications for teaching

Terminology

In planning how to incorporate the teaching of tense and aspect into a language syllabus, we need to begin from a clear understanding of how these grammatical systems function in English. Unfortunately, many textbooks and classroom grammar books demonstrate considerable confusion when it comes to this distinction and sometimes make generalizations that may not be helpful to students. The classroom classic, *Living English Structure* (Allen 1959), for example, merges tense and aspect and creates an array of tenses in an attempt to make English match the tense system of European languages. Therefore English is described as having a future progressive tense, a past progressive tense, and so forth. Close's excellent reference grammar (1975) gives a more accurate account of the facts of English usage. He writes:

There are two main tenses in English – present and past. Each tense can have a simple form, and each can be combined with either progressive aspect, with perfect aspect, or with both; thus

	Present	*Past*
a. simple	I play.	I played.
b. progressive	I am playing.	I was playing.
c. perfect	I have played.	I had played.
d. perfect-progressive	I have been playing.	I had been playing.

(Close 1975: 241)

Using Close's terminology we would thus describe a sentence like *I am studying German* as present tense, progressive aspect. We would describe *I was studying German* as past tense, progressive aspect. *I have been studying German* is present tense and both perfect and progressive aspect.

Basic meaning

To mistakenly describe the progressive as a tense leads one to look for a time distinction as basic to its function. Allen (1959) thus links the progressive to now. He talks of it as depicting the real present: now at this moment. In fact, as we have seen, it may be used with events that have past, present, or future time reference. To link the progressive to a view of activities is to get closer to its functions; however, it is often described as restricted to ongoing activity. But it is not an activity's ongoing aspect that calls for the progressive. We saw earlier than an ongoing activity can be described using either the simple form or the progressive aspect: *I pick up the pen, I am picking up the pen*. Hence the basic meaning of the progressive is in its depiction of an activity or event as incomplete, changing, temporary, and so on, and this is what our classroom presentation and practice should aim to establish.

Presentation

When classroom and textbook presentations link the progressive to time (now) and to ongoing activity, they may be responsible for introducing the common assumption that the progressive is a kind of narrative present. By analogy, then, the past progressive is assumed to be a narrative past: *Last Sunday, we were going to a party. We were leaving the house at six o'clock, and we were taking a taxi to our friend's house.* More typically, the progressive is used in free variation with the simple form in the interlanguage of ESL students, often never entirely assuming its correct place alongside the simple form and the perfect.

The analysis given here suggests that rather than limiting contexts for the practice of the progressive to ongoing activities, a wide range of actions can be used to illustrate the basic functions of the progressive, and these may have either past, present, or future time reference. The following are representative contexts:

A.   *Events and conditions of recent or temporary duration*

A.1.   Descriptions of people, scenes, and so forth.

> These people are wearing snow shoes.
> This man is carrying a gun.
> The woman is selling flowers.
> You are not looking well.
> The children are making a snowman.
> I am not wearing my contact lenses today.
> This car is carrying three passengers.
> We are staying at the Hilton Hotel.
> My shoes are wearing out.

A.2.   The weather.

> Is it still raining outside?
> It is snowing.
> The wind is blowing strongly today.

A.3.   Unfinished activities, not necessarily ongoing.

> The workmen are still repairing the bridge.
> They are having a sale at the bookshop this week.
> Mrs. Thomas is writing a novel.
> I'm taking Spanish this semester.

A.4.   Requests for explanations. (A temporary event is seen as leading to another event.)

> Who are these people waiting for?
> Why is this man carrying a gun?

Why is the girl crying?
Where are you going?

A.5. Comments that expect subsequent action.

The phone is ringing.	I'll get it.
It's raining.	I'll close the window.
The baby is sleeping.	I'll turn down the TV.
The water is boiling.	I'll make the coffee.

B. *Planned future events*

B.1. Reporting plans, arrangements, and so forth.

We are having dinner at 8 p.m.
We are having a holiday next week.
I'm leaving tomorrow.

B.2. Inquiring about plans.

What are you doing on Sunday?
What courses are you taking next semester?

C. *Incomplete events in the past*

C.1. Interrupted events.

What were you doing when the fire started?
The northbound train was traveling at 70 mph when it collided with a truck that was crossing the railroad tracks.

C.2. Temporary events in the past.

I wasn't feeling well yesterday.
We didn't see you at the cinema, because we were sitting downstairs.

Classroom activities used to depict the characteristic functions of the progressive can be varied. One well-planned course, for example, makes use of the writing of postcards (Figure 3) to contextualize the progressive in a situation where actions are seen to be temporary (Fowler, Pidcock, and Rycroft 1979). The same course bases a listening-comprehension exercise on a commentary on a sports event:

The rain is falling heavily here at Monza. Don Bracken is lapping at 237 kilometers an hour. He's leading Piero Angelo by eight seconds. Angelo is

Dear Fred,
We're all having a lovely time here. The sun's shining and we're enjoying every minute of our holiday. We aren't really doing anything at the moment. Nellie's lying on the beach beside me, and I'm writing this postcard. We're getting very brown. Nellie's got a beautiful tan and she's looking very attractive. Don't worry! She's missing you a lot!
                    See you soon.
                        Betty

Mr. Fred Appleyard,
23 Orchard Road,
Little Merking,
Middx.
INGLATERRA

Figure 3

trying to close the gap but Bracken's driving the race of his life today. Now they're in the straight and smoke is pouring from Bracken's engine. His manager is signaling to him desperately. He's coming in to the pit. The mechanics are working on the car and the smoke is dying down, but Bracken is losing precious time. Angelo's opening up a big gap...every second is vital.

This presents a series of actions, each seen to be of short duration and likely to change at any moment.

Conclusion

Contrary to what is often presented in popular grammar books, the progressive is not a tense (a grammatical form that depicts time) but an aspect (a grammatical form that depicts how an action unfolds). It is therefore not a tense for activities taking place now but a grammatical form that is based on a distinction between stative and dynamic situations and is used for actions and events that are regarded as incomplete or developing. We have suggested that this should be the distinction that guides our organization of the teaching of the progressive. This will lead to classroom activities and exercises that relate the progressive to situations in which actions and events are seen not on a time continuum, but as incomplete, temporary, or developing.

12 Introducing the perfect: an exercise in pedagogic grammar

The field of syllabus design and materials development for second-language teaching has been revitalized in recent years through the emergence of notional and functional approaches to language teaching. The question of selecting items for the realization of notions and functions remains problematic, however. This is because basic decisions concerning the choice of grammatical and lexical items still need to be made, despite the particular approach adopted. In a notional syllabus, both concept categories and functions form the focus of the syllabus. Concept categories include semantico-grammatical categories, such as concepts of time, motion, frequency, and duration. Functions include speech acts, such as requesting, ordering, describing, and informing. This chapter is concerned with one area of grammar within the field of concept categories, namely, the perfect; it examines the concept covered by the perfect as it might appear in an introductory language syllabus.

The perfect is variously described in the literature as both a tense and an aspect. In an attempt to clarify grammatical terms and concepts, Comrie (1976) argues that the perfect belongs to the aspectual rather than to the tense system of English. The tense system involves distinctions of time and is grammaticalized to give only two tenses: past and present. The aspect system involves distinctions that are separate from the time perspective. An event may be viewed for examples as *complete* or *incomplete* via the aspectual contrast of *nonprogressive* versus *progressive*. Thus in the contrast *He read / He was reading*, although both sentences are in the past tense, the first sentence involves nonprogressive aspect and the second, progressive aspect. The perfect evokes a retrospective view of an event; "it establishes a relation between a state at one time and a situation at an earlier time" (Comrie 1976: 64). Thus, in the contrast *He moved the chair / He has moved the chair*, the difference is not a difference of tense; it does not concern the *time* at which the moving of the chair took place, but a difference in the way the event described by the verb is viewed.

Grammarians typically identify four perspectives associated with the use of the perfect in English: (1) We regard an event as a state leading up to the present. *I have lived here for six years.* This view of events is common with verbs that are often used statively, such as *live, exit, own, be.* (2) We regard an event as occurring at an unspecified time within a time period extending up to the present. *Have you ever eaten frogs' legs?* This is the so-called indefinite past. (3) We regard events as repeated within a time period leading up to the present. *We have always eaten lunch together on Fridays.* (4) We regard an event as having results that extend to the present. *I have broken my watch.* This is the "resultative perfect." (See Leech 1971.)

Where should we start when we attempt to incorporate the perfect into our grammatical syllabus? Let us look at one possible approach, which is used in a recent film on methodology. Here is a transcript from the film, which deals with the teaching of the question forms of the present perfect. The teacher contextualizes the form by asking the students to perform actions in front of the class and then asks questions about the students' actions.

Teacher: (*To a student*) Come up here, Lim.
(*Student goes to the front of the class*)
Move the chair. (*Student moves the teacher's chair*)
Go back to your seat. She has moved the chair. She hasn't moved the desk. Has she moved the chair? Yes, she has. Has she moved the desk? No, she hasn't.
Come here, Foo. Touch the blackboard.
(*Student touches the blackboard*)
He has touched the blackboard. Has he touched the blackboard? Yes, he has. Has he touched the table? No, he hasn't. He hasn't touched the table.

And so on. The teacher calls other students to the front of the class and, using different objects (a book, a pen, etc.), demonstrates some of the other sentence patterns in which the present perfect can be used. It is a good classroom lesson in the terms in which it is thought out. The new form is taught through its association with a context and the students are actively involved in using the language. But what rules for the perfect are the students likely to have formed?

The context for the lesson was a series of complete actions performed by the students, a recounting of those actions by the teacher, and a series of questions about them. What verb forms did the teacher use? Looking back to our classification of the functions of the perfect we see that the perfect was used in the lesson in its resultative meaning much of the time: *Now the chair is in a different position.* The question form *Has he touched the table?*, however, illustrates a different function for the perfect, namely, the so-called indefinite past, which would be more common with *yet* (*Have you finished your homework yet?*) or with *ever* (*Have you ever...?*). But the resultative function of the perfect is the dominant impression we get from the lesson. The resultative perfect is used to describe an event in the past that has results extending to the present. Although all uses of the perfect involve a retrospective view of events (cf. Hirtle 1975) – a looking back to a period or event in the past and then returning to the point of orientation in time – the resultative perfect offers us a special way of looking at events whereby the results or consequences of an event are seen to extend up to the present moment. There is nothing unusual or extraordinary about the resultative perfect. It is a quite frequent use of the perfect and is seen in sentences like these:

What has happened to you?
An American Ambassador to China has just been appointed.
Jill has found an apartment at last.
I have come to Boston to attend the TESOL convention.
The president has said something about this recently.

It is the resultative perfect that reminds us that the perfect is not a tense but an aspect, a way of viewing events distinct from their time orientation. This is because another characteristic of the resultative is that it is an optional alternative to the simple past.

Resultative perfect	*Simple past*
What has happened to you?	What happened to you?
An American Ambassador to China has just been appointed.	An American Ambassador to China was just appointed.
Jill has found an apartment at last.	Jill found an apartment at last.
I have come to Boston to attend the TESOL convention.	I came to Boston to attend the TESOL convention.
The president has said something about this.	The president said something about this.

The fact that the resultative perfect can readily be replaced by the simple past is perhaps the reason why its additional, resultative meaning is difficult to grasp for the beginning student. Although the reporting or narrative function of the past tense is fairly easy to identify and is generally supported by time adverbs, the additional meaning conveyed by the resultative perfect is not easy to understand for a beginner. Thus it would be very difficult for the students in the class discussed earlier to understand anything but a reporting or narrative function for the perfect tense, as it was used by the teacher. In fact, it would have been more natural perhaps to have used the past rather than the perfect throughout the lesson, were it not for the fact that the lesson was supposed to be about the perfect! The teacher could have just as easily said:

Move the chair. She moved the chair. She didn't move the desk. Did she move the chair? Yes, she did. Did she move the desk? No, she didn't.

In selecting the resultative meaning for the perfect as an introduction to the perfect, we have not made a particularly helpful step toward establishing a function for the perfect in the learner's mind nor in reinforcing our prior teaching of the past tense. What we have probably succeeded in doing is to establish a rule like the following: The perfect tense is another way of describing past events. This rule will in turn account for students producing sentences like these:

Yesterday there has been a fire in the library building.
When I have got home last night I have felt ill.

Part of the problem is related to the fact that the same context or situation, that of narrating or reporting past events, has been used for the perfect as would normally have been used for the past. The syllabus designer's task is to minimize such conflicts by arranging the gradation of teaching items in such a way that new items are seen to be related to new functions, rather than being seen as alternative ways of doing things the learner can already do. Since the simple past is presumably already available for narration and for the reporting of past events – it is, in fact, one of the most statistically frequent verb forms for this function in discourse (Ota 1963) – the perfect, when it is introduced, should be linked with a function that is new to the students. Thus, as we saw earlier, although the language allows us the option of describing the same event in different ways through viewing it from a different mental view, this is not a luxury we can allow ourselves within a pedagogic grammar of English. Here we are justified in widening potential contrasts within the grammatical system of the language and of teaching limited options for talking about time and events. This suggests that we work from the premise of *one form for one function* for as long as possible. This has the additional advantage of providing a justification for the introduction of new language items, namely, that they are required for functions that cannot be performed by language items presently at the learner's disposal.

In introducing the perfect we will thus look for contexts that are different from those where the past is used. This can be done by starting with the first two of the functions listed previously, namely, (1) its use with verbs describing states leading up to the present and (2) its use with events occurring at unspecified times within time periods extending up to the present. Let us look at these two points in more detail.

1. *States leading up to the present.* The starting point is verbs like *live, be, like, know,* reinforcing the time span adverbially with *since, for,* or similar words.
   I have known John for six years.

Habitual or repeated events in this sense are also regarded as states:

I have worn glasses all my life.
I have studied French since 1975.

The distinction needed here is "continuation up to the present" with the perfect and "non-continuation" with the past. Thus, past-tense versions of the last two sentences above are not acceptable:

I wore glasses all my life.
I studied French since 1975.

It would also be possible to use the present perfect progressive in place of the perfect in these sentences:

I have been wearing glasses all my life.
I have been studying French since 1975.

However, following the principle of one form for one function, we would avoid this use of the present perfect progressive, reserving it for contexts where it is not an alternative for the perfect, namely, temporary events leading up to the present:

How long have you been waiting?

2. *With indefinite events.* Here the perfect is used with events occurring at unspecified times within a time period leading up to the present, reinforced adverbially with *ever, never, before, now*, and so on.
   Have you ever been to Florida?
   I have never eaten frogs' legs.

Leech (1971) draws attention to the fact that there is an implicit indefinite/definite contrast involved in the way the perfect leads into the simple past, in much the same way as indefinite articles lead to definite articles, reflecting the fact that in spoken discourse, conversation *starts* indefinitely and *then* progresses to definite reference. Thus:

Have you ever *been* to Florida?
Yes, I *went* there in 1975.

There are *a* number of letters on the table.
The top one is for you.

The basic contrast, however, is between actions described in a time period that excludes the present (Last month I *went* to the cinema only once) and events completed within a time period that includes the present (I *have been* to the cinema three times this month). Contexts for the past tense must be linked with complete time periods in the past, with events of either long or short duration:

I woke up at five o'clock.
I lived there for five years.

The major function of the past tense will then be the reporting of events in sequence, that is, narration:

We *got up* at six o'clock, *left* the house, and soon *arrived* at the railway station...

This provides later a link into the first introduction of the past perfect, which will be used for the description of events that are out of sequence:

When we got outside we realized we had forgotten to lock the door.

The resultative use of the perfect should be the last of its functions to be introduced, and this only when the regular meanings of the perfect and the past are firmly established. It will be initially taught for recognition, with direct explanation of its special, stylistic effect. Thus, to conclude with a maxim: Teach new functions for new forms, rather than new forms for old functions.

13 Lexical knowledge and the teaching of vocabulary

The teaching and learning of vocabulary has never aroused the same degree of interest within language teaching as have such issues as grammatical competence, contrastive analysis, reading, or writing, which have received considerable attention from scholars and teachers. The apparent neglect of vocabulary reflects the effects of trends in linguistic theory, since within linguistics this issue has only recently become a candidate for serious theorizing and model building (Leech 1974, Anthony 1975). This chapter considers the role of vocabulary in the syllabus, examining it in the light of the assumptions and findings of theoretical and applied linguistics. By considering some of the knowledge that is assumed by lexical competence, we can offer a frame of reference for the determination of objectives for vocabulary teaching and for the assessment of teaching techniques designed to realize these objectives. A word of caution is in order, however.

The theoretical concerns of linguists and others who study language are pertinent to syllabus design in two ways. First, since such disciplines have as their goal explanation of the nature of language, understanding of how language is acquired, and description of how language is used to carry out pragmatic functions in the real world, we can look to such disciplines as linguistics, psycholinguistics, or sociolinguistics for a more informed understanding of such questions as: What does it mean to know a word? How are words remembered? What are the social dimensions of word usage? Inevitably such information will turn out to be vastly more complex than we might intuitively have supposed yet will be tentative and inconclusive because of changes in knowledge and theory. Such information cannot be translated directly into teaching procedures.

It may, however, suggest in a general way the type of knowledge we expect of a learner, and by implication raise questions as to how such knowledge can be acquired through a teaching program. The development of teaching materials may also take place without direct application of a theoretical model, by reference to such factors as classroom effectiveness, learner interest, age of the learners. The model most desirable from a theoretical standpoint may turn out to be the least effective in actual use, because of the role of extralinguistic factors. So, for example, although rote memorization may not be a justifiable strategy on theoretical grounds, there may be learners who enjoy and succeed in learning material through memorization.

A second level of application is in the evaluation or interpretation of results obtained. When problems or failures arise we may have to refer to a model or theory to see if it can offer explanation. Alternatively the results we obtain through practical application of a theory may lead to revision of the theory itself. A consideration of recent work in theoretical or applied linguistics does not necessarily lead to the discovery of new and exciting ways to teach vocabulary. Rather it provides background information that can help us determine the status of vocabulary teaching within the syllabus. Let us begin by considering a number of assumptions concerning the nature of lexical competence and then look at some of the implications that can be drawn from them as a guide to syllabus design.

ASSUMPTION 1   *Native speakers of a language continue to expand their vocabulary in adulthood, whereas there is comparatively little development of syntax in adult life.*

A great deal of research has been carried out in recent years in the area of syntactic and semantic development in child language. Less attention has been given to vocabulary development, though this was extensively studied until the 1950s. Whereas in syntax the period of maximum development appears to be from age 2 to age 12, with only minor changes according to social role and mode of discourse taking place in adulthood, in vocabulary there is continued development beyond the childhood years, with adults constantly adding new words to their vocabulary through reading, occupation, and other activities. The primary period for conceptual development, however, is early childhood.

When we try to translate this information into statistical figures we cannot be precise, since measurement of vocabulary knowledge is difficult and only approximate. Watts suggests that the average child enters elementary school with a recognition vocabulary of 2,000 words, that at age 7 this has reached some 7,000 words, and by 14 the child should be able to recognize 14,000 words (Watts 1944). The vocabulary of adults has been variously estimated at between 10,000 for a nonacademic adult to over 150,000 for a professional scientist. College students are estimated to understand some 60,000 to 100,000 words (Mackey 1965: 173). These are estimates of the number of words we recognize the meanings of from the total lexical range of the language, which may be over 500,000 words (Watts 1944). Berry estimates that for spoken English the average person speaking on a telephone makes use of a vocabulary of only some 2,000 words (Mackey 1965).

ASSUMPTION 2 *Knowing a word means knowing the degree of probability of encountering that word in speech or print. For many words we also "know" the sort of words most likely to be found associated with the words.*

The speaker of a language recognizes that some words are common and familiar whereas other words are rare, unfamiliar, or even totally unknown to him or her. Our knowledge of the general probability of occurrence of a word means we recognize that a word like *book* is more frequent than *manual* or *directory*, and yet both these words strike us as more frequent than *thesaurus*. Given a list of words, with the exception of concrete nouns, a native speaker can classify them into "frequent," "moderately frequent," "not frequent," to a degree of accuracy reasonably close to their actual frequencies (Noble 1953, Richards 1974).

The speaker of a language recognizes not only the general probability of occurrence of a word but also the probability of words being associated together with other words. Knowledge of collocation means that on encountering the word *fruit* we can expect the words *ripe, green* (= not ripe), *sweet, bitter*; and that for *meat* we might expect *tender, tough*.

ASSUMPTION 3 *Knowing a word implies knowing the limitations imposed on the use of the word according to variations of function and situation.*

Our knowledge of vocabulary includes the recognition of the constraints of function and situation on word choice. This is seen in our recognition of *register* characteristics. We adjust our vocabulary to suit the demands of the situation. The following register restraints are often recognized (based on Chiu 1972):

temporal variation We recognize some words as being old-fashioned and others as belonging to contemporary usage. A *looking glass* to the Victorians is a *mirror* to us.

geographical variation What the British call a *tap* may be a *faucet* to an American.

social variation Middle-class British people prefer to call a *house* a *home*, and a *woman* a *lady*.

social role This influences the choice between a personal name, as in *Hi, John*, or the formal term, as in *Good morning, Mr. Smith*.

field of discourse Here we include factors that determine whether something will be described in the active voice (normal description) or the passive voice (scientific reporting) and whether we will use the first-person pronouns *I* or *we* or no pronoun.

mode of discourse This influences our choice of words that are suited to either the written or spoken mode. A *guy* or a *fellow* in speech is what a *person* or *gentleman* is in writing.

ASSUMPTION 4 *Knowing a word means knowing the syntactic behavior associated with that word.*

Our knowledge of a word is not stored only as a concept; we also associate specific structural and grammatical properties with words. The traditional division between *vocabulary* and *structure* is in fact a tenuous one, a fact that is recognized in our use of the term *structural words* for a number of frequent words in the vocabulary. Important information about the structural properties of words, which includes the types of grammatical relations they may enter into, is acquired by the learner as part of vocabulary learning. Accounts of language like those proposed by C. J. Fillmore (1968) relate the structural behavior of words to their semantic structure as reflected in case relations. A sentence in language is defined by a verb together with a number of cases, drawn from a limited set. The cases that are required in a particular sentence are determined by the verb of that sentence. The verb *break*, for example, as Nilsen illustrates, contains the features (O) (I) (A). (O) means the verb requires an object; (I) and (A) indicate that it may take instrumental and agent case in addition. If there is an agent, the agent becomes the subject. If there is no agent, but there is an instrumental case, the instrument is the subject. When there is neither an agent nor an instrument, the object becomes the subject. This is illustrated by Nilsen with the following examples.

1. Abdul broke the bicycle with a rock. + O I A
2. A rock broke the bicycle. + O I
3. The bicycle broke. + O

(Nilson 1971)

Case grammar tells us that for a certain verb, there is a range of associated syntactic units required to realize the cases associated with the verb. In some instances case relations enable us to predict the syntactic properties of words. Farsi points out, for example, that factitive verbs "which indicate a process such that at the end of the process a new object comes into being which was not present at the beginning, for example, *make, fabricate, construct, build, compose, draw, fashion, concoct, create*, can only be used transitively; they cannot occur intransitively; they cannot occur intransitively with the noun indicating the new resultant product as the subject of the sentence." We cannot have as subject *a house constructed, a chair made*, and so forth (Farsi 1974).

ASSUMPTION 5 *Knowing a word entails knowledge of the underlying form of that word and the derivations that can be made from it.*

When we learn a word we also learn the rules that enable us to build up different forms of the word or even different words from that word. With regular derivations, such as those for tense and person, the problems are not great. *Walked, walking, walks* are readily recognized as derived from *walk*. According to some linguists (Chomsky and Halle 1968), we also derive *solidity, solidify, solidly, solidness, consolidate* from the underlying form *solid*. The semantic relationship to the underlying form is preserved by the English spelling system; so for example, despite the differences in pronunciation between the first two syllables of *photograph, photographer, photographic*, the first two syllables are spelled identically in each word. If the spelling system of English were to be revised to more closely approximate the spoken language, these links between underlying forms and derived forms world be lost. Learning to be able to make such links is especially important in learning Malay, Indonesian, and many of the languages of the Philippines. The learner will less frequently encounter the base form of the word than one of its many derivations, and some training is required to be able to identify the base form, particularly when attempting to locate the meaning of the word in a dictionary. Hence when learning Indonesian, the learner would have to look in the dictionary under *bunga* (flower) for *berbunga, membunga, memperbungakan*, and *pembungaan*.

ASSUMPTION 6 *Knowing a word entails knowledge of the network of associations between that word and other words in the language.*

Words do not exist in isolation. Their meanings are defined through their relations to other words, and it is through understanding these connections that we arrive at our understanding of words. Some of these relations are seen in word association tests; there is a great deal of uniformity among typical responses:

Stimulus	*Typical response*
accident	car
alive	dead
baby	mother
born	die
cabbage	vegetable
table	chair
careless	careful

(Deese 1965)

Such responses suggest a number of different ways in which associative links between words are organized. For example:

by contrast or antonym	wet–dry
by similarity or synonym	blossom–flower
by subordinative classification	animal–dog
by coordinate classification	apple–peach
by superordinate classification	spinach–vegetable

(cf. Slobin 1971)

The same word can of course be seen as linked to many different words through different associative networks. *Giving* is linked both to *receiving* and to *taking. Old* is linked to *new* and to *young; good* to *bad* and to *poor.*

The responses to free association tests hence give much information about the psychological structuring of vocabulary in an individual and offer a way of investigating the syntactic and semantic relationships among words. Presumably, knowledge of this kind is inherent in language use, in helping us choose a word and in finding the right word for the context.

ASSUMPTION 7   *Knowing a word means knowing the semantic value of a word.*

One way of analyzing meaning is to break words down and categorize them according to a basic set of minimal semantic features, different combinations of which produce different words. Examples of such features would be *animate, living, human, nonhuman, inanimate.* A word like *man* contains the semantic features + *human* + *male.* The word *table* is + *inanimate* + *nonhuman.* These features impose restrictions on word usage. We can say *the table was damaged* but not *the table was hurt,* since *hurt* is associated only with animate subjects.

The meaning of a word in this sense is defined by its reference to a number of attributes, or minimal semantic features. Roget's famous *Thesaurus* is an attempt to classify words into general semantic features of this kind. A different dimension of the semantic value of words is seen in words like *famous,* so we may say *Churchill was a famous man* but not *Hitler was a famous man. Effeminate, shy, sentimental* are similar words in this category. The semantic value of many words can be determined by placing them on weighted semantic scales. The semantic-differential technique investigates meaning in this way using sets of polar opposites. For example, the word *father* could be evaluated on a set of terms in this way:

181

happy ....X... .... sad

hard ....X.. .... soft

slow ....X.. .... fast

In this way information both about the subjective values of an individual and the semantic structure of the lexicon can be studied. Use of an approach of this sort led to the *Cross-Cultural Atlas of Affective Meaning*, for which a cross-cultural study was made of reactions to a selection of words in terms of *evaluation* (nice–awful, good–bad, sweet–sour), *potency* (big–little, powerful–powerless, strong–weak), and *activity* (fast–slow, dead–alive, noisy–quiet) (Osgood 1964).

ASSUMPTION 8   *Knowing a word means knowing many of the different meanings associated with the word.*

The assumptions so far discussed suggest that *meaning* is a much richer concept than we often assume, and this is reflected in the fact that dictionary entries for words usually list a great variety of different or related meanings for each word, showing how the word takes its meaning from the context in which it is used. Kolers observes:

Word meanings do not exist in isolation in the reader's mind like so many entries in a dictionary. What a word means to the reader depends upon what he is reading and what he expects to read, the phrase, clause or sentence in which the words appear. The meaning of a word, that is to say, depends upon the thought that it is being used to express and the context of its expression. Whether one reads *unionize* as a verb in chemistry or a verb in labor relations depends upon many things other than its spelling and its symbol–sound relations. Indeed, a very large number of words in a dictionary have multiple meanings, and for some words the definitions are contradictory. For example *scan* means to glance at quick *and* to read in detail, and *cleave* to join and to separate. The reader, clearly, must construct a representation of what he is reading *about* if he is to appreciate the meaning of what he is reading. (quoted by Eskey 1973)

This emphasizes that words are not simply labels for things but represent "processes by which the species deals cognitively with the environment" (Lenneberg 1967:334). The dictionary entries for a word try to capture the most frequent ways in which a word realizes a particular concept; however, since this is always an active process of reconstruction, much of the way in which a particular meaning is formed cannot be recorded in the dictionary.

Implications

Let us now look at the assumptions that have been proposed and consider their implications for vocabulary teaching. The eight assumptions are briefly:

1. Native speakers of a language continue to expand their vocabulary in adulthood, whereas there is comparatively little development of syntax in adult life.
2. Knowing a word means knowing the degree of probability of encountering that word in speech or print. For many words we also know the sort of words most likely to be found associated with the word.
3. Knowing a word implies knowing the limitations imposed on the use of the word according to variations of function and situation.
4. Knowing a word means knowing the syntactic behavior associated with the word.
5. Knowing a word entails knowledge of the underlying form of a word and the derivations that can be made from it.
6. Knowing a word entails knowledge of the network of associations between that word and other words in the language.
7. Knowing a word means knowing the semantic value of a word.
8. Knowing a word means knowing many of the different meanings associated with a word.

Considering just these assumptions about word knowledge we get a picture of the complex learning task that is required in acquiring vocabulary. To what degree can teaching strategies accommodate these assumptions?

Assumptions 1 and 8 suggest that beyond the elementary levels of instruction, a major feature of a second-language program should be a component of massive vocabulary expansion. Though we cannot specify precisely the number of words a learner at a specific level should be able to recognize and use, it is clear that learners who are constantly adding to their vocabulary knowledge are better prepared both for productive and receptive language skills. Many language programs, however, assume that vocabulary expansion will be covered by the reading program. We can call this *indirect vocabulary teaching*, where vocabulary is acquired incidentally through the practice of other language skills. Mackey in his *Language Teaching Analysis* (1965) and Rivers in *Teaching Foreign-Language Skills* (1968) deal with vocabulary teaching only as it affects reading. An exception to this approach is taken by Bright and McGregor, who have a detailed chapter on *direct vocabulary teaching* in their *Teaching English as a Second Language* (1970). It is direct vocabulary teaching that is the focus here.

The need for a rapid increase in the learner's recognition vocabulary, as implied by assumptions 1 and 8, is the motivation behind Barnard's

Advanced English Vocabulary (1971), which teaches a 3,000-word vocabulary taken from a frequency analysis of university texts. The words
are carefully defined and explained in simple English, with several of
their important meanings given; they are then encountered in exercises
and reading passages. The implications of assumption 3 are taken up in
a range of textbooks recently published that familiarize the advanced
student with the vocabulary and language of particular registers (e.g.,
Lachowicz 1974, Mountford 1975). The most general register distinction that must be acquired is a feeling of the difference between written
and spoken English. Schonell et al. (1956) found that within the first
1,000 words-by-frequency in a count of spoken English, 15 percent were
not present in the first 1,000 words of written English. In the elementary
stages of language teaching, the distinction between spoken and written
English is minimized, and apart from occasional problems (such as the
use of *diligent* in speech, which really belongs to the register of written
English and report cards), there is little interference. Intermediate and
advanced learners, however, often inadvertently use a word in speech
that they have acquired from reading but that should be confined to a
written register. An example would be *I was most entertained by the
film* rather than something like *I really enjoyed the film*.

Lachowicz's *Using Medical English* is an example of a course that
teaches specialized vocabulary – it deals with the vocabulary of medicine
for students of intermediate proficiency. It is also of interest in relation
to assumption 6, since many of the vocabulary exercises are designed
to practice discrimination between members of lexical sets. The following is part of an exercise of this type:

In each of the following groups of words one word does not belong. The
other words have something in common which excludes this particular word.
Please underline the word that doesn't belong in the group.
1. swelling, lump, bump, mass, discoloration.
2. ribs, skull, spine, femur, bone, kneecap, hair.
3. stain, wart, blotch, discoloration, spot, mark.

(Lachowicz 1974: 30)

K. W. Moody (personal communication) has described a similar type of
exercise for establishing set discrimination:

Look at the following words.
foreman, operator, worker, supervisor, machinist

1. Which of the words in this list describe those who are responsible for the
   work of other people?
2. Which is the most general word in the list?
3. Which word says something about the kind of work done?

Further work.

a. You should have two words as your answer to 1.
   Which of the two would be the most likely in talking about work
   i. in an office?
   ii. on the construction of a new building?
   iii. in a service station for motor vehicles?
b. In which of these kinds of employment could you use *both* the words you wrote in 1?
   The army, a factory, the crew of an airliner, school teaching, the police
c. Which words would be used for
   i. a person who organizes the work of a group of typists?
   ii. a person in a factory who drills holes in pieces of metal?
   iii. a person who receives telephone calls in a large office?
   iv. the man in charge of a group of workers who are laying a telephone cable under a road?

Assumption 2 is dealt with in a number of exercises in Barnard (1971), and the rationale for collocation teaching is discussed in detail in D. F. Brown (1974), who analyzes exercises that can be used to give practice in the most frequent collocational groups of particular fields of writing, emphasizing, for example, that *intense* is likely to occur with reference to *heat, light, energy,* or *pressure.* The following is an exercise from Brown.

Choose the items that collocate most usefully with each verb. The number of lines left after each verb is a guide to the number of useful collocations possible.

1 to appeal ....   5 to conclude ....
   ....
   ....
   ....
2 to encourage ....   6 to intend to ....
   ....
   ....
   ....
3 to omit ....   7 to treat ....
   ....
   ....
   ....
4 to recognize ....   8 to consult ....
   ....
   ....
   ....

the library catalogue   go to Australia
that he is a good actor   to the public for money
finish this today   that man with the black hat
against the judge's decision   them to play more sport
to sign his name on the letter   to my friend for help

185

the slow student
several items from the list
all the tune
a doctor
the Advanced Learner's Dictionary
that there is no reason to punish him
him to learn from his mistakes
the last paragraph
the argument before tomorrow

him kindly
the government in its attempt to end
  unemployment
every fifth word
his claim to the land
the teacher with respect
the disease with a new medicine
marry next year
to their feelings

(Brown 1974)

Assumption 4 deals with the syntactic properties of words. Nilsen has proposed that case grammar has important applications in language teaching and suggests that case grammar allows the teacher to point out the common case relationships across languages. He illustrates that particular semantic categories (such as verbs of motion) require basically the same case frame: *agent, source, path, goal* and with transitive verbs, *agent, source, path, goal, object.*

John flew from *New York* to *Chicago* via *Philadelphia*
 A   S   G   P

has the same case frame as

John bussed *the football players* from *Ann Arbor* to *Detroit* via *Ypsilanti.*
 A   O   S   G   P

This example is intended to illustrate that two verbs of motion (*fly* and *bus*) have the same case framework except that the transitive verb requires object. The case frame (hence the syntax) of particular verbs is determined by their semantic categories (Nilsen 1971).

Farsi (1974), however, points out that the grammatical capacities of verbs cannot always be determined by their case relations. There is a great deal of lexical idiosyncrasy. For example, we can compare the following parts of semantically similar words with different syntactic properties:

head
The wound healed.
The medicine healed the wound.

cure
The patient cured.
The medicine cured the patient.

calm down
He calmed down.
It calmed him down.

soothe
He soothed.
It soothed him.

Although the insights of case grammar are useful, we do not as yet have a pedagogic grammar of English based on this approach. An understanding of case relationships and their consequent implications for syntax may, however, help the teacher interpret and more adequately explain certain errors, but there are many exceptions that even case grammar does not adequately deal with.

Assumption 5 is dealt with through direct teaching aimed at recognizing the basic forms of words they are combined with different inflexional and derivational suffixes. Praninskas (1972) found that words derived from *liberal* had a frequency of 46 occurrences across 5 different types of writing in the university texts she examined. In addition to the form *liberal* she found *liberalism, liberalize, liberalization, liberate, liberator, liberally.* Rapid identification of the base form of words is needed as part of an overall attempt to teach students how to infer meaning from words. A considerable portion of Croft's *Reading and Word Study* (1960) is devoted to this; and familiarity with the Latinate and Greek inflections of scientific terminology (cf. Flood 1960) should be dealt with in courses of scientific English.

Assumption 6 suggests that words are stored or come to mind according to associative bonds and that learning may be facilitated when such bonds are established. In a specific study of how second-language learners store vocabulary in short-term memory, Henning found that in the earlier stages of learning, words may be stored according to acoustic links (i.e., words that sound similar are stored together), whereas later learners used a semantic basis for storing words, storing words according to meaning links of the type discussed under 6. Henning notes:

The implications of the teaching of vocabulary are that strategies of encoding vocabulary in memory appear to change as a function of language proficiency. Low-proficiency language learners, although a test indicated they understood the meanings of the stimulus recognition items, appeared to encode them in memory on the basis of acoustic and orthographic similarities rather than by association of meaning. Therefore it would appear that they would benefit from selective listening, aural discrimination, songs, rhymes, affix drills and other exercises that point out similarities and differences of sound and spelling of words. For example, it might prove more helpful for learners at that level to discover the distinction between *whether* and *weather* than the distinction between *whether* and *if.* But learners at a high level appear to encode vocabulary in memory primarily on the basis of meanings. At that level learners might benefit more from synonym and antonym games and exercises, paired-associate compositions in which lists of related words are given the learner from which he is to prepare written or oral compositions. It is hoped that through continual drilling and exercises of this nature the language learner will begin to recognize not only a larger inventory of lexical items encountered, but be able to identify the acoustic and semantic families from which they come, and thus more efficiently progress in language proficiency. (Henning 1973: 193)

Some of the implications of assumption 7 are discussed by Bright and McGregor:

In our first language we pick up strong emotional associations within the home. But a second language is normally learnt in the less passionate atmosphere of the classroom, where physical violence, for example, about whether this is *mine* or *yours* does not normally arise. The result is a lack of emotional involvement in the language and hence great difficulty in seeing any meaning other than plain sense. *Obstinate* is understood to mean no more than *determined* – the writer's attitude of disapproval is missed. (Bright and McGregor 1970: 30)

Vocabulary teaching thus involves showing how a word can take on emotional connotation in a particular context. Perhaps one of the most useful exercises to deal globally with many of the aspects of word knowledge implied in the assumptions discussed here is the cloze exercise. Students fill in blanks to a passage from which words have been deleted. Subsequent classroom discussion of the different words offered allows the learner to acquire words in context and in relation to other words in the text and to the overall content of the passage (cf. Plaister 1973).

Conclusion

It has not been my purpose here to propose a classification of vocabulary teaching exercises. Most teachers will have their own preferred techniques for teaching the different aspects of vocabulary usage I have referred to. What I have tried to do, however, is to suggest that in preparing teaching materials we begin with a rich concept of vocabulary. The goals of vocabulary teaching must be more than simply covering a certain number of words on a word list. We must look to how teaching techniques can help realize our concept of what it means to know a word. As in all areas of the syllabus, an understanding of the nature of what we are teaching should be reflected in the way we set about teaching it. Vocabulary has been one area of the syllabus where this link between approach, method, and technique has been neglected.

14 Listening comprehension: approach, design, and procedure

Not to let a word get in the way of its sentence
Nor to let a sentence get in the way of its intention,
But to send your mind out to meet the intention as a guest;
That is understanding.

Chinese proverb, fourth century B.C.

In this chapter, we examine three dimensions involved in the teaching of listening comprehension. These are referred to as *approach, design,* and *procedure* (see Chapter 2). First we present an outline of some of what is known about the processes involved in listening. This is the level of approach, where assumptions about how listeners proceed in decoding utterances to extract meanings are spelled out. The next level is design, where an operationalization is made of the component micro-skills that constitute our competence as listeners. This in turn enables teaching objectives to be defined. At the third level, that of procedure, questions concerning exercise types and teaching techniques are examined. These three levels illustrate the domain of *methodology* in language teaching.

Approach

Message factors

Current understanding of the nature of listening comprehension draws on research in psycholinguistics, semantics, pragmatics, discourse analysis, and cognitive science (e.g., Clark and Clark 1977, Leech 1977, Schank and Abelson 1977, Marslen-Wilson and Tyler 1980, Clark and Carlson 1982, Dore and McDermott 1982). There is little direct research on second-language listening comprehension, however, and what follows is an interpretation of relevant native-language research. Three related levels of discourse processing appear to be involved in listening: propositional identification, interpretation of illocutionary force, and activation of real-world knowledge. The central question from both a theoretical and a pedagogical perspective concerns the nature of the units listeners make use of in understanding language. Do we listen for in-

189

tonation, stress, words, grammar, sentence, or some other type of language unit?

Much of the linguistic and psycholinguistic literature on comprehension suggests that propositions are the basic units of meaning involved in comprehension and that the listener's ultimate goal is to determine the propositions that an utterance or speech event expresses (Clark and Clark 1977, Foss and Haikes 1978). But propositions are represented indirectly in the surface structure of utterances. Listeners make use of two kinds of knowledge to identify propositions: knowledge of the syntax of the target language and real world knowledge. Syntactic knowledge enables the listener to *chunk* incoming discourse into segments or constituents. The following sentence would have to be chunked as in (1) rather than (2) in order to identify its propositional meaning:

I am informed that your appointment has been terminated.

1. I am informed/that your appointment/has been terminated.
2. I am/informed that your/appointment has/been terminated.

The ability to correctly identify chunks or constituents is a by-product of grammatical competence. Knowledge of the structure of noun phrases, verb phrases, and the grammatical devices used to express such relationships as complementation, relativization, and coordination in English allows us to segment discourse into the appropriate chunks as part of the process of propositional identification. Where segmentation is difficult, comprehension is also difficult.

But knowledge of the world is also used to help identify propositions, enabling listeners to sometimes bypass the constituent identification press. Hence, (1) below is understood as (2) because, in real life, this is a plausible reconstruction of likely events involving cats and rats:

1. and rat cat it chased the ate the
2. The cat chased the rat and ate it.

The following processes therefore appear to be involved in comprehension:

1. The listener takes in raw speech and holds an image of it in short-term memory.
2. An attempt is made to organize what was heard in constituents, identifying their content and function.
3. As constituents are identified, they are used to construct propositions, grouping the propositions together to form a coherent message.
4. Once the listener has identified and reconstructed the propositional meanings, these are held in long-term memory, and the form in which the message was originally received is deleted.

(Clark and Clark 1977: 49)

Permanent, or long-term, memory works with meaning, not with form. The propositional meaning of sentences is retained, not the actual words or grammatical devices that were used to express it. Thus, after hearing *Tom said that the car had been fixed and could be picked up at 5:00,* a listener is likely to remember only that the car is now ready to be picked up and not whether the speaker said *the car is fixed* rather than *the car has been fixed,* or *could be picked up* rather than *will be ready to be picked up.* Memory works with propositions, not with sentences.

What we have just illustrated is a semantically based view of how a listener decides what a sentence means. Leech distinguishes this view of meaning from a pragmatic perspective, that is, one that focuses on what an utterance means to a person in a particular speech situation. "The semantic structure of a sentence specifies what that sentence means as a structure in a given language, in abstraction from speaker and addressee; whereas pragmatics deals with that meaning as it is interpreted interactionally in a given situation" (Leech 1977: 1). Theories that describe how pragmatic meanings are understood derive from speech-act theory, conversational analysis, and discourse analysis (see Chapter 8).

Speech-act theory is concerned with the relationship between the form of utterances and their function in social interaction and rests on the distinction between propositional meaning and the illocutionary force of utterances. For example, the sentence *Helen likes chocolates* as a proposition attributes a certain quality to Helen, but does not tell us whether the sentence was uttered in order to offer an *explanation* of her obesity, a *suggestion* as to what to do with the chocolates, or a *denial* of a previous assertion. Speech-act and other interactional approaches to meaning assume that when we use language for communication, the meanings that are communicated are a function of the interactions between speakers and hearers meeting in specific circumstances for the achievement of particular goals. In arriving at an interpretation of the illocutionary force of an utterance (that is, in determining the speaker's intention), listeners call upon their knowledge of the situation, the participants, their purposes, goals, rights and duties, as well as the position of the utterance within the sequence of utterances preceding it. In an illuminating analysis of how the interpretation of talk is organized by context, Dore and McDermott observe that "in the course of organizing sensible moments with each other, people use talk as a social tool, relying on the social work they are doing together to specify the meaning of utterances" (1982: 375).

Grice proposed that one source of knowledge listeners make use of is their understanding of the nature and goals of conversation. He stated this knowledge in the form of maxims of conversational behavior, each illustrating the "cooperative principle" that dictates the sort of contributions people make during conversational interaction:

1. Maxim of quantity: Make your contribution just as informative as required.
2. Maxim of quality: Make your contribution one that is true.
3. Maxim of relation: Be related.
4. Maxim of manner: Avoid obscurity, ambiguity, prolixity. Be orderly.

(quoted in Clark and Clark 1977: 122)

Conversationalists, therefore, normally act on the assumption that remarks made during conversation will be relevant to the ongoing concerns of speaker and hearer. Thus, if I invite you to dinner, I assume that you will respond with a remark that is relevant to my purposes. I will try to interpret what you say as an acceptance or a refusal. But if you respond with *There's a white Cadillac on the corner of the street,* I will have great difficulty assigning this utterance to the category of reply I anticipated.

International views of meaning stress the crucial role inferencing and interpretation play in listening comprehension and remind us of the active and creative dimensions of listening. Work in cognitive science reveals an added dimension of this inferential process.

Script and schema theory (Schank and Abelson 1977) describes the role of prior knowledge in comprehension. For example, in understanding *I went to the dentist this morning. He gave me an injection and I didn't feel a thing,* the following prior knowledge is referred to:

1. We normally go to see a dentist when we need a check-up or when we have something wrong with our teeth.
2. Dentists typically check, drill, repair, or remove teeth.
3. This process is painful.
4. An injection can be given to relieve the pain.

This body of knowledge about a specific situation (at the dentist's), particular participants (the dentist, the assistant, the patient), goals of the situation (remedying a problem with the patient's teeth), and procedures (drilling a tooth, giving an injection) can be referred to as the *dentist's script.* Script or schema knowledge is what we know about particular situations and the goals, participants, and procedures commonly associated with them. Much of our knowledge of the world is organized around *scripts*, that is, memory for typical episodes that occur in specific situations. Our knowledge of dentist's scripts, cinema scripts, library scripts, drugstore scripts, school scripts, meal scripts, and so on, makes it possible to interpret a great deal of the language of everyday life. The information needed to understand many utterances is therefore not explicitly present in the utterance but is provided by the listeners from their repertoire of scripts. This means that many of the connections between events need not be specified when we talk about them, since they are already known and can be inferred. But if we lack a relevant script, comprehension may be difficult. For example, we have no available script that can be used to understand this sequence of events: *I climbed onto an elephant. The piano was out of tune. The rabbit tasted delicious.*

We are able to understand many utterances from our general awareness of how people achieve goals and from our assumptions that most human behavior is purposeful and directed toward particular ends. Non-native speakers, however, may lack many culturally specific scripts; their individual scripts may differ in degree and content from target-language scripts, and this poses additional problems for the non-native listener.

We are now able to expand the tentative model of the processes involved in comprehension:

1. The type of interactional act or speech event in which the listener is involved is determined (e.g., conversation, lecture, discussion, debate).
2. Scripts relevant to the particular situations are recalled.
3. The goals of the speaker are inferred through reference to the situation, the script, and the sequential position of the utterance.
4. The propositional meaning of the utterance is determined.
5. An illocutionary meaning is assigned to the message.
6. This information is retained and acted upon, and the form in which it was originally received is deleted.

Medium factors

The preceding discussion has focused on how meanings are understood in listening. But listeners confront another dimension of comprehension when processing speech. The act of speaking imposes a particular form on utterances, and this considerably affects how messages are understood. We call factors that result from this *medium factors*. Medium factors vary according to the nature of the discourse (whether planned or unplanned), the speaker's attitude toward the message or the listeners, and the situation in which the act of communication takes place (e.g., classroom, lecture room, or informal setting). We will consider nine such factors here, each of which influences the work listeners must do to process speech.

CLAUSAL BASIS OF SPEECH

Whereas the unit of organization of written discourse is the sentence, spoken language is generally delivered one clause at a time (Pawley, personal communication). The unit of conversational discourse is not the full sentence but the clause, and longer utterances in conversation generally consist of several clauses coordinated. Most of the clauses used are simple conjuncts or adjuncts, and Pawley points out that cases of complex clauses in conversation are rare. Clauses appear to be a major constituent in both the planning and delivery of speech. The frequent use of coordinating conjunctions is illustrated in this example from Stanley:

Um perhaps the most celebrated near miss was a twin reactor two reactors side by side in Tennessee in 1975, *and* that was due to a worker at the plant using a candle to test which way the air was flowing, underneath the control room, *and* it caught fire. *And* they had a very serious fire there for fourteen hours. They didn't know how to put it out... *And* it was only shut down in the end *and* a very you know, a major accident averted by an operator using a very unusual *and and* quite clever way of shutting it down by hand. (1980: 78)

REDUCED FORMS

In articulating clauses, speakers are guided by the need to express meanings efficiently. This means that words that play a less crucial role in the message may be slurred or dropped, and other words given more prominence (Brown 1977). In addition, consonants and vowels within words are affected by the position in which they occur. In speech there is not always time for the tongue to assume the ideal position required to articulate a sound. Consequently, patterns of assimilation are common, leading to the disappearance of word boundaries, to the omission of certain vowels and consonants, and to substitutions occurring for elements within words. Sentences also occur frequently in elliptical forms, with the deletion of such elements as subjects, auxiliaries, verbs, articles, and pronouns when context makes their presence redundant, as in *When will you be back? Tomorrow maybe* (instead of *Maybe I'll be back tomorrow*).

UNGRAMMATICAL FORMS

Because of the effort speakers put into planning and organizing the content of their utterances in ongoing time, grammaticality is often less relevant than ideational coherence. Consequently, ungrammatical forms and constructions are frequent. For example:

Big companies can only really make lots of money out of high technology centralized systems... And because of that *it* is tending to go into high technology solutions.

(lack of agreement)

And after that we arrived in a little town that there was no hotel anywhere
... (faulty clause construction)

PAUSING AND SPEECH ERRORS

An important component of human speech consists of the pauses, hesitations, false starts, and corrections that make up such a large portion of what we actually say. In natural speech, between 30 percent and 50 percent of speaking time may consist of pauses and hesitations, indicating some of the selection and planning processes speakers use. Pauses may be either silent pauses or filled pauses. Filled pauses contain items *uh, oh, hmm, ah, well, say, sort of, just, kind of, I mean, I think, I guess*, which indicate that the speaker is reaching for a word, or has found the word or an approximation of it.

RATE OF DELIVERY

Pausing also affects our perception of the pace of speech. The impression of faster or slower speech generally results from the amount of intra-clausal pausing that speakers use. If such pauses are eliminated, the impression of rapid speech is created. Fast and slow speakers are hence distinguished by the amount of pausing they use. Rivers cites the following figures:

Fast: above 220 wpm
Moderately fast: 190→220 wpm
Average: 160→220 wpm
Moderately slow: 130→160 wpm
Slow: below 130 wpm

(1981: 173)

RHYTHM AND STRESS

The rhythmic pattern of spoken English is another of its distinctive features. In many languages, the length of time required to pronounce an utterance depends upon the number of syllables in contains, since syllables are of about equal length. English, however, is a stress-timed language. Within an utterance, only particular syllables are stressed, and the remaining syllables in the utterance, no matter how many there are, must accommodate to the rhythm established by the stressed syllables, which recur at more or less regular intervals. According to Woods (1979), there is a major stressed syllable on the average of every 0.6 seconds in English. This means that the following sentences would take about the same amount of time to articulate, even though the number of syllables contained in each sentence is very different:

The CAT is INTerested in proTECTing its KITTens.
LARGE CARS WASTE GAS.

This adds yet another dimension to the listener's task, since listeners must be able to identify words according to the rhythmic structure within which they occur. They must be able to interpret words in stressed, mildly stressed, and unstressed forms, and not merely in their ideal forms as listed in a dictionary.

195

COHESIVE DEVICES

Speech shares with written discourse the mechanisms for marking grammatical ties within and between sentences, but many function differently in spoken discourse. The referents of cohesive markers such as *this*, *these*, and *you* are sometimes not readily identifiable in speech. For example:

Well *you* know, there was *this* guy, and here *we* were talking about, you know, girls, and all *that* sort of things...and *here's* what he says...

INFORMATION CONTENT

Since conversation involves both a speaker and a hearer, meanings are constructed cooperatively. A particular speaker does not say everything he or she wants to say in a single burst. Each speaker adds information a little at a time, often by repeating something of what has been said and then adding to it (Brown 1977). For example:

A: Are you pleased with the results?
B: Yes, I'm very pleased with them. They are better than I expected.

A: Is it impossible?
B: No, it's not impossible, just difficult.

Proposition markers such as *of course* and *really* may indicate the attitude of the speaker to preceding or subsequent propositions, and discourse markers such as *well, anyway, actually, of course*, and *now* signal the continuity between one utterance and another.

This means that the concept of coherence, as applied to conversational discourse, is very different from the way coherence is created in written discourse. Written discourse is planned, tightly organized, and generally the product of a single person. Spoken discourse is not preplanned, but is produced in ongoing time through mutual cooperation. Consequently, it presents meaning in a very different way from written discourse. Topics are developed gradually, and the conventions for topic development and topic shift are distinctive to the spoken register. Listeners must use cues such as *talking about that, reminds you of..., by the way, as far as that goes* to identify directions in topic development.

INTERACTIVE

Conversation is interactive. The listener's presence is indicated by gestures, movement, gaze, and facial expressions. Both speaker and listener send a variety of verbal and nonverbal signals back and forth indicating attention, interest, understanding, or lack of it (Murphy and Candlin 1979). The degree of formality or informality of the interaction may also be signaled by the presence or absence of idioms, humor, and colloquial expressions, or by the use of solidarity markers such as *you see* or *you know*.

Design

The factors we have just reviewed indicate some of the central processes of listening comprehension and ways in which spoken discourse differs from written text. The application of such information to the teaching of listening comprehension occurs in the design component of methodology; it enables the identification of component micro-skills that provide the focus for instructional activities. Design thus refers to the operationalization of information and theory into a form from which objectives can be formulated and learning experiences planned. The design phase in curriculum development consists of:

Assessment of learner needs. This refers to procedures aimed at identifying the type of listening skills the learner requires, according to situations and purposes the listener will encounter.

Isolation of micro-skills. From the information obtained from needs analysis and from an analysis of the features of the target-language discourse that the learner will encounter (e.g., conversation, lectures), particular listening skills are isolated that correspond to the listening abilities the learner requires. The product of this operation is a skills taxonomy.

Diagnostic testing. From proficiency or diagnostic testing, a profile is established of the learner's present listening abilities. Particular micro-skills from the skills taxonomy are then selected.

Formulation of instructional objectives. Using information from diagnostic or proficiency testing, instructional objectives for a listening comprehension program can be developed.

These procedures are essential before instructional activities can be selected or developed. Let us now consider each of these dimensions in turn.

Needs assessment

Needs assessment examines the purposes behind listening skills and analyzes the situations, activities, and tasks in which students will be involved as second-language learners. Listening purposes vary according to whether learners are involved in listening as a component of social interaction (e.g., conversation listening), listening for information, academic listening (e.g., lectures), listening for pleasure (e.g., radio, movies, television), or for some other reason. Needs-assessment procedures may involve interviews with learners, participant observation, questionnaires,

197

target-discourse analysis, literature surveys of related research, and other measures designed to obtain a profile of learner needs and to establish priorities among them.

Taxonomy of listening skills

Taxonomies of micro-skills involved in different types of listening are developed from a variety of sources, including needs analysis, discourse analysis, and related research. The analysis of listening processes and features of spoken discourse that were discussed in the first section of this chapter suggests that micro-skills such as the following are required for conversational listening:

Micro-skills: conversational listening
1. ability to retain chunks of language of different lengths for short periods
2. ability to discriminate among the distinctive sounds of the target language
3. ability to recognize the stress patterns of words
4. ability to recognize the rhythmic structure of English
5. ability to recognize the functions of stress and intonation to signal the information structure of utterances
6. ability to identify words in stressed and unstressed positions
7. ability to recognize reduced forms of words
8. ability to distinguish word boundaries
9. ability to recognize typical word-order patterns in the target language
10. ability to recognize vocabulary used in core conversational topics
11. ability to detect key words (i.e., those that identify topics and propositions)
12. ability to guess the meanings of words from the contexts in which they occur
13. ability to recognize grammatical word classes (parts of speech)
14. ability to recognize major syntactic patterns and devices
15. ability to recognize cohesive devices in spoken discourse
16. ability to recognize elliptical forms of grammatical units and sentences
17. ability to detect sentence constituents
18. ability to distinguish between major and minor constituents
19. ability to detect meanings expressed in differing grammatical forms/sentence types (i.e., that a particular meaning may be expressed in different ways)
20. ability to recognize the communicative functions of utterances, according to situations, participants, goals
21. ability to reconstruct or infer situations, goals, participants, procedures
22. ability to use real-world knowledge and experience to work out purposes, goals, settings, procedures
23. ability to predict outcomes from events described
24. ability to infer links and connections between events
25. ability to deduce causes and effects from events
26. ability to distinguish between literal and implied meanings
27. ability to identify and reconstruct topics and coherent structure from on-going discourse involving two or more speakers

28. ability to recognize markers of coherence in discourse, and to detect such relations as main idea, supporting idea, given information, new information, generalization, exemplification
29. ability to process speech at different rates
30. ability to process speech containing pauses, errors, corrections
31. ability to make use of facial, paralinguistic, and other clues to work out meanings
32. ability to adjust listening strategies to different kinds of listener purposes or goals
33. ability to signal comprehension or lack of comprehension, verbally and nonverbally

Diagnostic testing or detailed analysis of results of proficiency tests allows particular micro-skills to be further operationalized. Micro-skills relevant to academic listening include the following:

Micro-skills: academic listening (listening to lectures)
1. ability to identify purpose and scope of lecture
2. ability to identify topic of lecture and follow topic development
3. ability to identify relationships among units within discourse (e.g., major ideas, generalizations, hypotheses, supporting ideas, examples)
4. ability to identify role of discourse markers in signaling structure of a lecture (e.g., conjunctions, adverbs, gambits, routines)
5. ability to infer relationships (e.g., cause, effect, conclusion)
6. ability to recognize key lexical items related to subject/topic
7. ability to deduce meanings of words from context
8. ability to recognize markers of cohesion
9. ability to recognize function of intonation to signal information structure (e.g., pitch, volume, pace, key)
10. ability to detect attitude of speaker toward subject matter
11. ability to follow different modes of lecturing: spoken, audio, audio-visual
12. ability to follow lecture despite differences in accent and speed
13. familiarity with different styles of lecturing: formal, conversational, read, unplanned
14. familiarity with different registers: written versus colloquial
15. ability to recognize irrelevant matter: jokes, digressions, meanderings
16. ability to recognize function of nonverbal cues as markers of emphasis and attitude
17. knowledge of classroom conventions (e.g., turn taking, clarification requests)
18. ability to recognize instructional/learner tasks (e.g., warnings, suggestions, recommendations, advice, instructions)

The preceding taxonomies are suggestive of the sort of information that curriculum developers should aim to obtain from tests and other sources.

Diagnostic testing assessment

Diagnostic tests and assessment procedures give a detailed breakdown of how learners perform with respect to particular micro-skills. A good example of how detailed information on learner ability can be obtained from the use of a listening-proficiency rating scale is provided by an instrument developed by Brindley (1982). By means of interviews, a profile of the student's learning ability is built up, and the learner is classified into one of eight levels ranging from minimal to native-speaker-like. Brindley describes characteristics of a learner at the second level on the scale in the following way:

Listening comprehension
Able to understand enough to manage a very limited interchange about areas of immediate need. Can understand most predictable requests for basic personal and family information of the kind required by officials, though repetition often necessary if questions are not phrased in familiar form.
Can recognize a few basic intonation patterns (e.g., Yes/no questions).
Little understanding of syntax. Meaning deduced from juxtaposition of words and context. Still responds to isolated words in connected speech.
Can handle very short, simple, ritual social exchanges but rarely able to understand enough to keep conversation going of his/her own accord.
Can identify individual items in very short, simple, recorded passages relevant to needs. May get global meaning but would need more than one hearing. However misunderstandings frequent when s/he cannot see person speaking.
When s/he does not understand, can usually ask very simply for repetition.

Characteristic problems
Has great difficulty coping with subjects other than immediate priorities.
Finds longer utterances (especially those containing subordinate clauses) very hard to understand, owing to limitations on short-term memory load.
Often fails to understand questions which require other than a short, concrete answer (e.g., *why* or *how* questions).
Idiomatic expressions (even commonly used ones related to priority areas) normally not understood. Only understands when questions/statements are phrased in simplest, non-idiomatic form.
Has great difficulty using grammatical cues to extrapolate meaning. What seems clear to a native speaker would often be misinterpreted or seen as ambiguous by a listener at this level, owing to his/her inability to recognize the form and function of many syntactic structures.
May identify occasional words in a conversation between native speakers but could not identify topic.
Similar-sounding words/segments often confused, causing misunderstandings.

(Brindley 1982: 1)

Using information like this together with a skills taxonomy, it is possible to identify the micro-skills that would be most crucial for a learner at this level. Among the micro-skills that this type of learner lacks, for example, are:

200

1. ability to identify and reconstruct topics from ongoing discourse
2. ability to recognize typical word-order patterns in English
3. ability to recognize major syntactic patterns in English

By systematically comparing information in the skills taxonomy with the learner profile, it is now possible to formulate objectives for the target group of learners.

Formulation of objectives

Objectives translate the content identified in the skills selection process into a statement of what the student is expected to be able to do at the end of a course of instruction. Objectives defined this way are also known as *behavioral objectives* (Nicholls and Nicholls 1972). They serve as goals toward which the teacher should be aiming in a course, and therefore help determine the choice of appropriate methodology and classroom procedures. They also enable teachers to assess the extent to which learning has been accomplished. Basically, what is required is a clearly set out group of statements identifying what is to be achieved – methodology and the syllabus identify the means; objectives specify the ends. Objectives thus break down the micro-skills into descriptions of behavior or performance in terms that can be taught and tested. Objectives for the hypothetical target group identified above, for example, might be stated in the following terms:

1. The student will have a listening vocabulary of approximately 800 words, including dates, time, and numbers up to 100.
2. The student can recognize the different intonation patterns used for questions, statements, instructions.
3. The student can understand yes/no questions and Wh-questions on topics connected with home life, the family, school, free time, health, shopping, personal identification.
4. The student can understand common phrases used in short conversations and interviews on the above topics.
5. The student can identify the topics of conversations between native speakers on the above topics.
6. The student can understand utterances within an 800-word vocabulary in which the following grammatical constructions are used: sub V comp, sub V obj.
7. The student can understand utterances within an 800-word vocabulary containing subordinate and coordinating clauses.

From the formulation of instructional objectives we are now able to consider the development of instructional procedures and activities that enable the objectives to be realized. These are questions of procedure, that is, of techniques and exercise types.

Procedure

In teaching listening comprehension our aim is to provide opportunities for the learner to acquire particular micro-skills, those individual listening abilities that we have identified and used in specifying particular teaching objectives. In teaching listening we can manipulate two variables, both of which serve to develop ability in particular skill areas. We can either manipulate the *input*, that is, the language the learner hears, controling for selected features such as grammatical complexity, topic, and rate of delivery, or we can manipulate the *tasks* we set for the learner. Manipulation of either (or both) is directed toward developing particular micro-skills.

In examining procedures for teaching listening comprehension, we will focus on some general criteria that can be applied to the evaluation of exercises and classroom procedures and then look at techniques and procedures themselves.

Criteria for evaluating activities and exercises

In teaching listening skills our aim is to provide comprehensible, focused input and purposeful listening tasks that develop competence in particular listening abilities. The following criteria serve as a checklist in developing listening tasks (Stanley 1978, British Council 1981, McKeating 1981, Maley and Moulding 1981, Porter and Roberts 1981, Thomas 1982).

Content validity. Does the activity practice listening comprehension or something else? How closely does the input or task relate to the micro-skills that listening comprehension involves? Many listening materials contain activities that depend more on reading or general intelligence than on listening skills. The question of content validity raises the issue of whether the activity adequately or actually makes use of skills and behavior that are part of listening in the real world. Two related factors have to do with memory and purposefulness.

Listening comprehension or memory? We saw that a variety of processing activities in listening precede storage of information in long-term memory. Many listening activities focus on retrieval of information from long-term memory rather than on the processing activities themselves. An exercise involving listening to a passage and responding to true/false questions about the content of it typically makes use of memory rather than comprehension.

Purposefulness and transferability. Does the activity reflect a purpose for listening that approximates authentic real-life listening? Do the abilities the exercise develops transfer to real-life listening purposes, or is the learner simply developing the ability to perform classroom exercises? An activity that makes use of news broadcasts as input, for example, should reflect the reasons why people typically listen to news broadcasts, such as listening for information about events. Cloze exercises requiring the learner to supply grammatical words after listening to the news item do not reflect the purposes for which people listen to news broadcasts. It is not a situation that corresponds to any real-life listening purpose, and therefore involves a low degree of transfer.

Testing or teaching. Does the activity or set of procedures assume that a set of skills is already acquired and simply provide opportunities for the learner to practice them, or does it assume that the skills are not known and try to help the learner acquire them? A great many listening activities test rather than teach. For example, a set of true/false questions following a passage on a tape might indicate how much of the material the learner can remember, but this kind of activity in no way helps the learner develop the ability to grasp main ideas or extract relevant details. The amount of preparation the learner is given before a listening task is often important in giving a teaching rather than a testing focus to an activity. Pre-listening activities generally have this purpose. They activate the learner's script and set a purpose for listening. They may take the form of discussion, questions, or a short paragraph to read that creates the script, providing information about the situation, the characters, and the events. Activities that teach rather than test may require much more use of pre-listening tasks and tasks completed as the student listens than post-listening tasks.

Authenticity. To what degree does the input resemble natural discourse? Although much authentic discourse may be too disfluent or difficult to understand without contextual support, materials should aim for relative authenticity if they are to prepare listeners for real listening situations. Many current commercial listening materials are spoken at an artificially slow pace, in prestige dialects that are not typical of ordinary speech. They are often oral readings of written material articulated in a precise "acting" style, lacking the pauses and self-corrections of natural speech. Furthermore, the value of such materials must be examined in the light of Krashen's (1982) proposal that authentic learning experiences should provide an opportunity for *acquisition*; that is, they should provide comprehensible input that requires negotiation of meaning and that contains linguistic features a little beyond the learner's current level of competence.

Exercise types

In developing classroom materials and activities we can manipulate the input or the tasks. Input, for example, may be in the form of dialogue or monologue. Dialogue may be scripted or unscripted, between native speakers, between native and non-native speakers, or between non-native speakers. Difficulty in both dialogue and monologue may vary according to the rate of delivery, level of vocabulary, topic, information content, fluency (amount of pausing, errors), and coherence. Tasks may vary according to whether they require *global comprehension* (where the learner is required to attempt to understand the overall meaning) or *partial comprehension* (where only comprehension of specific items is required) (Blundell and Stokes 1981, Schecter 1984). Tasks may also vary according to whether they require a *mechanical, meaningful,* or *communicative* response (Paulston 1971). A task requiring a mechanical response, for example, would be a discrimination task where the learner is required to distinguish between two words or sounds and where comprehension is not required. A meaningful response would be one in which comprehension of the input is required, but no creative abilities are called into play as, for example, when a learner has to match one of two sentences to one he or she hears. A communicative response is one in which the learner has to create a suitable response on the basis of what is understood and where interpretation, adaptation, and the addition of new information are required. For example, the listener may hear a problem discussed and then have to suggest a solution. The criterion for selecting and evaluating tasks, however, is not their interest or ingenuity but the degree in which they relate to teaching rather than testing objectives. Among common task types in materials are:

Matching or distinguishing. Choosing a response in written or pictorial form that corresponds with what was heard (e.g., placing pictures in a sequence that matches a story or set of events; choosing a picture to match a situation, such as listening to a radio advertisement and finding the product from a set of pictures).

Transferring. Exercises of this type involve receiving information in one form and transferring the information or part of it into another form (e.g., listening to a discussion about a house and then sketching the house).

Transcribing. Listening, and then writing down what was heard. Dictation is the most common example of this activity.

Scanning. Exercises in which listeners must extract selected items by scanning the input in order to find a specific piece of information (e.g., listening to a news broadcast and identifying the name of the winning party in an election).

Extending. Exercises that involve going beyond what is provided, such as re-constructing a dialogue when alternate lines are missing or providing a con-clusion to a story.

Condensing. Reducing what is heard to an outline of main points, such as is required in taking notes.

Answering. Answering questions from the input. Different kinds of questions will focus on different levels of listening (e.g., questions that require recall of details, those that require inferences and deductions, those that require evaluation or reactions).

Predicting. Guessing or predicting outcomes, causes, relationships, and so forth, based on information presented in a conversation or narrative.

Applications

As an example of approach, design, and procedural elements of listening comprehension methodology, we will now show how a listening exercise that was presented to a materials development class at the University of Hawaii was adapted by the students in that class to give it a more relevant focus. This discussion also illustrates the sorts of activities that are useful in teaching workshops for teachers on developing materials for listening comprehension.

The text selected was *Have You Heard?* (Underwood 1979), which is described on the book's jacket as providing

listening comprehension practice for students of English as a foreign language who have had little opportunity to hear native English speakers. Each of the twenty units contains recorded extracts centered around a particular language function. The recordings are of spontaneous conversations in a range of accents and bring the students as close as possible to a real life situation.

The task set for the teacher trainees who were in this course was first to examine the text and the exercises in terms of content validity, testing, or teaching, and the other criteria discussed above. It was found that the existing exercises in the text mainly tested memory rather than listening comprehension, and many were found to have little relation to listening. In considering alternative exercises, the materials were first examined to determine the types of listening tasks and micro-skills that the conversational samples involved. From these, objectives and exercises were developed.[1]

Unit 1 of the text, for example, focuses on "people talking about things they like." The unit contains three short conversations on the topic by different people. The first is entitled "Felix talks about his job as a school-master." The following pre-listening information is given:

1 The exercises that will be presented here were prepared by Andrew Harper, Esther Soong, Phillip Pinsent, Holly Uyeda, Joel Wiskin, Florida Abe, Tereseta Kawamoto, and Pi-chong Su.

Felix shows his pleasure by mentioning the good things about his job. He begins by saying that he decided quite quickly about what he wanted to do as a job.

A few difficult vocabulary items are presented, then the teacher is instructed to play the type. True/false exercises, vocabulary exercises, and a transcription/dictation task follow. The conversational listening extract is as follows:

So there was no great lengthy process deciding what I was going to do – but I don't feel I've made a mistake – I enjoy it – I enjoy the company of other members of the staff in the staff room where they are colleagues of yours but you're not in a structured system where they are your boss or you are theirs – everyone is in the same boat – everyone is in the same level and yet – you don't actually work with one another – you just work with the same boys – and therefore I think that unlike an office situation – you get to know the ... the other members of the staff – as friends more than as workmates – and also I enjoy – the difference in the job – it isn't the same thing every year – in a yearly situation – you can do things a different way the second year, the third year – and I enjoy the differences it brings – every day – different classes, different age groups, different attitudes ... [transcribed from tape]

It was decided to replace all the exercises suggested in the text. In developing alternative exercises the trainees produced the following:

Objectives
Listen for general understanding of the gist of a conversation.
Identify the speaker's attitude toward a topic.

Micro-skills
Identify and follow the topic of a conversation.
Recognize vocabulary for expressing positive and negative attitudes.
Infer speaker's attitude from reasons given.
Infer meanings of words from context.

Pre-listening activities
Students work in groups and discuss what makes a job enjoyable or undesirable.
Students rank their findings.
Students discuss the advantages and disadvantages of school teaching.
(The goal of the pre-listening activities is to activate background knowledge or scripts and to prepare students for some of the vocabulary they will hear.)

Teaching procedure
1. On first listening, students are given a simple task. They are instructed to answer the following questions as they listen:
   a) What is Felix's job?
   b) How does he feel about his job? Does he like it or not?
   (By positing the task before the students listen to the tape, the listeners are given a purpose for listening, which forces them to focus on selected

information. They can also compare information they hear with information they obtained from their pre-listening group discussions.)

2. After listening to the tape and discussing their answers, the students are given a more specific task to be completed during a second listening:
Which of the following does Felix say are important for him about his job?

the salary	not having a fixed routine
the holidays	the power it gives
not having a boss	his colleagues

3. During a third listening, students answer true/false questions:
   a) It took Felix a long time to choose a job.
   b) Felix believes he chose the right job
   c) Felix says his job is like working in an office.
   d) Felix wants to change his job.
   e) Felix has to do the same thing every year.

4. The post-listening exercise involves deducing the meanings of words from the context in which they were used in the conversation:
What do these expressions in the conversation mean?
"To be in the same boat with other people"
"To enjoy the company of other people"

The exercises suggested by the trainees thus involve primarily pre-listening and "complete-while-listening" tasks, rather than the usual battery of post-listening exercises. They prepare the students for listening before listening begins and focus on a level of comprehension relevant to conversational listening.

Conclusion

The teaching of listening comprehension, or of any language skill, involves considering the objectives we are teaching toward and the micro-skills our procedures cover. An educated response is dependent, in turn, on how much of any attempt we have made to appreciate the nature of the listening comprehension process itself. Any informed methodology or teaching program looks both at techniques and classroom routines, and beyond them, to the broader principles that serve as their justification.

References

Abrahams, R. 1962. Playing the dozens. *Journal of American Folklore* 75: 209–220.

Adams, M. L. 1980. Five cooccurring factors in speaking proficiency. In James Frith (ed.), *Measuring Spoken Language Proficiency*. Washington, D.C.: Georgetown University Press.

Aguas, E. F. 1964. English composition errors of Tagalog speakers and implications for analytical theory. Doctoral dissertation, University of California, Los Angeles.

Albert, E. 1964. "Rhetoric," "logic," and "poetics" in Burundi: cultural patterning of speech behavior. *American Anthropologist* 66: 6. Revised and reprinted in Gumperz and Hymes (1972).

Allen, D., and R. Guy. 1974. *Conversational Analysis: The Sociology of Talk.* The Hague: Mouton.

Allen, P. 1977. Structural and functional models in language teaching. *TESL Talk* 8 (1): 5–15.

Allen, W. S. 1959. *Living English Structure.* London: Longman.

Allwright, R. L. 1975. Problems in the study of teachers' treatment of learner error. In Burt and Dulay (1975): 96–109.

Andersen, R. W. 1978. An implicational model for second language research. *Language Learning* 28 (2): 221–282.

Anderson, R. 1983. *Pidginization and Creolization as Language Acquisition.* Rowley, Mass.: Newbury House.

Anthony, E. M. 1963. Approach, method and technique. *English Language Teaching* 17: 63–67.

1975. *Towards a Theory of Lexical Meaning.* Singapore: RELC.

Apte, M. 1974. "Thank you" and south Asian languages: a comparative sociolinguistic study. In R. Cooper (ed.), *Language Attitudes 1, International Journal of the Sociology of Language* 3: 67–69.

Arabski, J. 1968. A linguistic analysis of English composition errors made by Polish students. *Studia Anglica Posnansiensia* 1(1) and 1(2): 71–89.

Asher, J. J. 1977. *Learning Another Language through Actions: The Complete Teacher's Guide.* Los Gatos, Cal.: Sky Oaks Productions.

Austin, J. 1962. *How to Do Things with Words.* Oxford: Clarendon Press.

Bailey, Kathleen M. 1983. Competitiveness and anxiety in adult second language learning. In H. W. Seliger and M. H. Long (eds.), *Classroom Oriented Research in Second Language Acquisition*, pp. 67–103., Rowley, Mass.: Newbury House.

Barnard, H. 1971. *Advanced English Vocabulary.* Rowley, Mass.: Newbury House.

Barnlund, D. C. 1975. Communicative styles in two cultures: Japan and the United States. In A. Kendon and M. R. Key (eds.), *Organization of Behaviour in Face to Face Interaction,* pp. 427–456. The Hague: Mouton.

Bates, E. 1976. *Language and Context: the Acquisition of Pragmatics.* New York: Academic Press.

Beebe, Leslie M. 1983. Risk-taking and the language learner. In H. W. Seliger and M. H. Long (eds.), *Classroom Oriented Research in Second Language Acquisition,* pp. 39–66. Rowley, Mass.: Newbury House.

Bhaskar, A. W. S. 1962. An analysis of common errors in P.U.C. English. *Bulletin of the Central Institute of English* (Hyderabad, India) 2: 47–57.

Bialystock, E. 1978. A theoretical model of second language learning. *Language Learning* 28(1): 69–83.

1981. The role of linguistic knowledge in second language use. *Studies in Second Language Acquisition* 4(1): 31–45.

Bley-Vroman, R. 1983. The comparative fallacy in interlanguage studies; the case of systematicity. *Language Learning* 33(1): 1–18.

Blundell, L., and J. Stokes. 1981. *Task Listening.* Cambridge: Cambridge University Press.

Bolinger, D. 1967. The imperative in English. In *To Honor Roman Jacobson: Essays on the Occasion of his 70th Birthday.* The Hague: Mouton.

1975. *Aspects of Language,* 2nd ed. New York: Harcourt Brace Jovanovich.

Borkin, A., and S. M. Reinhart. 1978. Excuse me and I'm sorry. *TESOL Quarterly* 12(1): 57–69.

Breen, M. P., and C. N. Candlin. 1980. The essentials of a communicative curriculum in language teaching. *Applied Linguistics* 1(2): 89–112.

Bright, J. A., and G. P. McGregor. 1970. *Teaching English as a Second Language.* London: Longman.

Brindley, G. P. 1982. *Listening Proficiency Descriptions.* Sydney: NSW Migrant Education Service.

1983. *Needs Analysis and Objective Setting in the Australian Migrant Education Program.* Sydney: NSW Migrant Education Service.

British Council. 1981. *The Teaching of Listening Comprehension.* ELT Documents. London: The British Council.

Brown, D. F. 1974. Advanced vocabulary teaching: the problem of collocation. *RELC Journal* 5(2): 1–11.

Brown, G. 1977. *Listening to Spoken English.* London: Longman.

Brown, H. D. 1980. *Principles of Language Learning and Teaching.* Englewood Cliffs, N.J.: Prentice-Hall.

Brown, P., and S. Levinson. 1978. Universals in language usage: politeness phenomena. In E. N. Goody (1978): 56–289.

Brown, R. 1973. *A First Language.* Cambridge, Mass.: Harvard University Press.

Brumfit, C. 1984. *Communicative Methodology in Language Teaching.* Cambridge: Cambridge University Press.

Brumfit, C. J., and R. K. Johnson (eds.). 1979. *The Communicative Approach to Language Teaching.* London: Oxford University Press.

Bruner, J. 1975. The ontogenesis of speech acts. *Journal of Child Language* 2(1): 1–20.

1978. Learning the mother tongue. *Human Nature* 1(9): 42–49.

References

Buckby, M. (ed.). 1981. *Graded Objectives and Tests for Modern Languages: an Evaluation*. London: Centre for Information on Language Teaching.

Burroughs, G. E. R. 1957. *A Study of the Vocabulary of Young Children*. Birmingham: University of Birmingham.

Burt, M. K., and H. C. Dulay (eds.). 1975. *On TESOL 75*. Washington, D.C.: TESOL.

Canale, M. 1983. From communicative competence to communicative language pedagogy. In J. C. Richards and R. Schmidt (eds.), *Language and Communication*. London: Longman.

Cancino, H., E. J. Rosansky, and J. H. Schumann. 1974. Testing hypotheses about second language acquisition: the copula and the negative in three subjects. *Working Papers in Bilingualism* 3: 80–96.

Candlin, C. N. 1976. Communicative language teaching and the debt to pragmatics. In C. Rameh (ed.), *Georgetown University Round Table on Languages and Linguistics*. Washington, D.C.: Georgetown University Press.

1978. Discoursal patterning and the equalizing of interpretive opportunity. Paper presented at the Conference on English as an International Auxiliary Language, East-West Center, Honolulu, April 1978.

Candlin, C. N., C. J. Bruton, and J. H. Leather. 1976. Doctors in casualty: applying components of communicative competence to specialist course design. *IRAL* 14: 3.

Cathcart, Ruth L., and Judy Olsen. 1976. Teachers' and students' preferences for correction of classroom conversation errors. In John Fanselow and Ruth Crymes (eds.), *On TESOL 76*, pp. 41–53. Washington, D.C. TESOL.

Chafe, W. 1970. *Meaning and the Structure of Language*. Chicago: University of Chicago Press.

Chaudron, C. 1977. A descriptive model of discourse in the corrective treatment of learners' errors. *Language Learning* 27(1): 29–46.

1979. Complexity of teacher speech and vocabulary explanation/elaboration. Paper presented at the 13th annual TESOL convention, Boston, March 1979.

1983a. Evaluating writing; effects of feedback on revisions. Paper presented at TESOL convention, Toronto, March 1983.

1983b. A method for examining the input/intake distinction. Paper presented at the 10th University of Michigan Conference on Applied Linguistics, Ann Arbor, October 1983.

1983c. Simplification of input; topic restatements and their effects on L2 learners' recognition and recall. *TESOL Quarterly* 17(3): 437–458.

Chiu, R. K. 1972. Measuring register characteristics: a prerequisite for preparing advanced level TESOL programs. *TESOL Quarterly* 6(2) 129–141.

Chomsky, N., and M. Halle. 1968. *The Sound Pattern of English*. New York: Harper and Row.

Clark, J. L. 1972. *Foreign Language Testing; Theory and Practice*. Philadelphia, Penn.: Center for Curriculum Development.

Cleark, H. H., and T. Carlson. 1982. Hearers and speech acts. *Language* 58(2): 332–373.

Clark, H. H., and E. V. Clark. 1977. *Psychology and Language*. New York: Harcourt Brace Jovanovich.

Clark, H. H., and P. Lucy. 1975. Understanding what is meant from what is said; a study in conversationally conveyed requests. *Journal of Verbal Learning and Verbal Behavior* 14: 56–72.

Close, R. 1959. Concerning the present tense. *English Language Teaching* 13.

1975. *A Reference Grammar for Students of English*. London: Longman.

Clyne, M. 1975. Intercultural communication breakdown and communication conflict: towards a linguistic model and its exemplification. Manuscript.

Cohen, A., and C. Hosenfeld. 1981. Some uses of mentalistic data in second language research. *Language Learning* 31(2): 285–314.

Cole, P. 1975. The synchronic and diachronic status of conversational implicature. In Cole and Morgan, eds. (1975).

Cole, P., and J. Morgan (eds.). 1975. *Syntax and Semantics, Volume 3: Speech Acts*. New York: Academic Press.

Comrie, B. 1976. *Aspect*. Cambridge: Cambridge University Press.

Cook, V. 1969. The analogy between first and second language learning. *IRAL* 7: 207–216.

Corder, S. P. 1967. The significance of learners' errors. *IRAL* 5: 161–169.

1978. Language learner language. In J. C. Richards (ed.), *Understanding Second and Foreign Language Learning*, pp. 71–92. Rowley, Mass.: Newbury House.

1979. Language distance and the magnitude of the learner task. *Studies in Second Language Acquisition* 2(1): 27–36.

Coulmas, F. 1979. On the sociolinguistic relevance of routine formulae. *Pragmatics* 3: 239–266.

(ed.). 1981. *Conversational Routine*. The Hague: Mouton.

Coulthard, R. M. 1975. Discourse analysis in English – a short review of the literature. *Language Teaching and Linguistics Abstracts* 8(2): 73–89.

1977. *An Introduction to Discourse Analysis*. London: Longman.

Cowan, J.R. 1974. Lexical and syntactic research for the design of EFL reading materials. *TESOL Quarterly* 8(4): 389–399.

Croft, K. 1960. *Reading and Word Study*. Englewood Cliffs, N.J.: Prentice-Hall.

Curran, C. A. 1972. *Counseling-Learning: a Whole-Person Model for Education*. New York: Grune and Stratton.

1976. *Counseling-Learning in Second Languages*. Apple River, Ill.: Apple River Press.

Dakin, J. 1969. The teaching of reading. In H. Fraser and W. R. O'Donnell (eds.), *Applied Linguistics and the Teaching of English*, pp. 107–111. London: Longman.

d'Anglejan, A. 1978. Language learning in and out of classrooms. In J. C. Richards (ed.), *Understanding Second and Foreign Language Learning*, pp. 218–238. Rowley, Mass.: Newbury House.

Day, R. A., N. A. Chenoweth, A. E. Chun, and S. Luppescu. 1983. Foreign language learning and the treatment of spoken error. *Language Learning and Communication* 2(2): 215–227.

Deese, J. 1965. *The Structure of Associations in Language and Thought*. Baltimore: Johns Hopkins Press.

1970. *Psycholinguistics*. Boston, Mass.: Allyn and Bacon.

References

De Silva, E. 1981. Form and function in Malaysian English. Masters thesis, University of Malaya, Kuala Lumpur.

Dickerson, L. J. 1975. The learner's interlanguage as a set of variable rules. *TESOL Quarterly* 9(4): 401–408.

Dickerson, L. J., and W. Dickerson. 1977. Interlanguage phonology: current research and future directions. In S. P. Corder and E. Roulet (eds.), *The Notions of Simplification, Interlanguages, and Pidgins*. Actes du 5ème Colloque de Linguistique Appliqué de Neufchâtel.

Dittmar, N. 1981. On the verbal organization of L2 tense marking in an elicited translation task by Spanish immigrants in Germany. *Studies in Second Language Acquisition* 3(2): 136–164.

Dore, J. 1975. Holophrase, speech acts, and language universals. *Journal of Child Language* 2: 21–44.

1977. "Oh them Sheriff": a pragmatic analysis of children's response to questions. In Ervin-Tripp and Mitchell-Kernan, eds. (1977).

Dore, J., and R. P. McDermott. 1982. Linguistic indeterminacy and social context in utterance interpretation. *Language* 58(2): 374–398.

Dulay, H. C., and M. K. Burt. 1974a. Errors and strategies in child second language acquisition. *TESOL Quarterly* 8(2): 129–138.

1974b. Natural sequences in child second language acquisition. *Language Learning* 24(1): 37–53.

Dulay, H. C., M. K. Burt, and S. D. Krashen. 1982. *Language Two*. New York: Oxford University Press.

Dundes, A., J. Leach, and B. Ozkok. 1972. The strategy of Turkish boys' verbal duelling rhymes. In Gumperz and Hymes, eds. (1972).

Dušková, L. 1969. On sources of errors in language learning. *IRAL* 7: 11–36.

Ervin, S., and C. E. Osgood. 1954. Second language learning and bilingualism. *Journal of Abnormal and Social Psychology*, Supplement 49: 139–146.

Ervin-Tripp, S. 1969. Comments on "How and when do persons become bilingual." In L. G. Kelly (ed.), *Description and Measurement of Bilingualism*. Toronto: University of Toronto Press.

1974. Is second language learning like the first? *TESOL Quarterly* 8(2): 111–128.

1976. "Is Sybil there?" The structure of American English directives. *Language in Society* 5(1): 25–66.

1977. "Wait for me, Roller Skate." In Ervin-Tripp and Mitchell-Kernan, eds. (1977).

Ervin-Tripp, S., and C. Mitchell-Kernan (eds.). 1977. *Child Discourse*. New York: Academic Press.

Eskey, D. E. 1973. A model program for teaching advanced reading to students of English as a foreign language. *Language Learning* 23(2): 169–184.

Estacia, C. 1964. English syntax problems of Filipinos. In *Proceedings of the Ninth International Congress of Linguistics*, pp. 217–223. The Hague: Mouton.

Ewer, J. R., and G. Latorre. 1969. *A Course in Basic Scientific English*. London: Longman.

Faerch, C. 1978. Language learning studies: a survey of some recent research

212

studies. *Occasional Papers: 1976–1977*. Department of English, University of Copenhagen.

1979. Describing interlanguage through interaction: problems of systematicity and permeability. Papers presented at the 17th International Conference on Polish-English Contrastive Linguistics. Boszkowo, Poland, May 1979.

Faerch, C., and G. Kasper (eds.). 1983. *Strategies in Interlanguage Communication*. London: Longman.

Fanselow, J. F. 1977. The treatment of error in oral work. *Foreign Language Annals* 10: 583–593.

Farhady, Hossein. 1982. Measures of language proficiency from the learner's perspective. *TESOL Quarterly* 16(1): 43–61.

Farsi, Ali Abdullah. 1974. Change verbs. *Language Sciences* 31: 21–23.

Faucett, L., M. West, H. Palmer, and E. W. Thorndike. 1936. *The Interim Report on Vocabulary Selection for the Teaching of English as a Foreign Language*. London: P. S. King.

Felix, S. W. (ed.). 1980. *Second Language Development; Trends and Issues*. Tubingen: Gunter Narr.

Ferguson, C. A. 1971. Towards a characterization of English foreigner talk. *Anthropological Linguistics* 17(1): 1–14.

1976. The structure and use of politeness formulas. *Language in Society* 5(2): 137–152.

Fillmore, C. J. 1968. The case for case. In E. Bach and R. T. Harms (eds.), *Universals in Language*. New York: Holt, Rinehart and Winston.

Fillmore, L. W. 1976. Cognitive and social strategies in language acquisition. Doctoral dissertation, Stanford University.

Fishman, J. A., R. L. Cooper, and A. W. Conrad. 1977. *The Spread of English*. Rowley, Mass.: Newbury House.

Flick, W. C. 1978a. Disfluency phenomena in L2 speech behavior. Paper presented at the Modern Language Association meeting, Minneapolis.

1978b. A multiple component approach to research in second language acquisition. Paper presented at the TESOL convention, Mexico City.

Flood, W. E. 1960. *Scientific Words: Their Structure and Meaning*. London: Oldbourne.

Foss, D. J., and D. T. Hakes. 1978. *Psycholinguistics: An Introduction to the Psychology of Language*. Englewood Cliffs, N.J.: Prentice-Hall.

Fowler, W. S., J. Pidcock, and R. Rycroft. 1979. *Incentive English* (Book 1). Middlesex: Nelson.

Fraser, B. 1975. Hedged performatives. In Cole and Morgan, eds. (1975).

1978. Acquiring social competence in a second language. *RELC Journal* 9(2): 1–26.

French, F. G. 1949. *Common Errors in English*. London: Oxford University Press.

Fries, C. C., and A. C. Fries. 1961. *Foundations for English Teaching*. Tokyo: Kenkyusha.

Fries, C. C., and A. E. Traver. 1942. *English Word Lists*. Washington, D.C.: American Council on Education.

Gaies, S. J. 1977. The nature of linguistic input in formal second language learning: linguistic and communicative strategies in ESL teachers' classroom language. In H. D. Brown, C. Yorio, and R. Crymes (eds.), *On TESOL 77.* Washington, D.C.: TESOL.

———. 1983. The investigation of language classroom processes. *TESOL Quarterly* 17(2): 205–217.

Garfinkel H. 1967. *Studies in Ethnomethodology.* Englewood Cliffs, N.J.: Prentice Hall.

Garvey, C. 1975. Requests and responses in children's speech. *Journal of Child Language* 2: 41–63.

Gass, S. 1983. Interlanguage syntax: state of the art: language transfer and language universals. Paper presented at the 17th TESOL convention, Toronto, March 1983.

Gatbonton, E. 1975. Systematic variations in second language speech; a sociolinguistic study. Doctoral dissertation, McGill University.

Gattegno, C. 1972. *Teaching Foreign Languages in Schools.* New York: Educational Solutions.

———. 1976. *The Common Sense of Teaching Foreign Languages.* New York: Educational Solutions.

Geertz, C. 1960. *The Religion of Java.* New York: The Free Press.

Genesee, F. 1982. Experimental neuropsychological research on second language processing. *TESOL Quarterly* 16(3): 315–321.

George, H. V. 1962. Teaching simple past and past perfect. *Bulletin of the Central Institute of English* (Hyderabad, India) 2: 18–31.

———. 1972. *Common Errors in Language Learning.* Rowley, Mass.: Newbury House.

Givon, T. 1979. *Understanding Grammar.* New York: Academic Press.

Godard, D. 1977. Same setting, different norms: phone call beginnings in France and the United States. *Language in Society* 6(2): 209–219.

Goffman, E. 1972. *Relations in Public.* New York: Harper and Row.

———. 1974. *Frame Analysis.* New York: Harper and Row.

———. 1976. Replies and responses. *Language in Society* 5(3): 257–314.

Good, C. 1979. Language as a social activity: negotiating conversation. *Journal of Pragmatics* 3: 151–167.

Goody, E. N. 1978. Towards a theory of questions. In Goody, ed. (1978): 17–43.

Goody, E. N. (ed.). 1978. *Questions and Politeness: Strategies in Social Interaction.* Cambridge: Cambridge University Press.

Gordon, D., and G. Lakoff. 1971. Conversational postulates. *Papers from the Seventh Regional Meeting of the Chicago Linguistic Society*: 63–84.

Green, G. 1975. How to get people to do things with words. In Cole and Morgan, eds. (1975): pp. 107–142.

Gregg, Kevin. 1984. Krashen's monitor and Occam's razor. *Applied Linguistics* 5(2): 79–100.

Grelier, S. n.d. Recherche des principales interférences dans les systèmes verbaux de l'anglais du wolof et du français. Dakar, Senegal: *Centre de Linguistique Appliquée de Dakar*, No. 31.

Grice, H. 1968. Utterer's meaning, sentences-meaning and word-meaning. *Foundations of Language* 4: 225–242.

———. 1975. Logic and conversation. In Cole and Morgan, eds. (1975).

Gumperz, J., and D. Hymes (eds.). 1972. *Directions in Sociolinguistics: the Ethnography of Communication.* New York: Holt, Rinehart and Winston.

Gumperz, J., and C. Roberts. 1978. *Developing Awareness Skills for Interethnic Communication.* Middlesex: National Centre for Industrial Training.

Halliday, M. A. K. 1973. *Explorations in the Functions of Language.* London: Edward Arnold.

1975. *Learning How to Mean: Explorations in the Development of Language.* London: Edward Arnold.

Hamayan, E. V., and G. R. Tucker. 1980. Language input in the bilingual classroom and its relationship to second language achievement. *TESOL Quarterly* 14(4): 453–469.

Hancher, M. 1979. The classification of cooperative illocutionary acts. *Language in Society* 8(1): 1–14.

Hatch, E. 1978. Discourse analysis, speech acts and second language acquisition. In W. C. Ritchie (ed.), *Second Language Acquisition Research: Issues and Implications.* New York: Academic Press.

(ed.). 1978. *Second Language Acquisition.* Rowley, Mass.: Newbury House.

1983. *Psycholinguistics: A Second Language Perspective.* Rowley, Mass.: Newbury House.

Henning, G. H. 1973. Remembering foreign language vocabulary: acoustic and semantic parameters. *Language Learning* 23(2): 185–196.

Henrickson, J. M. 1978. Error correction in foreign language teaching: recent theories, research and practice. *Modern Language Journal* 62: 387–398.

Heringer, J. 1972. Some grammatical correlates of felicity conditions and presuppositions. *Working Papers in Linguistics* (The Ohio State University) 11: 1–110.

Higgs, T. V. (ed.). 1984. *Teaching for Proficiency: the Organizing Principle.* Skokie, Ill.: National Textbook Company.

Higgs, T. V., and R. Clifford. 1982. The push towards communication. In T. Higgs (ed.), *Curriculum, Competence and the Foreign Language Teacher.* Skokie, Ill.: National Textbook Company.

Hirtle, W. H. 1967. *The Simple and Progressive Forms: an Analytic Approach.* Quebec: Laval University Press.

1975. *Time, Aspect and the Verb.* Quebec: Laval University Press.

Hok, R. 1963. Contrast: an effective teaching device. *English Language Teaching* 17: 3.

Holmes, J. 1978. Sociolinguistic competence in the classroom. In J. C. Richards (ed.), *Understanding Second and Foreign Language Learning.* Rowley, Mass.: Newbury House.

Holmes, J., and D. F. Brown. 1977. Sociolinguistic competence and second language learning. *Topics in Culture Learning* (August) 1977.

Hormann, H. 1970. *Psycholinguistics: an Introduction to Research and Theory.* New York: Springer-Verlag.

Hornby, A. S. 1954. *A Guide to Patterns and Usage in English.* London: Oxford University Press.

Hosenfeld, C. 1979. Cora's view of learning grammar. *Canadian Modern Language Journal* 35: 602–607.

References

Hyltenstam, K. 1977. Implicational patterns in interlanguage syntax variation. *Language Learning* 27(2): 383–411.

Hymes, D. 1967. Models of the interaction of language and social setting. *Journal of Social Issues* 23(2): 8–28. Revised and reprinted in Gumperz and Hymes, eds. (1972).

1972. On communicative competence. In J. B. Pride and J. Holmes (eds.), *Sociolinguistics*, pp. 269–293. Harmondsworth: Penguin.

Imai, M. 1981. *Sixteen Ways to Avoid Saying No.* Tokyo: Nihon Keizai Shimbun.

Ingram, D. E. 1982. Developing a language program. *RELC Journal* 13(1): 64–86.

Jacobson, R. 1976. Incorporating sociolinguistic norms into an ESL program. *TESOL Quarterly* 10(4): 411–422.

Jakobovits, L. A. 1969a. *A Psycholinguistic Analysis of Second-Language Learning and Bilingualism.* Urbana-Champaign, Ill.: Institute of Communications Research.

1969b. Second-language learning and transfer theory. *Language Learning* 19: 55–86.

1970. *Foreign Language Learning: a Psycholinguistic Analysis of the Issues.* Rowley, Mass.: Newbury House.

Jarvis, A. G., and S. J. Adams. 1979. *Evaluating a Second Language Program.* Washington, D.C.: Center for Applied Linguistics.

Johnson, F., and C. B. Paulston. 1976. *Individualizing in the Language Classroom.* Cambridge: Jacaranda.

Johnson, R. K. 1981. On syllabuses and on being communicative. *The English Bulletin* (Hong Kong) 7(4): 39–51.

1982. *Communicative Syllabus Design and Methodology.* Oxford: Pergamon.

Jupp, T. C., and S. Hodlin. 1975. *Industrial English.* London: Heinemann.

Kachru, B. (ed.). 1982. *The Other Tongue.* Urbana: University of Illinois Press.

Kasper, J. T. 1977. Foreigner talk input in child second language acquisition: its form and function over time. In C. A. Henning (ed.), *Proceedings of the Los Angeles Language Research Forum.* University of California, Los Angeles.

Keller, E. 1981. Gambits: conversational strategy signals. In Coulmas, ed. (1981): 93–114.

Keller-Cohen, D. 1979. Systematicity and variation in the non-native child's acquisition of conversational skills. *Language Learning* 29: 27–44.

Kellerman, E. 1978. Giving the learners a break: natural language intuitions as a source of predictions about transferability. *Working Papers in Bilingualism* 15: 59–93.

Krashen, S. D. 1973. Lateralization, language learning, and the critical period; some new evidence. *Language Learning* 23: 63–74.

1981. *Second Language Acquisition and Second Language Learning.* Oxford: Pergamon.

1982. *Principles and Practice in Second Language Acquisition.* Oxford: Pergamon.

Krashen, S. D., and R. Scarcella. 1978. On routines and patterns in language acquisition and performance. *Language Learning* 28(2): 283–299.

Krashen, S., and Tracy D. Terrell. 1983. *The Natural Approach.* San Francisco: Alemany Press.

Labov, W. 1972. Rules for ritual insult. In Sudnow, ed. (1972).

Labov, W., and J. Waletsky. 1967. Narrative analysis: oral versions of personal experience. In *Essays on the Verbal and Visual Arts.* Proceedings of the 1966 Spring meeting, American Technical Society. Seattle: University of Washington Press.

Lachowicz, D. J. 1974. *Using Medical English.* Saigon: University of Saigon.

Lado, R. 1957. *Linguistics across Cultures.* Ann Arbor: University of Michigan Press.

Lambert, W. 1961. Behavioral evidence for contrasting forms of bilingualism. In M. Zarechnak (ed.), *Monograph Series on Languages and Linguistics* 14. Washington, D.C. Georgetown University Press.

Larsen-Freeman, D. 1976a. An explanation for the morpheme acquisition order of second language learners. *Language Learning* 26: 125–134.

1976b. ESL teacher speech as input to the ESL learner. *Working Papers in Teaching English as a Second Language.* (Dept. of English, ESL section, UCLA): 45–50.

1978. Evidence of the need for a second language acquisition index of development. In W. Ritchie (ed.), *Second Language Acquisition Research.* New York: Academic Press.

Leech, G. N. 1971. *Meaning and the English Verb.* London: Longman.

1974. *Semantics.* Middlesex: Penguin Books.

1977. *Language and Tact.* Treer: University of Treer.

Lenneberg, E. H. 1967. *Biological Foundations of Language.* New York: Wiley.

Lightbown, P. M. 1983. Exploring relationships between developmental and instructional sequences in second language acquisition. In H. W. Seliger and M. H. Long (eds.), *Classroom Oriented Research in Second Language Acquisition.* Rowley, Mass.: Newbury House.

Littlewood, W. 1981. *Communicative Language Teaching.* Cambridge: Cambridge University Press.

LoCoco, V. 1976. A comparison of three methods for the collection of second language data. *Working Papers in Bilingualism* 8: 59–86.

Long, M. H. 1980. Inside the black box. *Language Learning* 30(1): 1–42.

1981. Input, interaction and second language acquisition. In H. Winitz (ed.), *Native Language and Foreign Language Acquisition. Annals of the New York Academy of Science* 379: 259–278.

1983. Process and product in ESL program evaluation. Paper presented at the 5th annual TESOL convention summer meeting. Toronto, Canada, July 1983.

Long, M. H., and C. Sato. 1983. Classroom foreigner talk discourse: forms and functions of teachers' questions. In H. W. Seliger and M. H. Long (eds.), *Classroom Oriented Research on Second Language Acquisition.* Rowley, Mass.: Newbury House.

Lozanov, G. 1979. *Suggestology and Outlines of Suggestopedy.* New York: Gordon and Breach.

Lyons, J. 1977. *Semantics 2.* Cambridge: Cambridge University Press.

217

References

Mackay, R., and J. Palmer (eds.). 1981. *Language for Specific Purposes*. Rowley, Mass.: Newbury House.

Mackey, W. F. 1965. *Language Teaching Analysis*. London: Longman.

Maley, A., and S. Moulding. 1981. *Learning to Listen*. Cambridge: Cambridge University Press.

Marslen-Wilson, W., and L. K. Tyler. 1980. The temporal structure of spoken language. *Cognition* 9: 1–71.

Matthews, P. 1972. Review of Jacobs and Rosenbaum, "Readings in English Transformational Grammar." *Journal of Linguistics* 8: 125–137.

McKeating, D. 1981. Comprehension and listening. In G. Abbot and P. Wingard (eds.), *The Teaching of English as an International Language*, pp. 57–80. London: Collins.

McLaughlin, B. T. Rossman, and B. McLeod. 1983. Second language learning: an information processing perspective. *Language Learning* 33 (2):135–159.

Medley, F. W. 1979. Identifying needs and setting goals. In J. K. Philips (ed.), *Building on Experience – Building for Success*, pp. 41–66. Skokie, Ill.: National Textbook Company.

Menyuk, P. 1969. *Sentences Children Use*. Cambridge, Mass.: MIT Press.

Mitchell-Kernan, C., and K. Kernan. 1977. Pragmatics of directive choice among children. In Ervin-Tripp and Mitchell-Kernan, eds. (1977).

Morrison, Donald M., and Graham Low. 1983. Monitoring and the second language learner. In Jack C. Richards and Richard W. Schmidt (eds.), *Language and Communication*. London: Longman.

Mountford, A. 1975. *English in Workshop Practice*. London: Oxford University Press.

Mulder, N. 1979. *Everyday Life in Thailand: An Interpretation*. Bangkok: Duang Kamol.

Munby, J. 1978. *Communicative Syllabus Design*. Cambridge: Cambridge University Press.

Murphy, D., and C. Candlin. 1979. Engineering lecture discourse and listening comprehension. *Practical Papers in English Language Education* (University of Lancaster) 2: 1–79.

Murray, D. M. 1980. Writing as a process: how writing finds its own meaning. In T. R. Donovan and B. W. McClelland (eds.), *Eight Approaches to the Teaching of Composition*, pp. 3–21. Illinois: National Council of Teachers of English.

Nemser, W. 1971. Approximative systems of foreign language learners. *IRAL* 9(2): 115–123.

Newmark, L. D. 1971. A minimal language teaching program. In P. Pimsleur and T. Quinn (eds.), *The Psychology of Second Language Learning*, pp. 87–96. Cambridge: Cambridge University Press.

Nicholls, A., and H. Nicholls. 1972. *Developing a Curriculum: A Practical Guide*. London: George Allen and Unwin.

Nilsen, D. L. F. 1971. The use of case grammar in teaching English as a second language. *TESOL Quarterly* 5(5): 293–299.

Noble, C. E. 1953. The meaning-familiarity relationship. *Psychological Review* 60: 89–98.

218

Noss, R. 1967. *Higher Education and Development in Southeast Asia: Language Policy*. Paris: UNESCO.

Nystrom, Nancy Johnson. 1983. Teacher-student interaction in bilingual classrooms: four approaches to error feedback. In H. W. Seliger and M. H. Long (eds.)., *Classroom Oriented Research in Second Language Acquisition*, pp. 169–189. Rowley, Mass.: Newbury House.

Ochs-Keenan, E. 1976. The universality of conversational postulates. *Language in Society* 5(1): 67–80.

Ogden, C. K. 1930. *Basic English*. New York: Harcourt Brace.

Olshtain, Elite, and Andrew D. Cohen. 1983. Apology: a speech act. In Nessa Wolfson and Elliot Judd (eds.), *Sociolinguistics and Language Acquisition*, pp. 18–35. Rowley, Mass: Newbury House.

Osgood, C. E. 1964. Semantic differential technique in comparative studies of culture. In A. K. Romney and R. G. D'Andrade (eds.), *Transcultural Studies in Cognition. American Anthropologist*, special publication 31, part 2.

Osgood, C. E., G. J. Suci, and P. H. Tannenbaum. 1957. *The Measurement of Meaning*. Urbana: University of Illinois Press.

Ostrander, S., and L. Schroeder. 1979. *Superlearning*. New York: Delta/Confucian.

Ota, A. 1963. *Tense and Aspect of Present-day American English*. Tokyo: Kenkyusha.

Page, B., A. Harding, and S. Rowell. 1982. *Graded Objectives in Modern Languages*. London: Centre for Information on Language Teaching.

Palmer, A., and T. Rodgers. 1982. Communicative and instructional considerations in language teaching. *Language Learning and Communication* 1(3): 235–256.

Palmer, F. R. 1965. *A Linguistic Study of the English Verb*. London: Longman.

Palmer, H. E., and F. G. Blandford. 1939. *A Grammar of Spoken English on a Strictly Phonetic Basis*. Cambridge: Heffer.

Palmer, H. E., and D. Palmer. 1959. *English through Actions*. London: Longman.

Paulston, C. B. 1971. The sequencing of structural pattern drills. *TESOL Quarterly* 5: 197–208.

　　1974. Linguistic and communicative competence. *TESOL Quarterly* 8(4): 347–362.

　　1980. The sequencing of structural pattern drills. In K. Croft (ed.), *Readings on English as a Second Language*. Cambridge, Mass.: Winthrop.

Pawley, A., and F. Syder. 1983. Two puzzles for linguistic theory: nativelike selection and nativelike fluency. In J. C. Richards and R. Schmidt (eds.), *Language and Communication*, pp. 191–225. London: Longman.

Pearson, E. 1983. Agreement and disagreement: a study of speech acts in conversation and ESL texts. Masters thesis, University of Hawaii.

Penfield, W. G., and L. Roberts. 1959. *Speech and Brain Mechanisms*. Princeton: Princeton University Press.

Peters, A. 1977. Language learning strategies: does the whole equal the sum of the parts. *Language* 53: 560–573.

Pica, T. 1983. Adult acquisition of English as a second language in different language contexts. *Language Learning* 33, 34: 465–498.

Pienemann M. 1984. Learnability and syllabus construction. In K. Hyltenstam and M. Pienemann (eds.), *Modelling and Assessing Second Language Proficiency*. Avon: Multilingual Matters.

Plaister, T. 1973. Teaching reading comprehension to the advanced ESL student using the cloze procedure. *RELC Journal* 4(2): 31–38.

Platt, J. T. 1977. English past tense acquisition by Singaporeans – implicational scaling versus group averages of marked forms. *ITL* 38: 63–83.

Platt, J., and H. Platt. 1975. *The Social Significance of Speech*. Amsterdam: North Holland.

Politzer, R. L. 1967. Towards psycholinguistic models of language instruction. *TESOL Quarterly* 2: 3.

Porter, P. A. 1983. How learners talk to each other; input and interaction in task-centered discussions. Paper presented at TESOL convention, Toronto, March 1983.

Porter, D., and J. Roberts. 1981. Authentic listening activities. *ELT Journal* 36(1): 37–47.

Prabhu, N. S. 1983. Procedural syllabuses. Paper presented at the RELC Seminar. Singapore: Regional Language Centre.

Praninskas, J. 1972. *American University Word List*. London: Longman.

Pratt, D. 1980. *Curriculum: Design and Development*. New York: Harcourt Brace Jovanovich.

Pratt, M. 1977. *Towards a Speech Act Theory of Literary Discourse*. Bloomington: Indiana University Press.

Quirk, R., S. Greenbaum, G. Leech, and J. Svartvik. 1972. *A Grammar of Contemporary English*. London: Longman.

Ravem, R. 1974. The development of Wh-questions in first and second language learners. In J. C. Richards (ed.), *Error Analysis: Perspectives on Second Language Acquisition*, pp. 124–155. London: Longman.

Richards, J. C. 1968. Language problems of Maori children. *Comment* (Wellington, N.Z.) 36: 28–32.

1974. Word lists: problems and prospects. *RELC Journal* 5(2): 69–84.

1975. Simplification: a strategy in the adult acquisition of a foreign language. *Language Learning* 25(1): 115–126.

1979. Rhetorical and communicative styles in the new varieties of English. *Language Learning* 29(1): 1–26.

1981. Form and function in second language learning: an example from Singapore. In R. Andersen (ed.), *New Dimensions in Second Language Acquisition Research*, pp. 153–164. Rowley, Mass.: Newbury House.

1984. Language curriculum development. *RELC Journal* 15(1): 1–29.

Ringbom, H. (ed.). 1983. *Psycholinguistics and Foreign Language Learning*. Abo (Stockholm): Abo Akedemi.

Ritchie, W. C. 1967. Some implications of generative grammar. *Language Learning* 17.

Rivers, W. M. 1968. *Teaching Foreign-Language Skills*. Chicago: University of Chicago Press.

1981. *Teaching Foreign Language Skills*, 2nd ed. Chicago: University of Chicago Press.

Rixon, S. 1981. The design of materials to foster particular listening skills. In

The Teaching of Listening Comprehension. ELT Documents 121: 68–106. London: The British Council.

Robinson, P. 1980. *English for Specific Purposes*. Oxford: Pergamon.

Roggendorff, J. 1980. Remarks made during an address to the Association of Foreign Teachers in Japan. Reported in *The Japan Times*, November 26, 1980.

Ross, J. 1970. On declarative sentences. In R. Jacobs and P. Rosenbaum (eds.), *Readings in English Transformation Grammar*. Waltham, Mass.: Blaisdell.

Sacks, H. 1972. On the analyzability of stories by children. In Gumperz and Hymes, eds. (1972).

Sacks, H., E. Schegloff, and G. Jefferson. 1974. A simplest systematics for the organization of turn-taking for conversation. *Language* 50(4): 696–725.

Sadock, J. 1970. Whimperatives. In J. Sadock and A. Vanek (eds.), *Studies Presented to Robert K. Lees by his Students*, pp. 223–238. Edmonton, Canada: Linguistic Research.

1972. Speech act idioms. *Papers from the Eighth Regional Meeting of the Chicago Linguistic Society*, pp. 329–339. Chicago, Ill.

1975. The soft, interpretive underbelly of generative semantics. In Cole and Morgan, eds. (1975), pp. 383–396.

Sampson, G. 1971. The strategies of Cantonese speakers learning English. In R. Darnell (ed.), *Linguistic Diversity in Canadian Society*. Edmonton, Canada: Linguistic Research.

Sanches, M., and B. Blount. 1975. *Sociocultural Dimensions of Language Use*. New York: Academic Press.

Sankoff, D. (ed.). 1978. *Linguistic Variation: Models and Methods*. New York: Academic Press.

Sato, C. 1981. Ethnic styles in classroom discourse. In M. Hines and W. Rutherford (eds.), *On TESOL 81*, pp. 11–24. Washington, D.C.: TESOL.

1983. Task variation in interlanguage phonology. Paper presented at 10th Michigan Conference on Applied Linguistics, Ann Arbor, October 1983.

Schachter, J. 1974. An error in error analysis. *Language Learning* 24: 205–214.

1983. A new account of language transfer. In S. Gass and L. Selinker (eds.), *Language Transfer in Language Learning*. Rowley, Mass.: Newbury House.

Schachter, J., and M. Celce-Murcia. 1983. Some reservations concerning error analysis. In B. Robinett and J. Schachter (eds.), *Second Language Learning*, pp. 272–285. Ann Arbor: University of Michigan Press.

Schachter, J., and W. Rutherford. 1979. Discourse function and language transfer. *Working Papers in Bilingualism* 19(1): 1–12.

Schank, R. C., and R. P. Abelson. 1977. Scripts, plans and knowedge. In P. N. Johnson-Laird and P. C. Watson (eds.), *Thinking: Readings in Cognitive Science*, pp. 421–432. Cambridge: Cambridge University Press.

Schecter, S. 1984. *Listening Tasks: For Intermediate Students of American English*. Cambridge: Cambridge University Press.

Schegloff, E. 1968. Sequencing in conversational openings. *American Anthropologist* 70: 1075–1095.

Schegloff, E., and H. Sacks. 1973. Opening up closings. *Semiotica* 8(4): 289–327.

References

Schenkein, J. 1978. *Studies in the Organization of Conversational Interaction.* New York: Academic Press.

Schmidt, R. W. 1975. Sociolinguistic rules in foreign language teaching. Paper presented at the Symposium on Sociolinguistic and Applied Anthropology, annual meeting of the Society for Applied Anthropology, Amsterdam, August 1975.

1983a. Interaction, acculturation and the acquisition of communicative competence: a case study of an adult. In N. Wolfson and E. Judd (eds.), *Sociolinguistics and Language Acquisition,* pp. 137–174. Rowley, Mass.: Newbury House.

1983b. The strengths and limitations of acquisition; a case study of an untutored language learner. *Working Papers* 2 (2): 87–114. Department of ESL, University of Hawaii.

Schonell, F. J., I. G. Meddleton, B. A. Shaw et al. 1956. *A Study of the Oral Vocabulary of Adults.* London: University of London Press.

Schumann, J. H. 1975. Affective factors and the problem of age in second language acquisition. *Language Learning* 25: 209–235.

1978. *The Pidginization Process: a Model for Second Language Acquisition.* Rowley, Mass.: Newbury House.

1981. Simplification, transfer and relexification as aspects of pidginization. Paper presented at the TESOL convention, Detroit, March 1981.

Scollon, R., and S. B. K. Scollon. 1981. *Narrative Literacy and Face in Interethnic Communication.* New Jersey: Ablex.

1983. Face in interethnic communication. In J. C. Richards and R. W. Schmidt (eds.), *Language and Communication.* London: Longman.

Scovel, T. 1971a. Getting tense in English: a linguistics for our time. *TESOL Quarterly* 5(4): 301–305.

1971b. A look-see at some verbs of perception. *Language Learning* 21:(1): 75–84.

1979. Review of Georgi Lozanov, "Suggestology and outlines of suggestopedy." *TESOL Quarterly* 13(2): 255–266.

1982. Questions concerning the application of neurolinguistic research to second language learning/teaching. *TESOL Quarterly* 16(3): 323–331.

Searle, J. 1965. What is a speech act? In M. Black (ed.), *Philosophy in America.* London and Ithaca: Allen and Unwin and Cornell University Press.

1969. *Speech Acts.* Cambridge: Cambridge University Press.

1975. Indirect speech acts. In Cole and Morgan, eds. (1975).

1976. The classification of illocutionary acts. *Language in Society* 5(1): 1–24.

Segalowitz, N., and E. Gatbonton. 1977. Studies of the non-fluent bilingual. In P. A. Hornby (ed.), *Bilingualism: Psychological, Social and Educational Implications,* pp. 77–90. New York: Academic Press.

Seliger, H. W. 1982. On the possible role of the right hemisphere in second language acquisition. *TESOL Quarterly* 16(3): 307–314.

1983. Learner interaction in the classroom and its effect on language acquisition. In H. W. Seliger and M. H. Long (eds.), *Classroom Oriented Re-*

search in Second Language Acquisition, pp. 246–267. Rowley, Mass.: Newbury House.

Selinker, L. 1969. Language transfer. *General Linguistics* 9: 67–92.

1972. Interlanguage. *IRAL* 10(3): 209–232.

Sinclair, J., and R. Coulthard. 1975. *Towards an Analysis of Discourse.* London: Oxford University Press.

Slobin, D. I. 1971. *Psycholinguistics.* Glenview, Ill.: Scott Foresman.

Smith, G. McB. 1969. Some comments on the English of eight bilinguals. In D. M. Lance (ed.), *A Brief Study of Spanish-English Bilingualism.* San Antonio: Texas A & M University Press.

Smith, L. E. (ed.). 1981. *English for Cross Cultural Communication.* London: Macmillan.

Snow, C. E. 1972. Mothers' speech to children learning language. *Child Development* 43: 549–565.

Stanley, J. A. 1978. Teaching listening comprehension. *TESOL Quarterly* 12(3): 285–296.

1980. Are listening materials just for listening to? *RELC Journal* 11(1): 78–88.

Steinberg, D. D. 1974. Semantics: a brief history from a psychological viewpoint. *Working Papers in Linguistics* 6(2): 111–118.

Stenson, N. 1974. Induced errors. In J. H. Schumann and N. Stenson (eds.), *New Frontiers in Second Language Learning.* Rowley, Mass.: Newbury House.

Stern, H. H. 1969. Foreign language learning and the new view of first-language acquisition. *Child Study* 30(4): 25–36.

Stevick, E. W. 1976. *Memory, Meaning, and Method.* Rowley, Mass.: Newbury House.

1980. *A Way and Ways.* Rowley, Mass.: Newbury House.

Stratton, F. S. 1977. Putting the communicative syllabus in its place. *TESOL Quarterly* 11(2): 131–141.

Strevens, P. 1978. The nature of language teaching. In J. C. Richards (ed.), *Understanding Second and Foreign Language Learning,* pp. 204–217. Rowley, Mass.: Newbury House.

Sudnow, D. (ed.). 1972. *Studies in Social Interaction.* New York: Free Press.

Svartvik, J. 1973. *Errata: Papers in Error Analysis.* Lund: C. W. K. Gleerup.

Swain, M. 1977. Future directions in second language research. In C. Henning (ed.), *Proceedings of the Los Angeles Second Language Research Forum.* University of California, Los Angeles.

Tarone, E. E. 1977. Conscious communication strategies in interlanguage: a progress report. In H. D. Brown, C. Yorio, and R. Crymes (eds.), *On TESOL 77.* Washington, D.C.: TESOL.

1979. Interlanguage as chameleon. *Language Learning* 29(1): 181–191.

1983. On the variability of interlanguage systems. *Applied Linguistics* 4(2): 142–163.

Tarone, E. E., U. Frauenfelder, and L. Selinker. 1976. Systematicity/variability and stability/instability in interlanguage systems. In H. D. Brown (ed.),

Papers in Second Language Acquisition, Special Issue 4 of *Language Learning*, pp. 93–134.

Terrell, T. D. 1977. A natural approach to the acquisition and learning of a language. *Modern Language Journal* 61: 325–336.

1982. The natural approach to language teaching: an update. *Modern Language Journal* 66(2): 121–131.

Thomas, J. 1983. Cross-cultural pragmatic failure. *Applied Linguistics* 4(2): 91–112.

Thomas, H. 1982. Survey review: recent materials for developing listening skills. *ELT Journal* 36(3): 192–199.

Tucker, G. 1978. Implementation of language teaching programs. In J. C. Richards (ed.), *Understanding Second and Foreign Language Learning*, pp. 204–217. Rowley, Mass.: Newbury House.

Twadell, W. F. 1973. Vocabulary expansion in the ESOL classroom. *TESOL Quarterly* 7(1): 61–78.

Ueda, K. 1974. Sixteen ways to avoid saying "No" in Japan. In J. C. Condon and M. Saito (eds.), *Intercultural Encounters with Japan: Communication, Contact and Conflict*. Tokyo: Simul Press.

Underwood, M. 1979. *Have You Heard?* Oxford: Oxford University Press.

Urmston Philips, L. 1976. Some sources of cultural variability in the regulation of talk. *Language in Society* 5(1): 8–95.

Van Ek, J., and L. G. Alexander. 1975. *Threshold Level English*. Oxford: Pergamon.

Vendler, Z. 1967. Verbs and times. *Linguistics in Philosophy*. Ithaca: Cornell University Press.

Wagner, M. J., and G. Tilney. 1983. The effect of superlearning techniques on the vocabulary acquisition and alpha brainwave production of language learners. *TESOL Quarterly* 17(1): 5–19.

Wagner-Gough, J., and E. Hatch. 1975. The importance of input data in second language acquisition studies. *Language Learning* 25(2): 297–308.

Watson, K. A. 1974. Understanding human interaction: the study of everyday life and ordinary talk. In R. Brislin (ed.), *Topics in Culture Learning*, pp. 57–67. Honolulu: East-West Centre.

Watts, A. F. 1944. *The Language and Mental Development of Children*. London: Harrap.

Weeks, T. E. 1979. *Born to Talk*. Rowley, Mass.: Newbury House.

Wells, G. 1981. Becoming a communicator. In G. Wells (ed.), *Learning through Interaction: the Study of Language Development*, pp. 73–115. Cambridge: Cambridge University Press.

West, M. 1953. *A General Service List of English Words*. London: Longman.

Widdowson, H. G. 1968. The teaching of English through science. In J. Dakin, B. Tiffin, and H. G. Widdowson (eds.), *Language in Education*, pp. 115–70. Oxford: Oxford University Press.

1978. *Teaching Language as Communication*. London: Oxford University Press.

Wilkins, D. A. 1976. *Notional Syllabuses*. London: Oxford University Press.

Wode, H. 1982. *Learning a Second Language*. Tubingen: Gunter Narr Verlag.

Wolfe, D. K. 1967. Some theoretical aspects of language learning and language teaching. *Language Learning* 17:(3) and 17:4.

Wolfson, N. 1983. Rules of speaking. In J. C. Richards and R. W. Schmidt (eds.), *Language and Communication*, pp. 61–87. London: Longman.

Woods, H. B. 1979. *Rhythm and Unstress*. Hull, Canada: Canadian Government Publishing Center.

Yalden, Janice. 1983. *The Communicative Syllabus: Evolution, Design and Implementation*. Oxford: Pergamon.

Yorio, C. A. 1980. Conventionalized language forms and the development of communicative competence. *TESOL Quarterly* 14(4): 433–442.

Zamel, V. 1982. Writing: the process of discovering meaning. *TESOL Quarterly*. 16(2): 195–210.

    1983. The composing processes of advanced ESL students: six case studies. *TESOL Quarterly* 17(2): 165–188.

Index